Leading a Business School

Business schools are critical players in higher education, educating current and future leaders to make a difference in the world. Yet we know surprisingly little about the leaders of business schools. *Leading a Business School* demystifies this complex and dynamic role, offering international insights into deans' dilemmas in different contexts and situations. It highlights the importance of deans creating challenging and supportive learning cultures to enhance business and management education, organizations and society more broadly.

Written by renowned experts on the role of the dean, Julie Davies, Howard Thomas, Eric Cornuel and Rolf D. Cremer, the book traces the historical evolution of the business school deanship, the current challenges and future sources of disruption. The leadership characteristics and styles of business school deans are presented based on an examination of different dimensions of their roles. These include issues of strategic positioning, such as financial viability, prestige, size, mission, age, location and programme portfolios, as well as the influences of rankings, sector accreditations, governance structures, networks and national policies on strategy implementation. Drawing on international case studies and deans' development programmes globally, the authors explore constraints on deans' autonomy, university and external relations, and how business school deans add value over the period of their tenures.

This candid and well-researched book is essential reading for aspiring business school leaders, those hiring and working with deans, and other higher education leaders.

Julie Davies is a Professor, Director of (E)MBA Health programmes and Deputy Director (Equality, Diversity and Inclusion) at the Global Business School for Health, a start-up business school, in University College London (UCL). She initiated and facilitated the International Deans' Programme (2008–2015).

Howard Thomas is a 'serial dean' having held deanships in Asia, Europe and North America. He is a well-regarded and highly cited scholar in the fields of strategic management and management education. He is an Emeritus Professor and former Dean at LKCSB, Singapore Management University, and currently a Special Advisor at EFMD Global.

Eric Cornuel has been President of EFMD Global since 2000. He is an acknowledged expert and authority on management education and a recipient of the Légion d'honneur for services to education. He is also a Professor at HEC, Paris, and the University of Louvain, Belgium.

Rolf D. Cremer has also been a successful 'serial dean' particularly in New Zealand, China and the Asia-Pacific as well as President of EBS, Wiesbaden. He initiated and facilitated the strategic Leadership Programme for Deans at EFMD 2017–2019. He is also the recipient of the Magnolia Award from the city of Shanghai. He is currently a Professor in the Frankfurt School of Finance and Management.

Leading a Business School

Julie Davies, Howard Thomas, Eric Cornuel and Rolf D. Cremer

Routledge
Taylor & Francis Group
LONDON AND NEW YORK

Designed cover image: Getty Images / sharply_done

First published 2023
by Routledge
4 Park Square, Milton Park, Abingdon, Oxon OX14 4RN

and by Routledge
605 Third Avenue, New York, NY 10158

Routledge is an imprint of the Taylor & Francis Group, an informa business

British Library Cataloguing-in-Publication Data
A catalogue record for this book is available from the British Library

ISBN: 978-1-032-01309-1 (hbk)
ISBN: 978-1-032-01310-7 (pbk)
ISBN: 978-1-003-17812-5 (ebk)

DOI: 10.4324/9781003178125

Typeset in Goudy
by codeMantra

Contents

Figures

Foreword

Leading a business school can be a daunting challenge particularly for academics with limited managerial experience or previous educational responsibilities. How many newly appointed deans have experienced great moments of euphoria (after having signed the contract of their new position) only to face, days or weeks after, the true complexity of the job and the real magnitude of their responsibilities.

A solid experience as the former dean/director of an MBA or PhD program may certainly help you in your new deanship position. However, it may not necessarily be enough since leading a business school is generally a broader and more complex task. From almost one day to another, you may suddenly find yourself responsible for the lives of hundreds – if not thousands – of people in your organization. Today, of course, there is a multitude of coaches ready to help. However, as many business school leaders have learnt on the job, a successful deanship journey starts with you taking the lead by quickly grasping the new educational context and unique culture of the School, setting a credible and inspiring direction, demonstrating fairness to all, getting the respect and support of the Faculty, energizing participants and staff, differentiating "commoditized" degree programs, getting better brand visibility in a very crowded educational market, dealing with the rankings and alumni's reactions, managing relations with donors, the media, government officials, sometimes managing complex relationships with other parts of the university, meeting the changing needs of the corporate world and... demonstrating results (in particular financial)!

The dean position comes with critical questions: What is expected of me? How do I share my vision and strategy for the School? What kind of leadership style is most appropriate to my new position? What priorities should I set for myself, my team and the School? What critical incidents should I anticipate? How much should I delegate? Who in the organization can I trust and who should be replaced? What stakeholders should I address first? Where can I find support?

Until today, it was impossible to find a practical, up-to-date and inspiring book that would address many of these issues. As the authors correctly suggest, "we know very little about what school deans do." The need was getting increasingly pressing as we are all facing an unprecedented VUCA (Volatile, Uncertain, Complex and Ambiguous) world, shaped by new technologies, changing geo-political and economic forces, more demanding stakeholders that make the job more challenging – but as some of us would argue – also more interesting.

Leading a Business School answers many of these questions and deflates the potential apprehensions often associated with the position. The book serves as a precious help and great inspiration for newly appointed as well as aspiring deans. *Leading a Business School* draws on the exceptional international and practical experience of first-class academics, including from several "serial" deans, who have worked in very complex environments and multicultural contexts set in different parts of the world. The book also builds on the great success of the "International Deans Program" launched jointly by EFMD and AACSB in 2004, and then run by EFMD together with ABS in the UK from 2008 to 2016. In 2017, EFMD redesigned the program and has been running it as a flagship program as part of its professional development for the past 6 years. *Leading a Business School* includes reflections and key learning points from the many participants who went through this program. It is further enriched with solid research, great observations and insights from the authors, various interviews with deans from different regions of the world, and several practical case studies.

Starting with the historical transformation of the business school deanship job, the book offers a new perspective on the challenges deans face today and closes on the opportunities offered by the business school of tomorrow. In between, it revisits the new role of deans and how they can add more value to their School and their various stakeholders by addressing the fundamental issue: What are business school deans expected to do? and providing practical and convincing answers to this question. The book also addresses many of the important "classic" and unexpected critical incidents we all face today including the challenges and opportunities created by the current global context and the use of new technologies.

As leaders of China Europe International Business School (CEIBS), we found this candid and well-researched book to be THE essential book for newly appointed and aspiring business school deans. Co-founded by the Chinese government and European Union (EU) in 1994, with Shanghai Jiao Tong University and the EFMD serving as its executive partners, CEIBS has made it into the global top tier with a brief history of just 28 years. No matter how veteran we consider ourselves to be as business school leaders, it has never been an easy task to steer a school that is uniquely positioned to educate responsible leaders versed in "China Depth, Global Breadth" and that aims to become the most respected international business school in the world. This book was a highly inspirational reading experience, since most of the challenges and complexities that we have come across are well covered here. Full of insightful observations, great wisdom, smart international perspectives and practical tips, we are confident that *Leading a Business School* will be your reference reading to make your deanship the richest and most enjoyable journey of your life!

Best wishes,
Dr Hong Wang and Dr Dominique Turpin
Presidents of CEIBS

CEIBS

Preface

This book is grounded in the authors' practical experiences, observations, reflections and research on business school leadership. It is also informed by an analysis of media reports, interviews and critical incidents recounted by business school deans globally. **Julie Davies** has worked in business schools for three decades and completed her doctorate at Warwick Business School on 'Hybrid upper middle manager strategizing practices: Linking archetypes and contingencies in the UK business school deanship'. She is currently Director of the MBA Health in the Global Business School for Health, a start-up business school in University College London. **Howard Thomas** is a Professor Emeritus of Strategic Management and Management Education and a Special Advisor at EFMD Global. He is a former Dean of Lee Kong Chian School of Business, Singapore Management University, Warwick Business School in the UK and the College of Commerce and Business Administration (now Business) at the University of Illinois-Champaign in the US. He is an acknowledged, highly cited scholar in the fields of strategic management and management education and has been awarded several fellowships and honorary degrees; most recently, he was awarded the Cooper Leadership Medal of BAM (the British Academy of Management). **Eric Cornuel** has been President of EFMD Global (the European Foundation of Management Development) since 2000. He has taught for over 20 years at management schools in Europe and Asia, and is an affiliate Professor at HEC, Paris and a Professor at the University of Louvain. His achievements have earned him numerous awards, including, in particular, the Magnolia Award of the City of Shanghai and the French National Order of the *Légion d'honneur* and several honorary professorships. He also served as Dean of KIMEP (the Kazakhstan Institute of Management, Economics and Strategic Research) from 1997 to 1999. He has written extensively about the future of responsible, impactful management education and his most recent book (2022), *Business School Leadership and Crisis Exit Planning*, was published by Cambridge University Press.

Rolf D. Cremer is a Professor and Academic Director (MBA/EMBA) at the Frankfurt School of Finance and Management. He is the Dean Emeritus of the China Europe International Business School (CEIBS), Shanghai, and from 2011 to 2013 was the President and CEO of EBS University for Business and Law, Wiesbaden. His experience in China and Asia-Pacific spans almost 30 years. He held deanships at the University of Macau, Massey University, New Zealand and returned to China as Dean and Vice-President of CEIBS. He also received an Honorary Doctorate from the European Business School, Wiesbaden. He is the recipient of the Silver Magnolia Award of the Shanghai Municipal Government for outstanding contributions to China in the field of higher education.

We hope that our insights into the evolution of business school deanship in different countries, contexts and cultures provide useful case studies and frameworks for leading and managing business schools. These are provided to help us to understand how individuals learn to become deans, make strategic choices, relate to others and develop over time in the role. This book examines critical incidents in media reports and lived experiences of business school leadership in order to identify key challenges and approaches for handling them in practice. Its logic is explained in the following flow diagram.

Outline of the Book: A Flow Diagram

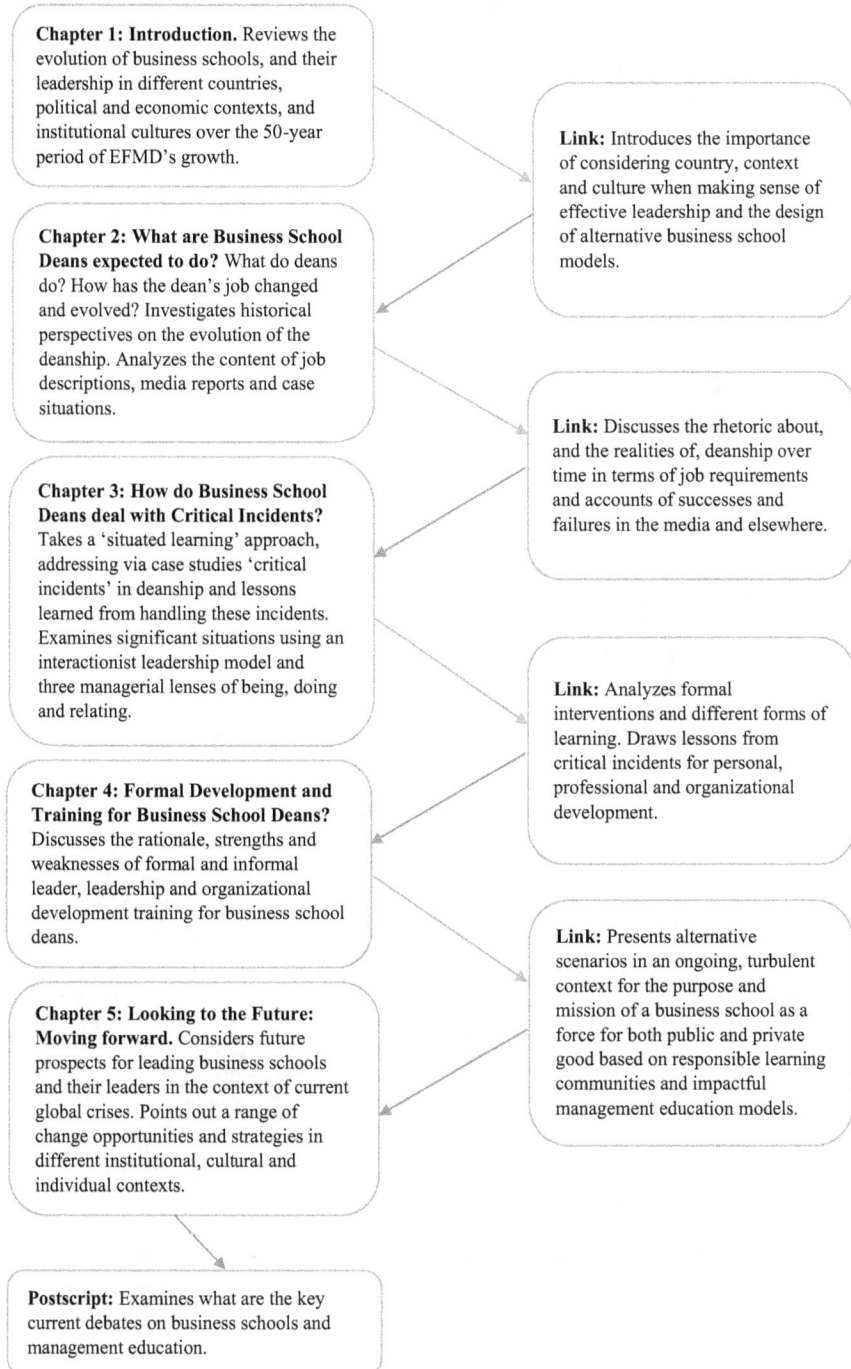

Chapter 1: Introduction. Reviews the evolution of business schools, and their leadership in different countries, political and economic contexts, and institutional cultures over the 50-year period of EFMD's growth.

Link: Introduces the importance of considering country, context and culture when making sense of effective leadership and the design of alternative business school models.

Chapter 2: What are Business School Deans expected to do? What do deans do? How has the dean's job changed and evolved? Investigates historical perspectives on the evolution of the deanship. Analyzes the content of job descriptions, media reports and case situations.

Link: Discusses the rhetoric about, and the realities of, deanship over time in terms of job requirements and accounts of successes and failures in the media and elsewhere.

Chapter 3: How do Business School Deans deal with Critical Incidents? Takes a 'situated learning' approach, addressing via case studies 'critical incidents' in deanship and lessons learned from handling these incidents. Examines significant situations using an interactionist leadership model and three managerial lenses of being, doing and relating.

Link: Analyzes formal interventions and different forms of learning. Draws lessons from critical incidents for personal, professional and organizational development.

Chapter 4: Formal Development and Training for Business School Deans? Discusses the rationale, strengths and weaknesses of formal and informal leader, leadership and organizational development training for business school deans.

Link: Presents alternative scenarios in an ongoing, turbulent context for the purpose and mission of a business school as a force for both public and private good based on responsible learning communities and impactful management education models.

Chapter 5: Looking to the Future: Moving forward. Considers future prospects for leading business schools and their leaders in the context of current global crises. Points out a range of change opportunities and strategies in different institutional, cultural and individual contexts.

Postscript: Examines what are the key current debates on business schools and management education.

In conclusion, we look forward to further debates and conferences about the changing nature of business school leadership as we continue to help our stakeholders tackle those grand challenges – and opportunities – that will arise in fast-moving, uncertain environments.

Julie Davies (London)
Howard Thomas (Stratford-upon-Avon)
Eric Cornuel (Brussels)
Rolf D. Cremer (Frankfurt)

Acknowledgements

We would like to thank participants on deans' development programmes at EFMD, CABS and AAPBS that we have contributed to and the following colleagues in particular (this list is by no means exhaustive) for their friendship and valuable insights into the business school deanship which we draw on in this book:

Barbara Allan, Gabriela Alvarado, Anand Anandalingam, Duncan Angwin, David Asch, Rachel Ashworth, George Bain, Mark Bannister, Nic Beech, George Benwell, Nick Binedell, Thomas Bieger, Julian Birkinshaw, Martin Boehm, Frank Bournois, Julia Balogun, Jordi Canals, Jérôme Chabanne-Rive, Jean Chen, Betty Chung, Tim Clark, Ian Clarke, Stewart Clegg, Simon Collinson, Nora Colton, Sue Cox, Andrew Crisp, Graeme Currie, Murray Dalziel, Samir Dani, Sandra Dawson, Arnoud De Meyer, Soumitra Dutta, Robert Dyson, Chris Earley, John Endicott, Ian Fenwick, Ewan Ferlie, Susan Fournier, Arthur Francis, Ken Freeman, Bob Galliers, Robin Gauld, Amanda Goodall, Thami Gorfi, Gregor Halff, Edeltraud Hanappi-Egger, Susan Hart, Charles Harvey, Ulrich Hommel, Toni Hilton, Per Holten-Andersen, Frank Horwitz, Jane Houzer, Sin Hoon Hum, Ahn Byung Ik, Santiago Iñiguez, Dipak Jain, Lily Kong, John Kraft, Angus Laing, Japhet S. Law, Marianne Lewis, Andy Lockett, Peter Lorange, Sherif Kamel, Alfred Kieser, Martin Kitchener, Nicola Kleyn, Ryuji Konishi, Robert MacIntosh, Jean-François Manzoni, Katy Mason, Sharon Mavin, Colin Mayer, Robert McIntosh, Peter McKiernan, Heather McLaughlin, Bob McNabb, Simon Mercado, Martin Meyer, Huw Morris, Morris Mthombeni, Katrin Muff, Piet Naudé, David Norburn, John North, David Oglethorpe, Enase Okonedo, Judy Olian, Sergio Olavarrieta, Michael Osbaldeston, Michael Page, Federico Pasin, Michel Patry, Kai Peters, Andrew Pettigrew, Paul Phillips, Zoe Radnor, Carl Rhodes, Johan Roos, Alfons Saquet Rovira, Leisa Sargent, John Saunders, Adrian Saville, Mark Smith, J-C Spender, André Spicer, Barbara Sporn, Rajendra Srivastrava, Ken Starkey, Nils Stieglitz, Chris Styles, Mark P. Taylor, Anne Tsui, Dominique Turpin, Daneel

Van Lill, Susan Vinnicombe, Stephen Watson, Robin Wensley, Greg Whit-well, David Wilson, Robina Xavier, Baback Yadzani, Lin Zhao.

We would particularly like to recognize the contributions of Dipak Jain, a very distinguished former dean and most recently, President (European) of CEIBS, and Kai Peters, a very well-regarded European dean. Virginie Heredia-Rosa and Matthew Wood, editor of Global Focus and Operations Director at EFMD, also provided valuable insights, inspiration and support.

Julie would like to thank her parents, Aziz, Isabella and Arianna – 'at the still point of the turning world' (T S Eliot) while Howard richly appreciates the continuing strong support of the Thomas family and especially his wife, Lynne – 'they are always there for me'.

Finally, we would like to thank those individuals who worked tirelessly to improve this book. Our excellent and highly professional colleagues Paula Parish (Greenwood Editorial) and Julia Greenslade (Howard's PA in Stratford-upon-Avon) were absolutely outstanding and performed in a stellar manner. Our publishing editor at Routledge (Rebecca Marsh) was a constant source of advice and guidance. Without their constant efforts, this book would not have crossed the finishing line.

Finally, we hope you enjoy the book and look forward to receiving your comments and feedback.

1

The Evolution of Management Education (1972–2022)

EFMD's Journey, Changes in Business Models and Deanship Roles

Introduction

As we explore deanship roles and leadership styles in this book, we must ground this exploration in the context of how business schools have evolved, particularly in the British and European context and culture. For that reason, we examine in this and later chapters how deanship roles have changed along with the range of challenges and issues that have been faced as business schools have adapted to environmental, economic and social factors over the last 50 years. In essence, management education's past – and its historical development – shapes the present and future pathways of its evolution.

EFMD (the European Foundation for Management Development) came into being in 1971 through the merger of the International University Contact for Management Education (IUC) and the European Association of Management Training Centres (EAMTC). Since then, EFMD has stressed its role as Europe's forum for high-quality networking and worldwide co-operation in management education and development. According to Hubert (1996, p.27), its establishment had three main purposes:

- To serve as a bridge between management practice and management learning
- To dedicate itself to a worldwide exchange of experience and ideas
- To represent management development to third parties

DOI: 10.4324/9781003178125-1

The EFMD volume *Training the Fire Brigade* (1996) outlined the evolution of the European Foundation for Management Development (EFMD) and sought to identify some of the key issues that had driven management education over the first 25 years (1971–96) of its existence. The volume, a compendium of essays, allowed the essay writers, including George Bain (LBS), Peter Lorange (IMD) and Claude Rameau (INSEAD), to explore the future of management education in relation to the economic and political context of the European environment.

As noted by Van Schaik (1996, p.13) (at that time the President of EFMD), it has clearly sought to link the corporate world and the world of education and hence be a catalyst and a 'broad church', encouraging debate and dialogue between corporations and institutions of management education and learning. Consequently, it has consistently tried to attract a significant proportion of corporate members.

Van Schaik (1996, p.14) further suggested that 'one of the most fundamental properties (of business schools) will be that their students will know how to handle the unexpected, how to handle life'. He went on to add that 'on top of technical skills – which have become a *sine qua non* … new managers more than ever should abhor rigid concepts and thrive on the art of improvisation'.

Van Schaik also clearly specified his vision for the role and purpose of EFMD in the management education environment:

> It should endeavour to continue to be a *trait d'union*, a link, between the corporate world and the world of education; it should continue to build and explore a network of personal and business relationships that enables it to contribute to the process of high-quality, practical, 'true to life' education … and finally, it should continue to cement its relationship with governments and public bodies that are involved in the process of management and education.

The academic/business linkage has been a strong influence in the evolution, role and strategic positioning of the business school in the European context. Since its founding, EFMD has constantly focused on combining European educational experience and ideas with meaningful impact on management practice and learning. It has also emphasized an international perspective in building its approaches to the growth of high-quality management education.

Indeed, by the early 1990s, European business schools had gained respect and growing influence in the global management education community. For example, Professor Pedro Nueno, trained at Harvard Business School and a European pioneer at IESE (Barcelona), EFMD and CEIBS (Shanghai), and Claude Rameau, a former Dean of INSEAD, emphasized that the distinctive identity and internationalism of Europe and the range of different European approaches to management should be a catalyst for transformation and change in management education.

During the first 25 years of its existence, the International Programmes Unit of EFMD promoted a range of international alliances and research centres including Euro-China, Euro-India, Euro-CIS, Euro-Arab and Euro-Palestine. This unusually wide-ranging international footprint attests to both influences acting on it and its own pioneering intent to transform the educational infrastructure of rapidly emerging economies such as China and India through co-operation with experts from European schools.

The Euro-China initiative, for example, led directly to the establishment of the first independent international business school in China (CEIBS – the China-Europe International Business School) in 1994. With subsequent investment, this school is now a very significant and important Asian school with broad international recognition in the rankings, notably most recently reaching seventh ranking in the FT's 2021 global MBA ranking (*Financial Times*, 8th February, 2021).

Fragueiro and Thomas (2011) provide a comprehensive 'map' of the management education landscape in Europe, showing the breadth of the marketplace and its heterogeneous nature. They also demonstrate how London Business School, IMD (Lausanne), and INSEAD (France) internationalized their schools significantly in the 1990s through the influence and leadership of George Bain, Peter Lorange and Antonio Borges, respectively. They and other European leaders also persuaded the *Financial Times* (FT) to develop its business school rankings to counteract the formidable strength of US rankings from *Business Week*, the *US News and World Report* and the *Wall Street Journal*.

Almost every country in Europe now has a set of national business school champions, and many are internationally ranked. France, the UK, Spain and Switzerland have probably led the growth of international schools, although other countries, such as Germany, are now producing an increasingly important set of business schools (e.g., ESMT, Berlin, Cologne, Frankfurt, Mannheim and Munich in Germany and Aalto, B.I., Copenhagen and Stockholm in Scandinavia).

What, then, are the characteristics of European management schools? What makes them distinctive? How do they differentiate themselves from well-regarded North American business school models? How are they managed and led?

Is There a Distinctive European Management Model?

It is argued, for example, in both the EFMD (1996) volume and in Thomas (2012), that the European identity and model of management education has been shaped by a range of environmental characteristics that differentiate the European scene from North American and Asian contexts and cultures.

- Europe and the EU is a large trading area involving many cultures and countries. Its diversity means that European trading corporations have learned how to expand and develop their businesses across borders. They have wide experience of international business and international relations.

- European companies have grown in size and have become leaner and fitter through European and international competition. As a consequence, many large, influential multinational European corporations have emerged and gained a strong reputation in the global marketplace.

- There is significant governmental and public-sector influence on the conduct of business and business policy in most European countries. Europeans tend to accept a broader role for government in business and society.

- Europeans generally favour socially responsible capitalism over what is sometimes characterized as unbridled market capitalism. Centrist models of social democracy (embedded in the rule of law) are more common in the European political environment than in the United States.

As a result, European business and, in turn, European management education has developed a balanced relationship with government and society, with governments often being important funders of higher education. In this context, business grows not only economically and technically but also gains social responsibility and legitimacy. The European culture and environment encourage greater social empathy and more direct co-operation with government to improve poverty and social welfare with an emphasis on inclusive growth and human and economic progress.

However, just as there is no common 'North American model' in management education, neither is there a common 'European model'. But there are issues, explained below, which differentiate and characterize the key elements of European management education.

- The belief in socially responsible management education is endemic. It is stressed by agencies such as the GRLI (Globally Responsible Leaders Initiative), EABIS (European Academy for Business in Society), PRME (Principles for Responsible Management Education) and RRBM (the Responsible Research in Business and Management Community), which have been carefully nurtured by EFMD while endorsing the sustainable development goals of the UN Global Compact. In particular, the RRBM Initiative began with the founder's article (Anne Tsui, 2015 on 'Socially

Responsible Leadership' in *Global Focus*. This led EFMD to support the founding of RRBM with a core founding set of 20 or so scholars. Their overarching aim was to address the two major problems of business school research, namely, its credibility and its practical, societal impact.

- The development of close linkages between business schools and corporate organizations and the consequent strong bridges between management education and practice fuelled a rapid expansion of executive education and life-long learning models in Europe. This has led to a greater focus on experiential, action-based, project-oriented learning, often providing clear evidence of the successful implementation of promising management practices in business.

- Internationalization and globalization are clearly very important to large European corporations (and to the EU as a trading bloc) as they expand their markets and corporate influence globally. Similarly, European business schools such as INSEAD (in Singapore and, more recently, Abu Dhabi), Nottingham (in China and Malaysia) and CEIBS (in Shanghai) provide evidence of how European schools have rapidly built an international footprint – and profile – to mirror the international growth perspectives of European businesses.

- The Bologna Process and European Accord in management education has also considerably strengthened the structure and functioning of European management education through the creation of common structures for degree-level management education. The resulting simple credit transfer process across courses taken in different European management education institutions has strongly facilitated co-operation and network-building among these institutions. Indeed, this has led to a largely European development of high demand, so-called pre-experience master's programmes, as well as network alliances such as CEMS (the Committee of European Management Schools), which have built a sense of creative identity and image for European schools.

- EFMD's EQUIS business school accreditation process (started in 1997) demonstrates its strong emphasis on high-quality management education. The CLIP programme shows a similar emphasis on quality assurance in corporate and executive education, while EOCCS is a more recent online accreditation. By 2020, EFMD had given EQUIS accreditation to over 200 schools worldwide.

- There is currently a much greater emphasis on cross-European educational networking for the development of interdisciplinary teaching and research programmes (e.g., Erasmus) and high-quality faculty development. Thus, the quality, and impact, of European research output is well recognized on the world scene.

Hence, it can be argued that European management educators and deans have adopted a more inclusive leadership style, with a somewhat less analytically rigorous perspective on management education than is common in, for example, the United States. They often believe in a closer linkage with practice and focus on a balanced view of management and leadership.

Paul Danos (2011), then Dean of Tuck Business School at Dartmouth College in the United States, expressed this in the following terms in discussing the philosophy of the well-regarded IE business school (Instituto de Empresa) in Madrid and its then Dean, Santiago Iniguez:

> His is a world where the professor is a teacher first, and the weight of research and practical experience in that teaching depends on each situation. That contrasts with the classic US model where research professors are seen as the prime teaching asset, and research itself fosters expertise about the world of practice.

Europeans tend to view formal analytic and strategy models and technical skills as valuable and sensible but also argue that such analytically, and scientifically, rigorous approaches may be too heavily emphasized in current curricula. This, in turn, may lead to the production of scientific research of little practical managerial relevance.

An emphasis on softer skills, more socially responsible management, and on vision and communication skills for engaging employees are viewed as critical and important attributes. Indeed, Europeans believe strongly in a balanced philosophy in management education involving an appropriate mix of course and project work to develop skills of analysis, synthesis and criticism. Through this process, the differentiation between European and other models of management education becomes clear and provides welcome diversity in models and management approaches in management education.

Our aim here is to identify the timelines and provide insights into the key events in EFMD's evolution, focusing particularly on the last two decades. We examine the following questions in relation to challenges and business models, as well as the role of the dean:

- What have been the key roles, achievements and activities in EFMD's evolutionary history?

- What were the key challenges and issues in management education discussed after the first 25 years of EFMD's development?

- What have been the key themes and challenges to management education more recently? How have they changed?

- What were the key challenges and themes noted in the research carried out in 2011–13, after 40 years of EFMD's development?

- What challenges and unresolved issues are still regarded by key constituencies as critical to the future of management education, particularly following major global crises such as the 2008/09 financial crisis and the more recent global pandemic?

The Timelines and Achievements in EFMD's History

The detailed material presented in Table 1.1 represents the key milestones and critical events in EFMD's history and emergence as a key thought-leader and authority in the field of management education. Table 1.2 provides a listing of the current regular schedule of member conferences offered by EFMD.

The history illustrated in Table 1.1 demonstrates clearly the success of EFMD in building and managing its relationship with education institutions and in monitoring the quality and content of business school faculty and curricula. From the outset, EFMD has promoted the Annual Deans and Directors' of Business Schools Meeting and the Annual EFMD Conference as networking events for its members. Over time it added the MBA Directors Meeting (1988), the EFMD Guide to MBA Programmes (1990), the Executive Education Network (1992) and the External Relations Network (1994) to reflect the educational diversity of business schools, as well as their research and quality assurance programmes. It also provides training in leadership for their administrative Deans/Directors as well as research Directors and Associate Deans.

More recently, EFMD launched a number of global initiatives, such as the Global Leadership Responsibility Initiative (GLRI) and, in association with AACSB International, the Global Foundation for Management Education (GFME), which focuses on leadership challenges both for society as a whole and for different regions and cultures.

A clearly important strategic move was EFMD's early alliance with the European Institute of Advanced Studies in Management (EIASM) (located also in Brussels and originally funded by the Ford Foundation) in order to enhance research quality and to professionalize the disciplines of management research. Together, they subsidized the development (by the early 1990s) of the European Marketing Academy, the European Finance Association, the European International Business Association, the European Accounting Association, the European Business Ethics Network and the European Foundation for Entrepreneurship Research.

Table 1.1 EFMD timeline

1972	EFMD foundation (merger of EAMTC/IUC)	First EFMD Annual Conference (Barcelona)
1973	193 members	First Deans & Directors Meeting
		First Banking Development Programme
1975	First European Case Development Workshop	
1978	First MBA Directors Meeting	
1980	China Europe Management Institute (CEMI) starts: First International Project	
	First Corporate Members Meeting (hosted by Shell)	
1983	EU commissions EFMD to develop/implement modular MBA in Beijing	
1984	China/EU (CEMP) EFMD develops executive programme for managers in Beijing	
1985	Launch of European Women's Management Development Workshop	
1986	European Enterprises Employment Project	
1987	Launch of European Business Ethics Network	
1989	Launch of first Case Writing Competition and Awards	
1990	First EFMD guide to MBA programmes	
	CEMI offers MBA and executive courses in China	
1991	Euro-Algerian Cooperation programme	
1992	Euro-CIS programme	
	Executive Education Network	
1994	CEIBS (China Europe International Business School) – joint venture in Shanghai	
	External Relations Group launched	
1995	Launch of EQUAL (European quality link for management education)	

(Continued)

Table 1.1 (Continued) EFMD timeline

1996	25th anniversary of EFMD (publication of book *Training the Fire Brigade*); launch of Euro-Arab Management School
1997	Launch of EQUIS (European (EFMD) Accreditation System) with 18 pioneer schools
	EFMD governance: two V.P.s – one each for business schools and corporates
1998	EFMD HQ at Rue Gachard, Brussels
	Launch of European Management Education Report
1999	Publication of European Executive Education Directory
	EQUIS accredits first school outside Europe – HEC, Montreal, Canada
2000	450 members
	New EFMD Director General – Professor Eric Cornuel
	New initiative on first degree programmes announced
2001/2	Corporate activities – Corporate Special Interest Groups
	CLIP programmes launch (quality improvement)
2002	Launch of GLRI (Global Leadership Responsibility Initiative)
2003	First New Deans Seminar (leadership training)
	Outstanding Doctoral Research Awards (ORDA) announced
2004	Launch of GLRI – in partnership with UN Global Compact
	Establishment of GFME (Global Foundation for Management Education)
2005	Launch of EPAS: programme accreditation system (led to EFMD accredited 2020)
	511 members
2006	Launch of Global Focus magazine (available in Chinese, English, Russian and Spanish)
	Launch of EFMD Advisory Services

(Continued)

Table 1.1 (Continued) EFMD timeline

2007	Launch of IDP (International Deans Programme)
	EQUIS accredits 100th school
	Development of PRME (Principles for Responsible Management Education)
2008	Launch of Excellence in Practice (EIP) awards
	700 members
2010	First conference in MENA region
	First conference in Africa region
	752 members
2011	EFMD Asia established
	Launch of EDAF (Deans Across Frontiers)
2012	EFMD GN (Global Network) formed – offices in Brussels, Geneva, Hong Kong, Miami and Prague
2013	FORGEC – EFMD projects in Cuba
2014	Launch of BSIS (Business School Impact System) in partnership with FNEGE (France)
2015	Formation of AHRMI (HR network)
	Formation of RRBM (Responsible Research in Business & Management) (2014/15)
	862 members
2016	EOCOS launched (online programme accreditation): higher ed. EFMD global career services launched
2017	Executive Academy launched
2018	EFMD South East Asian Initiative (business school partnerships in, e.g., Vietnam (European Management University, Vietnam))
	First EFMD GN Central & East European Conference
	912 members
2019	937 members

(Continued)

Table 1.1 (Continued) EFMD timeline

2020	EFMD Global Virtual Career Fairs (by Higher Ed) – launch of EFMD fellows
	EFMD accredited
2021	Launch with GBSN of 'Going Beyond' Awards
	Launch of EFMD Communities of Practice (e.g., Doctoral Community)
	Rendanheyi (RDHY) Certification System
2022	EFMD 50th Anniversary
	Executive Academy: Professional Development Portfolio
	New Cuban Project (e.g. Forint, Intercambio de Expertos)
	972 members

All of these have prospered and contributed to enhancing the quality of European management research and stimulated the founding of journals such as the *European Management Journal* and the *European Journal of Marketing*. EFMD also set up its own research committee in 2010, which held the first Conference on the Future of Management Education in 2012 in Zurich, Switzerland, and has continued to organize research and thought leadership seminars on a regular basis.

EFMD has had relatively less success in building its corporate membership despite promoting a wide range of corporate activities (corporate membership reached a peak proportion of 40% of all members in the mid-1980s). For example, it launched the first Corporate Members Meeting in 1980; the public sector management initiative (1982), the European enterprises employment project in 1986 and the Best Practice Project (1995), which further reinforced EFMD's desire for a strong corporate focus. This led to the LINK programme (2001), supporting the formation of corporate special interest groups (2001) and the CLIP quality improvement standards and subsequent best practice workshops for executive education (from 2002 to 2006). It also prompted EFMD to launch a practice-oriented, highly regarded publication, *Global Focus*, in 2005, with the sole aim of explaining through readable short articles new ideas in management practice. It has published a wide range of material regularly since that date. In addition, in 2008, EFMD joined with the Graduate Management Admissions Council (GMAC) to produce a corporate recruiters survey.

Table 1.2 List of current EFMD conferences

Annual Conference

Conference for Deans and Directors General

Conference on Bachelors Programmes

Conference on Masters Programmes

MBA Conference

Doctoral Programmes Conference

EFMD@Solvay: Job Fair and Conference for PhDs in Business and Management

Career Services Conference

Entrepreneurship Education Conference

Executive Development Conference

MARCOM, External and Alumni Relations Conference

Americas Annual Conference

Asia Annual Conference

Central and East Europe Conference

Middle East and Africa regions Conference

Strategic Leadership Programme for Deans

Admissions Institute for New Professionals

EFMD-EURAM Research Leadership Programme

EFMD-HUMANE Summer School

EFMD-HUMANE Asia Pacific School

EFMD-HUMANE Winter School

Throughout its existence EFMD has insisted that its governance, and particularly its Board, should have a balance between corporate and business education members. In 1997, the Board, for the first time, instituted the practice of having two Vice-Presidents, one from the business school side and one from the corporate side, an innovation that has continued to the present day.

One area of real strength for EFMD has been its internationalism, gained through its various partnerships with the European Union and the European Commission, starting with the initial China Project in 1983/84 (the China-Europe Management Institute (CEMI)). This led subsequently to the joint-venture project (already noted) to form the China Europe International Business School (CEIBS) in Shanghai in 1994.

EFMD has also collaborated with the European Union on a wide range of other overseas projects. These international projects and partnerships have gradually built a strong global footprint for EFMD and created its deserved reputation as the most internationally oriented of the professional management education organizations. This resulted in the opening of an EFMD office in China in 2009 and the first EFMD conferences in both the Middle East and Africa in 2010. More recently, EFMD has collaborated to develop business schools in Cuba and Vietnam. It has rebranded itself as EFMD-Global to reflect its global mindset and profile, and has opened offices in Geneva, Hong Kong, Miami and Prague in addition to its long-time presence in Brussels.

In its history, EFMD has also wrestled with the issue of quality and accreditation standards for management education. It started somewhat tentatively in 1986/87 with the formation of the Strategic Audit Unit, which sought to help schools to improve institutional quality and competence on a consulting basis through expert peer team visits and analyses. In 1995 the EQUAL network initiative (an alliance with organizations such as ABS (the Association of Business Schools, UK), AMBA (the Association of MBAs, UK), and AACSB (the Association of Accredited Schools of Business International, USA) was formed to specify international quality assurance standards and approaches. It was not long after this that the EFMD Board decided, in 1997, to launch its own European accreditation system (EQUIS), paralleling AACSB's more North America-focused programme, with a group of 18 pioneer schools. In 1999, it accredited its first school outside Europe (HEC Montreal in Canada) and now has accredited around 200 schools worldwide.

In 2004, it augmented EQUIS with EPAS (subsequently renamed as EQUIS Accredited), a programme (not an institutional) accreditation scheme, and has recently launched Deans Across Frontiers (EDAF) to improve quality standards in less developed areas of the world. It has also promoted accreditation for management development and executive education programmes through the CLIP scheme (2002–06). And, in recognition of developments in online technology-enabled learning, it established high-quality assurance standards through its EOCCS (EFMD Online Course Certification System) initiative. Similarly, it has focused on addressing the significant impact and reach of business schools through its highly regarded BSIS (Business Schools Impact) initiative, developed in association with FNEGE, a French foundation in the area of management education.

EFMD has adopted a broad focus on environmental issues, sustainability, the social and societal dimension of management and public sector management. This reflects European views of capitalism, which embrace social democratic models rather than the models of free-market capitalism common in North America. It has also, since 2004, promoted principles for responsible management education, endorsed by the GLRI, PRME, EABIS and RRBM communities centring on the UN's sustainable development goals and linked these to accreditation requirements. More recently in 2012 EFMD produced a draft manifesto for management education that has nurtured the growth of the RRBM community (Responsible Research in Business and Management) since its energetic founding by Professor Anne Tsui (Notre Dame and Arizona State Universities, USA) and a former President of the US Academy of Management).

What Challenges for Management Education Were Identified after 25 Years of EFMD? What Roles Were Suggested for EFMD's Future?

By 1996 – the 25th anniversary of EFMD – it had clearly fulfilled a number of its goals. It had established a distinctive European network with a global footprint encompassing a range of initiatives in the Middle East, India, China, and Central and Eastern Europe. This international diversity, both regionally and culturally, has been reinforced by its relentless desire to embrace the constant challenge of attracting corporate and public-sector managers as members alongside deans and leaders of educational institutions.

Even so, the contributors to the 1996 volume specified a number of key challenges facing EFMD at that time. They included the following (with relevant quotes from 1996):

- Embracing liberal management education

- Focusing on change innovation and entrepreneurship in our educational approaches

- Promoting globalization and European models of management education

- Addressing the realities of competition and strategic change

- Adapting to societal/stakeholder needs

- Recognizing that inertia and complacency may create business school failures

Embracing the Ideas and Principles of a Liberal Education

In his 1996 essay, Charles Handy, an eminent management educator and philosopher, reflected that:

> our business schools are, for the most part, set in the context of a university or institute where psychology, politics, philosophy and history are almost certainly part of the established faculty. It was a mistake, I now believe, to have established our business schools as a race apart from so much else in education.
>
> (Handy, 1996, p.11)

Handy's critique is an emphatic plea for grounding management education in the tradition of a liberal education, with less time spent on the more formulaic, mechanical and specialized aspects of the management task. He views (p.208) some management schools as instrumental and unexciting. He believes that they should make learning fun, a process of discovering new worlds rather than an unexciting exploration of the mechanics of the management process.

Focusing on Change Innovation and Entrepreneurship

George Bain (1996, p.89), at that time Principal of London Business School, concerned himself with strategic change and identified three main trends in the business environment: the increasing pace of change (through technology, entrepreneurship and global competition); the increasing scope and intensity of global competition; and the increasing stakeholder pressure on organizations (to address performance standards beyond economic criteria to embrace social, environmental and ethical aspects). He pointed out that each of these has implications for strategy and operations.

The first of these implications is that companies will need to compete on clearly understood strategic capabilities, innovatory ideas and core competences in the context of the need for rapid and flexible strategic change. He predicted that corporate structures would become leaner with fewer command and control processes and much flatter organizational structures. This would have clear implications for management education and for training managers in the core skills and capabilities necessary for managing change.

The second implication is that there will be a need for continuous learning, as the 'shelf life' of an MBA will shorten quite considerably. Managerial careers will be less predictable and managers will become more mobile.

The third is that there will be a focus in management education, particularly executive education, on lifelong learning and issues associated with topics such as leadership skills in problem identification and corporate vision, and cognitive abilities in the sense-making process through contextual, cultural, global and emotional intelligence.

Promoting Globalization and European Models of Management Education

Claude Rameau (1996, p.57), at that time Dean at INSEAD, reinforced the global aspect of change and the advantages of European management education:

> Europe and European management should be an inspiration for the rest of the world. It is more diverse, it is richer, it now has more experience than the rest of the world can offer, including the United States. The business schools should take advantage of that and EFMD should take the leading role in offering all of it to the world.

Giovanni Agnelli (1996, p.117), the then chairman of Italy's FIAT group, also believed that it is important to address 'the formation of a distinctly European culture and approach in the field of business and management'.

Addressing the Realities of Competition, Growth and Strategic Change

Dramatic growth, in the context of developing new industries in Europe, requires 'a radical rethinking of current management paradigms' (Prahalad, 1996, p.109). Hamel (1996, p.113) argued that the 'race to the future, to create the new (emerging) industries ...[means] we are standing on the verge of a new industrial revolution dealing with genetics, materials, and, more than anything else, information'. He continued: 'as we look to the future, we have to consider a totally new way of looking at competition'.

Hamel and Prahalad, well-respected pioneers in the strategy field, both strongly believed that the curricula in management education had become trapped in somewhat obsolete textbooks and in stories of past corporate experiences, i.e., case studies. New management theories, business models and paradigms would be needed in the new growth environment.

Hamel (1996, p.113) commented: 'What we continue to teach in the business schools is a little bit like being a mapmaker in an earthquake zone. Never before has the gap between our tools and the reality of emerging industry been larger.' He also criticized business schools for their alleged corporate blindness:

> For years most business schools assumed their product was the MBA. It's not; it's competitiveness. The only contribution business schools can make to society is to improve competitiveness and, therefore, the potential for wealth creation. How many business schools look at what they do through the perspective of: 'What is the contribution we made last year to competitiveness?'

Adapting to Societal/Stakeholder Perspectives

Peter Lorange (1996, pp.141, 142), the then President of IMD, also challenged the role of business schools in the future. At that time, he believed that business schools would still exist in the next 25 years (i.e., up to 2021/22) but that their foci would have to change. More than anything else, he implored business schools (and EFMD) to try new ideas and be inquisitive about them:

> We should help regions, countries, organizations to develop. We should look at curious phenomena and situations and ask more about them. Why for example, should Manila in the Philippines be cited as having the best managed 'company' in South East Asia for several years running (San Miguel) despite the other Asian 'Tigers'. What can we learn from this?

His overall theme was that new business school models are needed. Business schools, for example, should be more open and inquisitive about problems of inequality in society and seek to improve human and moral values in society.

Recognizing that Inertia and Complacency May Create Failure

Michael Osbaldeston (1996, pp.215, 216) also addressed themes considered by Hamel, Prahalad and Lorange. He asked: 'Why might business schools not be as successful as they might wish to be in the future?' He suggested that inertia may be a real issue: 'It could be a combination of the difficulty of escaping from your past, with an inability to create the future, or contentment with a track record of past and current performance'.

Beyond inertia, complacency with the status quo might also be a pressing issue, with faculty sometimes being the impediments to change: 'Our core competence is invested in the faculty; so if we recruit the right people, then surely the right people will deliver the right business school of the future.' However, he then commented: 'Sadly, faculty often hold strong views and well-formed recipes about good education and research. They often do not see the need to reinvent the future.'

At this point, it is important to question whether any or all of the key issues and challenges stressed in 1996 were addressed in the next 15 years of EFMD's evolution.

- What changes were made?
- What lessons were learned?
- What issues remained?

Next, we examine these questions during the 2010/12 period following the global financial crisis using evidence from a research study commissioned by EFMD on promises fulfilled and unfulfilled in management education.

What Happened to Business Schools Following the Global Financial Crisis: Promises Fulfilled and Unfulfilled in Management Education

Despite continued success, the business school had faced continued critical fire (e.g., Bennis & O'Toole, 2005; Jacobs, 2009) over its legitimacy as a serious, academic discipline (e.g., Nussbaum, 1997) and over its failure to reach its original promise and ambitious goal of the professionalization of management (e.g., Khurana, 2007). Yet, while business schools have failed to turn management into a profession, they were somewhat more successful in recasting it as a science (Schlegelmilch & Thomas, 2011, p.478), even though Mintzberg (2004) strongly believed that management is in fact neither a science nor a profession but rather an art or craft.

An important criticism, particularly since the global financial crisis in 2008, has seen business schools charged with complicity in stressing the value of financial engineering approaches in business curricula and failing to emphasize the importance of morality and ethical perspectives in business decision-making. The question was posed whether business schools were responsible, at least partially, for the economic problems that resulted from the crisis.

As Rakesh Khurana (2007) noted in his important review of American management education, by the late 1970s and early 1980s concerns began to emerge from practitioners and academics (e.g., Herbert Simon and Henry Mintzberg) about the overly scientific focus of business schools and the impact of management research on practice. Many of the challenges and issues stressed by authors in EFMD's 1996 volume had not been fully resolved. In particular, the dominant US logical positivist paradigm of management education (with somewhat obsolete case studies and management discipline-oriented curricula) still prevailed, with the design of newer business models reflecting innovation and change not in evidence. Management education had seemingly not fulfilled its evolutionary promises and deans and leaders had not embraced innovation, or change, or addressed the growing global competition in the business marketplace.

Yet, at around the same time European management schools such as HEC, IESE, IMD, INSEAD and LBS had established their growing influence in global management education (see Thomas [2012] 'What is the European Management School Model?', *Global Focus*, 6 pp.18–21). It was suggested that they had stressed elements which were more reflective of more balanced, less positivist European management education traditions including action-learning, practice-engaged research, customized executive education and, most importantly, a focus on international linkages, activities and research. It was clear by around 2010 that not only was there already a European identity and style in management education but also a rapidly evolving Asian identity and style exemplified in schools such as NUS, Nanyang and SMU in Singapore and Fudan, CEIBS and HKUST in China and Hong Kong.

Nevertheless, despite such European and Asian model innovations, criticism of business schools and management education continued in the first decade of the 21st century in an unabated fashion. The conventional judgement was that the dominant business school model was definitely in transition and business schools were at a 'turning point' in their evolution. Management educators had failed to address many of the challenges identified by Khurana and scholars such as Bain and Lorange in the 1996 EFMD volume.

The concerns of some of the most eloquent critics should be recognized as we reflect on the unmet promises of management education and assess whether in the second decade of the 21st century business schools would go on to develop a more diverse range of educational models. We outline the main areas of criticism below:

- Jeff Pfeffer and Christina Fong (2002) at Stanford had suggested that business schools were too market-driven and that management research had fallen short of good scientific traditions.

- Henry Mintzberg (2004) continued to argue that management is an art, not a science, and that the emphasis on analytical methodology and science in business schools was misplaced. He maintained that the traditional MBA curriculum is too narrow and specialized and ignored the development of leadership and management skills.

- The late Sumantra Ghoshal (2005) (London Business School) pointed out the moral and ethical decline of business and argued that business schools had been guilty of propagating and teaching amoral theories that destroyed sound management practices.

- Edwin Locke and J.C. Spender (2011) amplified Ghoshal's arguments and showed how the business schools' focus on numbers, mathematical modelling and theories, and specifically those based on financial economics, had led to rational choices which ignored important issues of culture, managerial behaviour and ethics. They concluded that market capitalism had evolved into 'casino capitalism', largely absent of a moral and ethical compass, in which the lack of financial morality and ethical leadership partially fuelled the global economic crisis of 2008.

Indeed, business schools were more widely blamed not only for their influence on the global financial crisis but also for ethical business failures such as Enron and WorldCom in the United States and Parmalat in Europe.

Rakesh Khurana (2007) has observed that a manager's role has shifted over time from addressing the 'higher aims' and objectives as professional stewards of a firm's resources to that of 'hired hands' operating only on the basis of contractual relationships. A key consequence of this demoralization and de-professionalization of managers is that the self-interest of relevant parties had taken the place of a proper ethical and moral compass and that the principle of trust that was central to the operation of market capitalism had been abandoned.

There was a dominant view that the ethical tradition in business life was in danger of erosion by the institutionalization of management education and business schools in their current form. Others, including Chris Grey (2005) of Warwick Business School in the UK and Paul Schoemaker (2008) in the

Wharton School in the United States, argued that business schools had become 'finishing schools' for elites to prepare for well-paid positions in finance and consulting without requiring them to examine the ethical and moral challenges of leadership and reflect on their broader roles in society.

It was felt, therefore, following the financial crisis, that there was an urgent need for management educators to engage in a period of sustained reflection about the purpose of management education. Important questions included the following:

- What is business for?

- What are business schools for? What is their purpose? Are they schools for business or schools for management?

- Who are the key stakeholders in management education?

- Should the curriculum of management education emphasize greater breadth and a holistic perspective encompassing the study of disciplines, theories, models, cultures and humanities which embraced traditions of analysis, criticism and synthesis?

An emerging school of thought was also becoming popular which advocated that the business school is a human institution embracing humanistic and societal values (endorsed by Eric Cornuel, CEO of EFMD) and that management is a creative art and not a deterministic science. Hence, it was argued that it is important to view management education from a wide range of stakeholder perspectives – society, business, government, students and employers.

In short, their position was that the sole purpose of firms is not to maximize shareholder wealth. Rather, firms must deploy their power in a socially responsible manner in balancing the competing interests of different stakeholders. It was stressed that it was imperative to examine the broader stakeholder perspective as an alternative to the dominant paradigm in management education in a systematic fashion.

Consequently, Howard Thomas and a research team examined the relative influence of stakeholders, individuals and organizations, the issues they focused on, the lessons not learned and the potential for change in management education models and approaches.

Their research study, sponsored by EFMD in 2011/12, involved a series of in-depth interviews with a set of stakeholders to develop a more comprehensive and informed view. Around 35 interviews lasting between two and three hours each were conducted taking in the informed views of stakeholders from academia, professional bodies, media, business and students. Interviewees were asked to focus on the time period from EFMD's formation in 1971–2010 and also to consider the likely future scenarios for management education.

Who Are the Key Stakeholders in Management Education?

As one interviewee stated: 'You'd think that in order of priority it should be students and employers at the top … but it doesn't always work out that way in practice.'

Students were often seen as key stakeholders because of the relationship between businesses as consumers of skilled graduates and business schools as suppliers of this resource. As such, businesses and employers emerged among the foremost stakeholders as a result of their position in the labour market as customers seeking skilled managers.

This perception of management education as a supply chain arrangement reinforced the position of students at the very core of management education. This maintained the view that business schools must serve to develop skilled individuals who provide significant added value to business. However, our interviews also revealed that business schools were subject to competing academic pressures, not least to function as a legitimate academic department, while keeping the customers happy:

> [It] leads to an academic dilemma because if you treat the student as a customer then you are compromising the academic side of the business … somehow business schools have to balance the idea of being an academic institution but also being a business that is selling bodies to companies.

This response summarizes the constant tensions that exist between teaching and research, with what amounts to a balancing act – an academic dilemma – for business schools to negotiate. A common comment made by deans and academics was the following: 'Is it still the case that we as business school deans continue to enact Steven Kerr's (1975) notorious folly of hoping for excellence in teaching while rewarding research activity?' Certainly, it was pointed out that the evidence from the ground shows that students are not key stakeholders, and it appears that the problem described by Kerr still remains.

Hence, faculty, business and students emerge as important stakeholders, with faculty clearly dominant in terms of their influence over management education and yet students still deemed to be a key stakeholder. Do the needs of students for quality instruction come second to the academic pursuits of faculty in their ivory towers?

The detailed responses of our interviewees reveal two different spheres of stakeholder influence: a supply-driven model and demand-driven model of management education over the last 20 years.

The first of these is a supply-driven perspective, where the preferences, terms and conditions of employment and institutional factors mean that faculty call the shots and determine what is taught to students and the areas of research that are pursued. Respondents noted that faculty have shaped and continue to influence teaching in management education. With a high level of control over the governance of instruction and also of what gets taught in business schools, it is easy to see why faculty are perceived as perhaps the most influential stakeholders. Hence, we regard this as a form of supply-driven management education.

What also emerged from the research data was a viewpoint that both business and students are perceived as playing a highly influential role in management education. This view represents a demand-driven perception of management education. This was especially evident in executive and post-experience courses, possibly because stakeholder interests are much more closely aligned, with each student being essentially a representative of business as both an employee and agent of business.

Therefore, in a demand-driven perspective, the sphere of influence shifts from academic influences to those driven by consumer demand from both student and business stakeholders. In this scenario, the mechanisms of influence for students are that they pay fees – as one respondent commented 'extortionate fees'. This means that they are positioned to influence how and where courses are delivered and also express a demand for specific course content (such as, perhaps, finance, management accounting and consultancy skills).

Further, in a climate of economic recession such as that which followed the financial crisis, and a general trend of state austerity reducing or freezing funding for higher education, the bargaining power and 'willingness to pay' of fee-paying students and businesses is strengthened. We should expect the relative influence of students and businesses to increase as they push for 'value-for-money' from management education and pay the bills for business schools.

In contrast, the comparatively low perceived influence of rankings and auditors as stakeholder voices was initially somewhat surprising but it told only part of the story; there was a link between these stakeholders and the supply- and demand-driven models of management education discussed above.

On the one hand, media rankings (such as those published in the *Financial Times*) have continued to follow the customer, for example, by providing information on average earnings following graduation and the number of alumni in employment. This reinforces the shift of influence over courses and education towards students or, at least, away from faculty. On the other hand, the concerns of auditors who monitor academic value, such as EQUIS and AACSB, the key professional organizations in the management education field, can be seen as more closely aligned with a supply-driven model, with their concerns anchored to academic quality goals.

However, many deans and university administrators viewed rankings as an increasingly important performance metric and potentially a signal of reputation of management education (note: the rankings era clearly started with the first *Business Week* rankings of MBA programmes in 1987). They also pointed to the 'tyranny of the rankings era', and noted that Professor Khurana (2007) had consistently argued that rankings have a dysfunctional relationship with management education by focusing attention on financial issues like the increase in earnings of graduates or school image rather than on either academic or teaching quality concerns or addressing the need for improved problem-solving approaches by businesses. With these rankings increasingly in place as reputational metrics, a number of business school deans argued forcefully that they were increasingly being judged on their performance by alumni and university presidents or vice-chancellors in relation to the rankings. They believed that they should be reviewed on the educational quality of investments in faculty and new courses as well as subsequent improvements in teaching and research activities, rather than the 'image' metrics obtained from media rankings.

Which Issues Did Key Stakeholders Stress?

Apart from rankings pressures, it is not surprising that deans faced with far-reaching and high-paced change in the macro-environment tended to stress the significant influences of technology, globalization and competition on their strategic positioning. Yet they stated that there have been relatively few game-changing innovations in curricula design and rather incremental innovations in business models despite the increasing influence of information technology, new or emerging subject areas in management education, globalization, the changing role of faculty and the growing influence of competition and performance measures. Next, we try to explain why this might be.

Information Technology (IT)

The most commonly cited innovation in management education was the influence of information technology, and its potential role in delivering distance and e-learning. However, precisely what impact IT-driven innovation had on management education was a contested issue among the respondents in the study.

There was consensus that while much has changed in terms of IT capabilities and the range of technology available, the assessment of how it had changed management education indicated quite a modest change in the adoption of technology-enabled learning. The evidence from our interviews suggested that the role of technology had involved more cautious developments through incremental change. Some schools had launched distance learning courses, typically not as stand-alone programmes but in terms of scalable forms of teaching and assessment for management subjects (often in the core areas of accounting, finance and more quantitative subjects). Alongside this cautious approach to new technology, respondents reported that there had been relatively minor developments in curricula with respect to technology-enabled learning and relatively few faculty had been trained in the productive use of online learning in teaching.[1]

Subject Areas in Management Education

Over the period, there had been relatively minor developments in management education approaches and models. Indeed, no radical innovation or innovative new paradigm had emerged according to respondents. They suggested that curricula had changed incrementally around a fairly stable status quo academic platform.

Hence, management education maintained its reliance on core disciplines but had incorporated some newer topics. However, these often occurred within the established disciplinary silos that existed in many schools with perhaps the exception being the design of newer courses in ethics, CSR and entrepreneurship.

More recently, there was a sense that some deans would have liked to see more creative, multi-disciplinary, integrated programmes, but a concerted drive towards this ambitious goal had not emerged.

Globalization

Globalization and its influence had been stressed by many authors, notably Professors Michael Porter and Pankaj Ghemawat at HBS in an AACSB report in 2011. The sense was that adjustments had been made to curricula, but there were still considerable improvements and challenges that would probably arise in the future from having more overseas students than ever before as participants in business school programmes (as well as home students similarly beginning to take advantage of studying abroad for an academic term or year). At the same time, the international diversity of faculty was seen to be increasing, which was a positive sign for renewed curriculum development in the international management area.

The Role of Faculty

The evolving role of faculty was thrown into question, particularly in light of new technological advances and globalization. There was a growing consensus that a combination of who, where, what and how we teach was shifting away from so called 'talk and chalk' and towards different combinations of traditional teaching, online and interactive media. Consequently, respondents questioned whether the role of faculty needed to change, especially where the requirements of the marketplace suggested a more demand-driven than a supply-driven model of management education.

Competition and Performance

Alongside the pressures from a global theatre for management education, respondents also signalled changes in the competitive dynamics of management education. This took the form of increasingly strong market challenges from for-profit and private organizations including the Apollo Group, Hult, Kaplan and corporate universities. The rise in these providers in the market would provide strong challenges as well as opportunities and threats for incumbent institutions.

Summary of Interview Findings

The research revealed that much had changed in awareness about IT, new subject areas in management (e.g., CSR, ethics), the importance of globalization and the evolving role of faculty. Further, increased competitive pressures presented a more complex scenario for business schools to cope with. Yet these challenges, whilst predicted by deans in the 1996 volume, were still being faced in 2012 and had not been adequately handled by either administrators or deans.

In addition to these factors, a continued growth in student numbers and a rise in the prominence and scale of accreditation and professional bodies such as

AACSB and EQUIS were all driving changes in the relationships and relative influence of stakeholders. However, with these changes clearly emerging, and increased competitive pressures, it is important to examine what lessons were not learned by respondents in the first decade of the 21st century.

Which Lessons Were Not Learned?

There were several areas where stakeholders believed there were so-called 'blind spots' in management education. These blind spots occurred in three key areas.

The first questioned the impact of business schools on business, government and society. How impactful had management teaching and research been in relation to business and societal priorities? Deans and academics pointed to the tensions between academic rigour and practical relevance in the management discipline and questioned how the rigour-relevance gap could be bridged. They stated that, crucially, management education cannot always meet stakeholder expectations if it is perceived to be torn between becoming a legitimate academic subject (with high-quality theoretical research), establishing management as a 'true' profession and providing inspiring teaching while conducting research that is perceived to be of little value for solving real life, applied managerial problems.

The second was a concern that the inertia that exists in established academic structures and reward systems in management education inhibits the capacity of institutions to deal with the pace of change in businesses and organizations. Put simply, there are barriers to strategic change that needed to be resolved in order to achieve quicker and more flexible, agile change management in business schools. Indeed, the shortcomings of providing largely theory-driven management education without business model innovation were captured by Mintzberg's (2004) adage 'managers not MBAs' as problems in changing the culture and practices of management education.

In particular, stakeholders pointed out that well-regarded scholars such as Drucker and Mintzberg argued for a far greater understanding of the practice of management as opposed to the alleged narrow, short-term approaches adopted by our students, in which management education was structured around disciplinary silos, which offered no, or limited, integration across management concepts for students. Institutions were designed to deliver teaching in silos that had grown up from the various business disciplines but had largely failed to present an integrated view of the processes and practices of management.

Therefore, a third element in lessons not learned suggested that there was a serious blind spot in being able to deliver more transformational models of integrated management education, let alone developing a repertoire of practical management skills that could be taught in a more enlightened fashion.

Overall, the evidence implied that there was a lack of focus on practice, too much teaching in silos with no integration, a narrow focus on rational managerial behaviour and academic research, all of which reduced the effectiveness of management education in teaching the 'Art of Managing'.

Consequently, overcoming the blind spots in the interface between research and teaching, improving the quality of teaching as well as the content of management curricula and business models would clearly help management educators to develop better managers and business leaders through more focused knowledge development and dissemination processes.

Can Deans/Leaders Change Management Education?

Given the sometimes conflicting evidence in the 2011/12 survey, the diverse viewpoints of stakeholders and the many issues and lessons not learned that they identified, it is appropriate to ask whether more radical change would be possible in re-designing management education and its models. Why had the challenges of change, competitive pressure and innovation resulted in largely incremental strategic change?

More positive evidence emerging from the survey demonstrated a common and refreshing desire to revitalize curricula and encourage diversity in teaching and learning approaches, although little effort had been made to address those concerns. In addition, there was a felt need to understand, from the lessons of history, how business schools got it wrong during the global financial crisis and to stimulate rankings and accreditation agencies to focus more deeply on schools' educational distinctiveness and programmes rather than, particularly via rankings, building on a value proposition that stressed growth in graduate salaries and reputation. Yet there was little evidence of attempts to achieve more disruptive, transformational change.

What is evident is that business schools occupy a difficult position in attempting to straddle the conflicting goals of academic legitimacy and identity and management practice where, arguably, the needs of neither are met! Crainer and Dearlove (1998) caricature this predicament, with business schools portrayed as schizophrenic organizations that must demonstrate their capacity as bona fide academic institutions, generate knowledge to provide solutions to management problems and at the same time perform as businesses.

Alternative models had nevertheless been suggested for strengthening the perceived legitimacy of business schools in the eyes of management practitioners and other stakeholders. These include stakeholder models such as the Copenhagen Business School's Public Management Initiative, schools advocating a pragmatic professional model and schools oriented towards a liberal management education with an arts/humanities or knowledge-based focus. However, few had yet gained significant traction.

But the key question from the survey evidence is whether business schools will, in the future, exhibit a willingness to change and adopt new approaches to management education. One problem that is central to answering this question is the quality of leadership by deans with respect to faculty and staff in business schools. The main issue here is the 'management of autonomy'.

How should deans mediate a decision-making process and serve as a bridge between the interests of external stakeholders and faculty? Collegiality, in terms of critical debate and open communication by faculty, and persuasion should dominate bureaucratic control if strategic change is to be successfully implemented by deans in business schools. Mintzberg (1998) confirms that covert forms of strategic leadership might be preferred in academic environments. A metaphor for such a leader might be the conductor of an orchestra. Translation into the business school environment implies little direct supervision from deans but rather 'protection and support' that creates legitimacy and reputation for the business school.

The second associated problem, and criticism, that was often raised involved a deficit of strategic leadership in many business schools. Deans have been variously described as 'jugglers', 'dictators', 'doves of peace' and 'dragons'. Their roles are seen as multi-faceted, stressful and often characterized as similar to middle managers squeezed for resources, at least in the university context, between university presidents and demanding faculty members. Further, deans face short tenures (the median tenure of a business school dean is four to five years), ambitious goals and critical challenges as they lead schools through their future evolution. As a consequence, particularly of time pressure, many deans have probably 'muddled through' and made incremental, minor changes to their existing business schools' models and scenarios. (This was confirmed by the responses from academics in the research sample who focused narrowly on improving the status quo.)

There are a few deans who have the experience, time, the courage, determination and resilience to follow through their chosen path and succeed with their chosen strategic direction. Success is personified by leaders such as Bain, Borges and Lorange in their transformational tenures at LBS, INSEAD and IMD respectively in the 1990s. They reached the quality level described by Jim Collins (2001) as Level 5 leaders who possess 'a paradoxical combination of personal humility and professional will'. These are the great leaders who leave behind lasting legacies.

The evidence from this research study on ways forward was discussed alongside the concerns of EFMD's Board and this led EFMD to produce and publish a manifesto (based on some of the early research evidence) on 'The Future of Management Education' (24 January, 2012), reflecting a more European-style of business school which could be achieved by deans adopting five clear principles as follows:

- **Transformational Change**

    Business schools will have to change the way they operate. They should take a multiple stakeholder perspective in the design of their programmes and research activities. Schools should be transformed into moral institutions that perpetuate strong values, a clear vision and open processes in governance and strategic change.

- **A More Holistic Approach to Management Education**

    Business schools should incorporate a more integrated and liberal view of management education in which knowledge of the humanities, culture and history can be integrated into the principles of responsible management and form a framework for cross-disciplinary thinking. This implies that issues of ethics, moral responsibility and sustainability 'should be embedded in the core curricula of management education as well as in the broader practices of schools'.

- **Sustainability**

    'Sustainability, with its ecological, social and economic dimensions' requires those in management education to 'carefully consider cultural and developmental differences when dealing with sustainability issues'.

- **Critical Thinking and Whole Person Learning**

    Critical thinking must be designed to emerge from the tension between learning about humanistic principles and the more professional, analytic business subjects such as accounting, finance and marketing. Students must learn how to absorb skills of both analysis and synthesis but also develop a personal willingness to reflect on issues and incorporate self-criticism into the learning process.

- **Accreditations (such as EFMD Quality Improvement System)**

    Accreditations must be updated to reflect the advent of multiple stake-holder perspectives and a more holistic approach to management education. They must also recognize that 75–80% of all business school students are participants in undergraduate programmes. The focus on the MBA by many business schools (largely because of MBA-based reputational media rankings) has diverted attention from undergraduate business education.

The evidence through 2013 from EFMD's scholars and surveys, namely the *Training the Fire Brigade* 1996 volume and the 2011/12 survey (Thomas et al., 2013a, 2013b), indicated that although many of the (existing) challenges and issues remained the same, there was a real willingness among stakeholders/deans to re-think and consider changes in management education models.

Using Open Innovation on Ourselves: The Global Business Education Jams and the Future Transformation and Change Options for Business Schools

Therefore, after the publication of the *Promises Unfulfilled* and *Securing the Future* volumes (2013, 2014) that followed the 2011/12 survey, the work of Howard Thomas and his colleagues continued (with strong support particularly from EFMD as well as AACSB and GMAC). They also gained support from (global) companies (such as IBM and J&J) and other businesses to engage in an open innovation process to further debate and re-imagine the future of management education through the Business Education Jam. This process would address many of the issues and challenges identified in 1996 and 2011/12 and were exemplified in the 2012 EFMD manifesto.

While our scholarly lenses often focus on firm strategic challenges and changes in the disruptive business world, we chose to turn our focus instead to that of our own industry 'management education', and the likely disruptions facing business schools. Leveraging the open innovation concept of a 'jam', global forums of stakeholders were created with a free-flowing convergence of ideas and considerations for the future business model of business education (Carlile et al., 2016).

Overview of the Business Education Jam

The concept of open innovation has been explored by strategy scholars and practised by business leaders seeking to obtain external input especially in light of the complexity of global business systems. The concept of a 'jam' comes from jazz musicians who come together to play unprepared music, often creating new ideas in the process. The Business Education Jam process embodied that tradition by bringing together a diverse and creative group to bounce ideas, skills and concepts around to ignite open innovation in our industry.

Innovation is becoming more open as organizations require more contextual and market relevance given the increasing stakes of evolving a market-based strategy and business model (Chesbrough, 2003). While leaders of business schools often converge for conferences that discuss ideas and trends, many have been critical of their lack of radical innovation and transformation following the traditions established in business education in the 1960s.

The Business Education Jam has been a significant and continuing open innovation project which started in 2014/15. This collaborative project has been the work of a research team led by Howard Thomas at the Questrom School of Business at Boston University. It started in earnest to rethink the business model and the requisite assumptions for future models of business and management education.

The first jam, a 'crowd-sourcing jam', took place in 2014 in Boston over 60 consecutive hours. Thousands of people around the world, including researchers, scholars, students, thought leaders and executives, were all united in a unique virtual environment to re-imagine the distinctive models of business schools. Digital discussion forums sparked a multitude of conversations, collaborations and potential themes of interest. Quick poll surveys gave a real-time look at where participants stood on issues such as programme length and the value of an MBA. Thousands of participants across the globe logged on and contributed more than 7,000 posts to the ten discussion forums which had clearly emerged from the findings of the 2011/12 EFMD research: Supporting 21st Century Competencies; Increasing the Value of Management Education; Engaging New Generation Students & Employees; Producing Research with Impact; Fostering Ethical Leadership; Cultivating Innovation & Entrepreneurship; Driving Learning Experiences; Harnessing Digital Technology; Challenging the Business Model of Education; and Evaluating Policy & Rankings.

Following the success of the initial jam in 2014/15, smaller, global jams around the world were launched, to not only spread the open innovation idea, but also better understand the unique regional challenges and ideas in our industry outside of North America and Europe. This set of regional jams was conducted in South Africa, United Arab Emirates, Austria, China, Mexico, Tanzania, Singapore, Canada, Japan and Egypt with great success.

It emerged that the dominant North American model of management education had been imitated widely and adapted to reflect differences in national norms, cultures and contexts. We noted, in particular, that there were strong influences from government and civil society on the conduct of business schools globally. We found clusters of types of business schools such as the North American group, the UK and continental Europe, Scandinavian models, South-East Asian clusters, Indian and South American clusters operating in diverse regional economic and social contexts.

These discussions increasingly focused on socially responsible changes and purposeful challenges, which indicated strong views about the value of, and different rationales for, management education in addressing the needs of a broad set of countries, cultures and contexts. Some discussants and scholars also put forward alternative models of business schools based on greater civic and corporate engagement, the inclusion of humanities as well as closer interdisciplinary integration within the university (e.g., with other professional schools such as engineering, medicine and law).

It was clear from all the jam debates that there should be a much broader appreciation of different management education models in existence globally. While Western developed economies may have provided fundamental structures and models for business schools, they can certainly learn from developing and emergent economies that have prepared for and confronted economic, health, climate and sustainability crises that have required more inclusive and socially responsive forms of capitalism. Indeed, we noted that a wider discourse about purposeful social capitalism was possible that went beyond Western models of shareholder capitalism.

Yet, there was considerable consensus in the jams about creating socially responsible leaders with a clear moral and ethical compass. These leaders would need to develop a more holistic perspective of management education based on a balanced tri-sector collaboration and partnership between business, government and society. This would allow business schools to re-assert their influences on the many, diverse interests of their ecosystem stakeholders. It was also felt that thought must be directed to the design of meaningful models of liberal, responsible management education to produce humanistic global leaders and citizens in a socially responsible and sustainable framework.

Conclusion

Little did we know, in late November 2019, that the upcoming global pandemic would, through its crisis-oriented context, provide a hugely disruptive and challenging impact on business schools and stimulate urgent innovative and transformative changes to business school models of strategy and operations.

But some of these challenges would not be of the 'one size fits all' variety, and would be far more specific, meaningful and potentially transformational than those identified in either the 1996 or 2011/12 studies, or even in the jams.

To further advance business education, prompted by the pandemic transformation, we need a comprehensive dialogue that recognizes the critical nature of national and regional challenges which the global economy will face as the pandemic evolves as being a necessary prerequisite for designing a range of future business school scenarios and models. The final chapter therefore examines, given our detailed discussion of the largely incremental nature of business school evolution over 50 years, how business schools should now respond to the disruptive challenges of the pandemic and address associated issues of technological change, digitization, inclusive growth and the role of governance and tri-sector collaboration in revitalizing and re-shaping business school models for their future evolution in a somewhat ambiguous and volatile environment (the so-called 'new normal'!).

Note

1 We will see, later in this chapter, how IT enabled radical changes to course delivery during the pandemic of 2020/21.

References

Agnelli, G. (1996) in EFMD (1996) *Training the fire brigade: Preparing for the unimaginable*. Brussels: EFMD Publications, p.117.

Bain, G. (1996) in EFMD (1996) *Training the fire brigade: Preparing for the unimaginable*. Brussels: EFMD Publications, p.89.

Bennis, W.G. and J. O'Toole (2005) How business schools lost their way. *Harvard Business Review*, 83(5), pp.96–104.

Carlile, P.R., S.H. Davidson, K.W. Freeman, H. Thomas and N. Venkatraman (2016) *Re-imagining business education: Insights and actions from the business education jam*. Bingley: Emerald Publishing.

Chesbrough, H. (2003) *Open innovation: The new imperative for creating and profiting from technology*. Cambridge, MA: Harvard Business School Press.

Collins, J.C. (2001) *Good to great: Why some companies make the leap … and others don't*. New York: Harper Collins.

Crainer, S. and D. Dearlove (1998) *Gravy training: Inside the world's top business schools*. Oxford: Capstone Press.

Danos, P. (2011) Foreword, In S. Iniguez (Ed.), *The learning curve*, pp.xiv–xv. London: Palgrave Macmillan.

EFMD (1996) *Training the fire brigade: Preparing for the unimaginable*. Brussels: EFMD Publications.

Fragueiro, F. and H. Thomas (2011) *Strategic leadership in the business school: Keeping one step ahead*. Cambridge: Cambridge University Press.

Ghoshal, S. (2005) Bad management theories are destroying good management practices. *Academy of Management Learning and Education*, 4(1), pp.75–91.

Grey, C. (2005) Chapter 5 in *A very short, interesting and reasonably cheap book about studying organisations*. London: Sage.

Hamel, G. (1996) in EFMD (1996) *Training the fire brigade: Preparing for the unimaginable*. Brussels: EFMD Publications, p.113.

Handy, C.B. (1996) in EFMD (1996) *Training the fire brigade: Preparing for the unimaginable*. Brussels: EFMD Publications, p.11.

Hubert, T. (1996) in EFMD (1996) *Training the fire brigade: Preparing for the unimaginable*. Brussels: EFMD Publications, p.27.

Jacobs, M. (2009, April 24) How business schools have failed business. *Wall Street Journal*, p.A13.

Kerr, S. (1975) Folly of rewarding A, while hoping for B. *Academy of Management Journal*, 18(4), pp.769–783.

Khurana, R. (2007) *From higher aims to hired hands: The social transformation of American Business Schools and the unfulfilled promise of management as a profession*. Princeton, NJ: Princeton University Press.

Locke, E.C. and J.C. Spender (2011) *Confronting manageralism*. London: Zed Books.

Lorange, P. (1996) in EFMD (1996) *Training the fire brigade: Preparing for the unimaginable*. Brussels: EFMD Publications, pp.141–142.

Mintzberg, H. (1998) Covert leadership: Notes on managing professionals. *Harvard Business Review*, 76(6), pp. 140–147.

Mintzberg, H. (2004) *Managers not MBAs*. Harlow: Pearson Education.

Nussbaum, M.C. (1997) *Cultivating humanity: A classical defence of reform in liberal education*. Cambridge, MA: Harvard University Press.

Osbaldeston, M (1996) in EFMD (1996) *Training the fire brigade: Preparing for the unimaginable*. Brussels: EFMD Publications, pp.215–216.

Pfeffer, J. and C.T. Fong (2002) The end of business schools? Less success than meets the eye. *Academy of Management Learning and Education*, 1(1), pp.79–95.

Prahalad, C.K. (1996) in EFMD (1996) *Training the fire brigade: Preparing for the unimaginable*. Brussels: EFMD Publications, p.109.

Rameau, C. (1996) in EFMD (1996) *Training the fire brigade: Preparing for the unimaginable*. Brussels: EFMD Publications, p.57.

Schlegelmilch, B.B. and H. Thomas (2011) The MBA in 2020: Will there still be one? *Journal of Management Development*, 30(5), pp.474–482.

Schoemaker, P.J.H. (2008) The future challenges of business: Re-thinking management education. *California Management Review*, 50(3), pp.119–139.

Thomas, H. (2012) What is the European Management School Model? *Global Focus*, 6(1), pp.18–21.

Thomas, H., M. Lee, L. Thomas and A. Wilson (2013a) *Securing the future of management education*. Bingley: Emerald Publishing.

Thomas, H., L. Thomas and A. Wilson (2013b) *Promises fulfilled and unfulfilled in management education*. Bingley: Emerald Publishing.

Tsui, A. (2015) Re-connecting with the business world: socially responsible scholarship. *Global Focus*, 9(1), pp.36–39.

Van Schaik, G. (1996) in EFMD (1996) *Training the fire brigade: Preparing for the unimaginable*. Brussels: EFMD Publications, pp.13–14.

2
What Are Business School Deans Expected to Do?

Introduction

In this chapter, we provide insights into the norms expected of business school deans. We examine vision, mission and values statements and compare job titles and descriptions in different countries, institutional contexts and cultures. Historically, there has been a role shift from deans as educators in collegial models of management education to deans as executives in more managerialist systems, subject to marketplace exigencies (Thomas, 2013, 2014; Thomas et al., 2013a, 2013b., 2014b). We also draw on business school sector, national, university, business school and individual perspectives to understand deans' predicaments in university-based, stand-alone, public, private, non-profit, family/private equity owned and merged business schools.

Metaphors are helpful to distinguish deans' identities as boundary spanners, diplomats, stewards, jugglers, tightrope walkers, buffers and umbrellas in the squeezed middle as hybrid scholar-managers, executives and entrepreneurs. Deans experience losses as they transition into the position and craft their preferred identities (Brown et al., 2021). We discuss academic and non-traditional types of deans who exercise various degrees of freedom to navigate the 'oil and water' (Simon, 1967) of management scholarship and practice to establish their legitimacy and impact.

A growing concern for media rankings, branding and the bottom line in achieving targets in the 'performative university' (Jones et al., 2020) means that the character of business school deans is tested in challenging circumstances in dealing with social and technical tensions, centralization, compliance, integration in parent universities and differentiation to be positioned competitively. Deans now also find themselves on a burning platform of culture wars, grand challenges, casualized workforce, IT platforms and edtech companies such as AWS Educate.

DOI: 10.4324/9781003178125-2

We highlight the most time-consuming activities for deans (AACSB, 2021), including working with central administration, strategic planning, developing academic programmes, managing accreditations, fundraising, corporate engagement, faculty development, communications, budget planning, faculty and student recruitment and retention and risk/crisis management. Historical accounts of deans' achievements, publications by deans on business school leadership (e.g., articles in EFMD's *Global Focus*) and media reports announcing new deans, successes, scandals and exits offer interesting sources for studying deans' dilemmas in dealing with people, processes and partners, career trajectories, enjoyment, attrition and exhaustion in the role. Examples of serial and long-serving deans and of those who suddenly exit exemplify job-hopping, distinguished, disgraced deans and those in denial. We note that the arrival of a new university vice-chancellor/president can be an especially stressful and precarious time for business school deans.

Finally, this chapter considers deans' views during the COVID-19 pandemic and in the context of greater government policy focus on STEM disciplines (science, technology, engineering and mathematics). We also consider the pipeline for business school deans and their vital role in not only supporting national productivity, institutional revenues, business school standards, wider social impact, their personal legitimacy and generativity – a concern for 'establishing and guiding the next generation [which includes] productivity and creativity' (Erikson, 1950). Nowadays, courage is required for deans to deal with geo-political realities, disciplined imagination, knowledge about trends and networking. Business school deans need to be role models in nurturing inclusive and respectful cultures, guarding against 'rot at the top' (Kets de Vries, 2021) in the governance structure.

Vision, Mission and Values Statements

Clearly, vision, mission and values statements guide deans' behaviours. We synthesized the vision, mission and values statements of ten global business schools: CEIBS, Columbia Business School, Fundação Dom Cabral, Indian Institute of Management, INSEAD, Lagos Business School, Melbourne University Faculty of Business & Economics, Tsinghua University School of Economics and Management, Warwick Business School and Wits Business School. The vision statements all mentioned aspiring to be leading, world-class, the most respected, a premier business school globally by creating and disseminating deep and high-impact knowledge (about general management practices), innovation and transformational ideas through teaching and research. The visions referred to developing business professionals and organizations with high ethical standards, critically evaluating and influencing policy design, corporate governance and business practices for positive, progressive and sustainable impact on our stakeholders and society locally and globally.

Excerpts from mission statements amongst this group of business schools include a renewed focus on purpose, impact, goals, services, market and location:

- To educate responsible leaders versed in 'China Depth, Global Breadth'. (CEIBS)

- To advance knowledge and cultivate leaders for China and the world. (Tsinghua University School of Economics and Management)

- A community of people committed to creating and transmitting management and business knowledge based on a Christian conception of the human person and of economic activity and relevant to Nigeria and Africa at large. We strive to be a world-class business school which will have a significant impact on the practice of management. (Lagos Business School)

- Bring together people, cultures and ideas to develop responsible leaders who transform business and society. (INSEAD)

- Educating and developing leaders and builders of enterprises who create value for their stakeholders and society at large. Developing new scholars and teachers, creating and disseminating pathbreaking knowledge, concepts, and tools which advance the understanding and practice of management. (Columbia Business School)

- To contribute to the sustainable development of society by educating, developing and building the skills of executives, entrepreneurs and public managers. (Fundação Dom Cabral)

- To develop innovative and ethical future leaders capable of managing change and transformation in a globally competitive environment and to advance the theory and practice of management. (Indian Institute of Management)

- We enable individuals and organizations to be global leaders through the creation, application and dissemination of business and economics knowledge. (Melbourne University Faculty of Business & Economics)

- To provide a transformational learning experience, enabling our stakeholders to realize their full potential. (Warwick Business School)

- To graduate agile and ethical leaders who are a force for positive change locally and globally. We will achieve this through empowering education, relevant research and impactful public discourse. These will be informed by the principles of critical thinking, innovation and sustainability. (Wits Business School)

Figure 2.1 Most frequent words in values statements for ten b-schools.
Source: Authors.

The most frequent words in values statements for the ten schools emphasize learning, integrity, respect, community and excellence (Figure 2.1):

Deans' (e.g., Stanford Graduate School) farewell reflections when stepping down also indicate what is perceived to matter officially. These include, for example, innovations, collaborations and community engagement as well as sustainability, rankings and accreditations (e.g., Durham Business School), capital projects, curriculum redesign, fundraising, greater diversity in the student body and research centres (e.g., Wharton). The challenge for business school deans is to fit the expectations of what a business school dean should be doing in the eyes of key stakeholders while ensuring stretch goals to address changes in work and society more broadly locally, regionally, nationally and globally.

Job Titles

We use the generic term 'dean' to refer to an individual who has the most significant authority for a tertiary level academic unit which offers business and management studies. Originally, the term was applied to the leader of 10 soldiers or monks. It was subsequently adopted in schools and universities to describe leaders with administrative duties. While a span of control of ten direct reports may still be optimal for a dean, the complexity, pace and scale of the business school leader's role has increased significantly over time.

The title for an individual who is leading a business school, school of business, school of management or equivalent has gradually evolved and varies in different parts of the world. Before the massification of higher education, a senior insider who was a top scholar might have been quietly elected or invited to chair a department of management for a few years, possibly pre-retirement, before the position rotated democratically to another seasoned full professor.

At Wharton, the title 'director' rather than dean was used in the 19th century and up until the 1930s. A 'president' heads Copenhagen Business School and Hult International Business School and a 'managing director' leads HEM Business School, Morocco. In France, 'director general' is commonly used, while one of the grandest sounding titles, 'Rector Magnificus', is held in the Netherlands such as in Nyenrode Business University. More recent titles for UK and Australian business school leaders include 'executive dean' and 'pro-vice-chancellor' (possibly with a pan-university specialism such as entrepreneurship). The University of St. Andrews has had (deputy) 'co-heads' of the School of Management in the past and the University of Sydney Business School appointed 'co-deans'. Acting and interim deans are also interesting appointments, especially when there are successive temporary deans, raising questions about whether the head of the university (rather than the dean) is directing or micromanaging a school's strategy.

The Open University in the UK has an Executive Dean of the Faculty of Business and Law and a Head of the Business School. In Monash University there is a Dean of the Faculty of Business and Economics who is also Head of the Business School. Exeter Business School is led by a Pro-Vice Chancellor and Executive Dean. The range of disciplines for which the dean (or equivalent) is responsible may include the law school, economics, governance (Murdoch University), social sciences (Aarhus University), technology (ESMT, Berlin), hospitality (SC Johnson College of Business, Cornell University), and an explicit focus on society (Glasgow Caledonian University; TIAS School for Business and Society).

Despite the 'squeezed middle manager' portrayal of deans, one university vice-chancellor (equivalent to president) stated that he views his business school dean as a mini vice-chancellor. In contrast, Peter Lorange was the owner, President, and CEO of the Lorange Institute of Business Zürich, and sold his own business school to become the European campus of CEIBS. The title, or equiv-alent, of business school dean, therefore, belies a range of different role types, from compliant administrator to strategic business unit leader and academic entrepreneur.

There is also a proliferation of titles such as pro-dean, vice, senior deputy, dep-uty, assistant, associate, academic and other deans as well as chief academic officer within senior leadership teams of business schools. Ginsberg (2011) talked about armies of 'deanlets' and 'deanlings' in his polemic about the all-administrative university.

It is interesting to compare the founding dean of a particular school with more recent successors. For example, Arthur Earle, a Canadian businessman and the first Principal of London Business School (LBS) in 1964 responded to an ad-vertisement for the position that sought an 'egghead tycoon'. A sign of his busi-ness acumen is that Earle negotiated administrative autonomy for LBS within the University of London. Over half a century later, the ninth dean of LBS, François Ortalo-Magné, is described as Head and CEO. He is responsible to the governing body for guiding the School's direction, shaping its values and standards, and balancing 'current priorities with future investment' to help 'the School's major constituents achieve their objectives'. Although the titles have changed for the head of LBS, the balancing act that incumbents must fulfil remains.

It is interesting to see instances of a deanship being advertised and the new appointment becoming a faculty dean and then appointing a dean or head of the business school. This indicates that the job of leading a faculty is too large for one individual to focus sufficiently on the business school within it. There is a risk in such cases of a vacuum being created, with a faculty dean being a member of the university's senior executive team and 'going native' while the head of the business school has little discretion over financial investments in the business school and the sub-brand. On the one hand, this means that the role of the business school dean has been enlarged with pan-university respon-sibilities while at the same time diminished, with a business school head no longer reporting to the head of the university.

In contrast, we might assume that deans of stand-alone business schools ex-ercise considerable autonomy as they do not manage cash cows that cross-subsidize other disciplines, which is common in universities. At the same time, they are more vulnerable to the vicissitudes common to executive education markets, as we have seen in Ashridge Business School, Henley Business School and Thunderbird School of Global Management before they merged with more financially stable partners.

It is interesting that Symonds (2009) portrays a golden age 'when becoming the dean of a major business school was like winning the lottery. It meant a comfortable gig with good pay, prestige, the opportunity to mix with the great and good of business, politics and academia and, perhaps best of all, the kind of job security enjoyed now only by popes.' Indeed, historically the chair of a department of management in some institutions was once a modest part-time role, primus inter pares, with an internally elected scholar (typically a professor) emerging among equals to take on the deanship on a rotating basis. Typically, before the age of rankings in kinder and gentler times, budgets were not devolved and business school deans focused on management education rather than on business school branding.

As well as changes over time in the level of comfort and precarity in the role of dean, there are clearly different risks in different types of business schools in various parts of the world. In universities where deans are civil servants and there is less hype about paying premium salaries, transitions into and out of the deanship may be relatively smooth. For example, in some contexts, the deanship is a government appointment for three years or a comfortable pre-retirement pension-boosting end-of-career career move. In other cases, the business school deanship has become a high-stakes, highly pressured but precarious executive position. One dean we interviewed described himself as a 'hired gun' to overhaul a business school and moved on after three years.

We see examples of global recruitment campaigns led by executive search firms using glossy brochures in search of a high profile 'corporate savior' (Khurana, 2002) dean, only to be followed by announcements of sudden departures, like national football managers who are unceremoniously fired for losing a World Cup football match. The *Washington Post* (Anderson, 2013) reported how Doug Guthrie at GWU Business School was charged with driving the school into the top 25 and praised for extending the school's presence in China. He was subsequently fired as dean although he remained as a tenured professor (before moving to Apple University). This arose as a result of disagreements over lower-than-expected surpluses from the business school because of the dean's investments in online education. This dramatic incident indicates the types of challenges faced by many business school deans who are responsible for the university's 'cash cow' and charged with climbing the business school rankings despite a lack of financial investment by the central university in the business school.

Lessons drawn from such incidents lead us to advise individuals (particularly outsiders) who are considering a new role as the head of a business school to undertake due diligence. One headhunter (executive search firm consultant) observed that the business school deanship is the most oversold position in the university, and interviews for business school dean are the ones that candidates are most likely to withdraw from when they realize this. Aspiring deans need to explore their own reporting lines, governance structures, financial arrangements and contractual terms in relation to performance expectations. Some candidates for a deanship insist before they accept a position that they report directly to the head of the university. Others have been appointed and quit when they feel demoted following internal mergers that result in them reporting to a college dean within the university rather than to the overall head of the institution. Even for deans who have carefully negotiated their terms and conditions, these can be reneged on if they are not in writing and the trigger of a new boss can overturn existing arrangements and lead to early exits for deans.

Clearly, deans can experience induction crises once they do take on the role. Two highly successful deans took six months to a year to take up new appointments and used this time to undertake institutional research, interviewing their colleagues, reading minutes, and consulting with others so that they could present a strategy and 'hit the ground running' when they officially arrived in their new roles.

One model of a business school deanship we do not advocate is that of the 'lone ranger'. A critical early decision for a newly appointed dean is to consider the structure of his or her senior management team and to determine who they can trust within their group of informal advisors. One externally appointed dean bitterly regretted allowing an unsuccessful internal candidate for the deanship to remain in the dean's team as he subsequently realized that this individual could not be trusted. The dean's senior team might include positions such as a chief operating officer, chief finance officer, pro-deans for research, engagement and impact, for external affairs, faculty development, teaching and learning, associate deans for business development, regional engagement, undergraduate programmes, postgraduate taught programmes, doctoral and research programmes, equity diversity and inclusion, director of executive education, as well as heads of groups organized by discipline.

Clearly, the shape of the dean's team partly depends on how it complements the incumbent's strengths and limitations. Some deans focus on fundraising and business development, others see themselves as champions of the faculty while others may position them more as dean of students. Following a highly successful executive career, Ken Freeman, Dean Emeritus of Boston University's Questrom School of Business, was mindful in overseeing faculty promotions that he included a full professor in meetings with individuals. At Warwick Business School, a former Chairman, Robin Wensley, was subsequently appointed as Deputy Dean. In NUS Business School Singapore, the Dean, Bernard Yeung, also appointed his interim predecessor, Hum Sin Hoon, as Deputy Dean and this continued following the appointment of Andrew Rose as Dean.

Leading a stand-alone private business school like INSEAD is clearly different in many respects from a full-service business school in a comprehensive civic university located in a remote region. Some deans can move apparently seamlessly from research-intensive business schools to modern teaching-focused universities. Kai Peters moved from being Dean of the research-intensive Rotterdam School of Management to heading a standalone executive education charity in rural Ashridge as CEO, to a role as Chief Academic Officer in Hult International Business School (family owned with international campuses), to becoming Pro-Vice-Chancellor of the Faculty of Business & Law at Coventry University, a large undergraduate public sector teaching-focused institution. Transferable skills in business development and income generation can help deans to move from one type of business school to another. For other individuals, it is a matter of 'horses for courses', with some highly cited deans confining themselves to research-intensive business schools primarily as research leaders, while other deans very much see themselves primarily as full-time administrators and choose to work in institutions that play to their strengths. Unfortunately, several financially successful deans without top publications have left their positions suddenly when a new research-active boss arrives and expects the dean to be a top scholar. Curiously, in one graduate school the well-cited dean oversaw a financial deficit and was far less successful in generating financial surpluses than his predecessor who lacked either a doctorate or publications.

As the well-respected Indian management scholar and educator Sumantra Ghoshal commented at Davos in 1995, 'the smell of the place' (Ghoshal, 1995) is critical for how people perform in organizations. He argued that 'dominance as a management (and communication) style is not good in any circumstances'. If deans adopt this approach in business schools, they create cultures like 'downtown Calcutta in summer', sapping workers' energy through constraints, compliance, controls and contracts. Instead, Ghoshal called for leaders to create organizational cultures that are reminiscent of walking in a Fontainebleau forest in the springtime, i.e., based on discipline, stretch, support and trust, with employees excited and intrinsically motivated to aim for higher goals.

Job Descriptions and Person Specifications for Business School Deanships

Figures 2.2 and 2.3 indicate the job requirements and person specification for a Faculty Executive Dean in the Open University Business School in the UK which is 50 years old and specializes in distance learning. The focus appears to be on delivering against academic objectives and consulting internally. The

Figure 2.2 Job requirements for the Open University Faculty of Business & Law deanship.
Source: Authors.

Figure 2.3 Person specification – Open University Faculty of Business & Law deanship.
Source: Authors.

job and personal profiles (Figures 2.4 and 2.5) for the Dean of Lee Kong Chian School of Business at Singapore Management University appear more dynamic in a much younger business school. It is also triple-accredited but better funded by the government, with firm ambitions to be a leading business school in Asia that is innovative and entrepreneurial. The third example (Figures 2.6 and 2.7) illustrates job and personal profiles for a faculty deanship in a large unaccredited new university in the UK. The span of control and responsibilities are larger with a much stronger managerialist focus on meeting targets and controlling expenditure.

'Academic', 'collaborate', 'innovative', 'leader', 'research', 'strategist' and 'visionary' are key words in the appointment material that describes the job profile with a reference to public value, while fundraising is low in the list of priorities. There is a strong focus on a collaborative culture at SMU.

Figure 2.5 indicates the importance of experience in academic administration, leadership and management in a complex environment. It highlights commitment to Singapore and Asia, government relations and the ability to articulate foresight about the future of management education. There is also a reference to inclusivity.

Figure 2.4 Job profile for the LKCSB deanship at Singapore Management University. Source: Authors.

Figure 2.5 Personal profile expected for the LKCSB deanship, Singapore Management University. Source: Authors.

Figure 2.6 Job profile – Plymouth University Executive Dean, Faculty of Business & Law. Source: Authors.

Figure 2.7 Personal profile, Plymouth University Executive Dean, Faculty of Business & Law. Source: Authors.

In dissecting job descriptions, it is useful to consider the formal statements made about the seniority of a role in the case of university-based business schools, which is indicated by whether they report to the head of the institution. In some cases, following restructuring into larger schools, faculties or colleges, the deanship has been 'demoted' to no longer report to the most senior person in the organization, while others have been promoted to become head of the newly formed entity. In the former case, business school deans have quit a university because they do not want an added layer of bureaucracy.

Historical Accounts of Deanships

As an example of the changes for deans over almost 150 years, we can look at the evolution of the deanship from the founder and the roles of successive deans at Wharton, even though this is a US-based, private, well-endowed business school that has a particularly quantitative economic focus that is not typically found in Europe. Early deans in 19th century collegiate or university-based business schools were men, often with industrial and/or military experience. For example, in 1881, Joseph Wharton was a Quaker and US entrepreneur and industrialist (the largest shareholder in Bethlehem Iron Company) who founded the world's first collegiate school of business in the University of Pennsylvania, with a strong interest in Taylor's scientific management and the natural sciences (Wharton Magazine, 2007). Edmund James, Wharton's first director (1883–96), completed his PhD in Germany and was appointed Professor of Public Finance and Administration as well as Professor of Political and Social Science in the Department of Philosophy. Simon Patten, the second director (1896–1912), an economist, believed that there would soon be sufficient wealth to satisfy people's basic needs provided there was social action to achieve these goals. He introduced 'practical philanthropy' into the curriculum. However, his forceful anti-war views resulted in his premature retirement.

The interests of Wharton's deans over time indicate how business school deans generally can make a difference. For example, Roswell McCrea strengthened the school's ties with government administrators in Philadelphia, which illustrates the importance of civic engagement and public value. During and post-World War II, Canby Balderston led a fundraising campaign to construct Wharton School's first building. William McClellan worked with university trustees to raise the profile of the School within the University, which emphasizes the status of business and management education in relation to other more traditional disciplines such as STEM disciplines. Subsequently, Emory Johnson required faculty and students to specialize in a professional subject which provided depth. Joseph Willits emphasized the importance of economic research in business studies, which was questioned in the 2008 Global Financial Crisis (Currie et al., 2016), and provides a dilemma for some deans today, who may decide to shift economists into a department of economics (e.g., Warwick University chose to develop a strong department of economics alongside a strong business school). Alfred Williams became President of the Philadelphia Federal Reserve Bank after his deanship, mirroring the former Dean of Rotman School of Management, University of Toronto, Tiff Macklem, who subsequently became Governor of the Bank of Canada.

Later deans reformed the curriculum, particularly in entrepreneurship (Willis Winn), strengthened interdisciplinary programmes and inter-school degrees (Donald Carroll) with an undergraduate degree in management and technology, improved the quality of admissions and built a conference centre (Russell Palmer). Thomas Gerrity ensured programmes reflected the importance of technology. In the 21st century, following his roles as deputy and interim dean, Patrick Harker created Wharton West in San Francisco and the AI West Learning Laboratory, forged alliances with INSEAD and Singapore Management University (SMU), and completed the largest fundraising campaign in any business school, the Campaign for Sustained Leadership. He also established Knowledge at Wharton and Wharton School Publishing. He had completed a PhD in civil and urban engineering, held a joint appointment as Professor of Electrical and Systems Engineering, and was a co-principal investigator on a $6m Sloan Foundation project to study productivity and technological impacts in financial services. Additionally, he served as a trustee of Goldman Sachs Trust and the Board of Goldman Sachs Hedge Fund Partners, as well as a Diocesan Finance Council, was on Juniper Bank's advisory board, and a founding member of the Board of the National Leadership Roundtable on Church Management. Later, he became a White House Fellow, Special Assistant to the Director of the FBI and Editor-in-Chief of the top journal *Operations Research*.

Following his deanship, Harker became a university president and then President and CEO of the Federal Reserve Bank of Philadelphia. Harker was succeeded as Dean of Wharton by Thomas Robertson, a Scottish-born marketing professor and former Dean at Emory Business School and Deputy Dean of London Business School and a board director of the Carlyle Group. At Wharton, he implemented a new MBA curriculum, a new public policy initiative, created modular courses in ten countries, a research and teaching campus in Beijing, and designed a portfolio of global online courses. He was followed by Geoffrey Garrett (O'Donnell, 2020) who served on the boards of advisors of the Indian School of Business and the Tsinghua University School of Economics and Management. He is now on his fourth deanship, having completed two deanships in Australia, each of less than two years. Subsequently, Erika James, Wharton's first woman and first African-American dean to lead Wharton was appointed in 2020 following one previous deanship. This indicates growing diversity of incumbents in the deanship as seen in Europe and an example of an individual born outside the country where they are now living.

Deans can look to past and current business school pioneers for inspiration on leaving lasting legacies beyond iconic skyscrapers such as those at IE Business School, UCL School of Management, and Warwick Business School. Vignettes of business school deans provide themes on entrepreneurship education, using technology in teaching, the impact of businesses in society, and changing governance and educational/business models within business schools that are helpful to inform current debates. We believe that despite differences in ownership, governance and status, all business schools present common challenges for deans, even where the business school benefits from considerable public funding. Whether in a standalone or university-based business school, deans must balance attention to management practice and management scholarship as well as the operational challenges of sustaining financial well-being, values and innovations to enhance careers and reputations. For example, the Dean at Sasin School of Management in Bangkok created the new position of Chief Impact Officer (Fenwick, 2020).

In the United States, founders and early deans of well-established business schools declared the importance of business and business schools in society, a sentiment that is commonly expressed today. For instance, Joseph Wharton created the first collegiate business school in the world to prepare graduates to become 'pillars of the state, whether in private or public life' (University of Pennsylvania, n.d.) with broad and in-depth knowledge. It was designed originally 'to create a liberally educated class of leaders for American society' (Sass, 1982). Roswell McCrea, an early dean at Wharton, continued to support the faculty's studying of social problems in Philadelphia and strengthened ties with the city's government administrations (Wharton, n.d.).

Wallace Donham was the second dean of Harvard Business School for 23 years following World War I, the Great Depression and the start of World War II. In this turbulent era, he inherited a school with precarious finances but was productive and innovative in establishing the School's mission, residential campus, case method teaching based on his legal experience, *Harvard Business Review* and field-based research based on strong links between the faculty and practice. Donham had worked in industry and was a skilled negotiator and fundraiser. He provided an intellectual culture in which faculty members could be innovative. He also wrote prolifically on ethics, responsibility and business as a profession linked to improving society. Post deanship, Donham continued his scholarship in human relations and mentored new generations of faculty members (Blagg, 2019).

Even in well-endowed private US business schools, the persistent challenge for deans is brokering and bridging gaps between the academy and organizational practice. Simon (1967, p.1) quite sensibly asked 'Can we use our knowledge of organization theory to improve our own institutions?' He realized, however, that:

> Organizing a professional school or an R & D department is very much like mixing oil with water: it is easy to describe the intended product, less easy to produce it. And the task is not finished when the goal has been achieved. Left to themselves, the oil and water will separate again. So also will the disciplines and the professions. Organizing, in these situations, is not a once-and-for-all activity. It is a continuing administrative responsibility, vital for the sustained success of the enterprise.
>
> (1967, p.16)

If a dean's job is about continually 'mixing oil with water', we might assume that it is helpful to appoint a dean whose DNA includes the ability to move frequently between academic disciplines and professional functions in organizations. IE Business School presents an interesting case. It was founded in Madrid as a graduate school and achieved multi-disciplinarity through acquiring a university to establish IE University in 2009. Lee Newman, the Dean of IE Business School, completed an interdisciplinary PhD in psychology and computer science, founded and sold two tech start-ups, previously founded IE's School of Human Sciences and Technology and was hired as dean for his strategic vision, team leadership, ability to anticipate trends and innovate (IE Business School, 2021). Academic credentials and entrepreneurship, strategic leadership and the ability to build effective teams are key expectations in the IE deanship, illustrating Simon's (1967) argument about mixing research and practice.

Moreover, IE Business School exemplifies some of the advantages that Antunes and Thomas (2007) pointed out in European business schools, such as the importance of 'reflective, integrative and action-based learning, public sector management and public policy issues [with] ... a greater sensitivity to international relations' than in other parts of the world. On the other hand, even these private schools lack the endowments, rapid first-mover advantage and international brand recognition of elite US business schools.

It is interesting that following business school mergers in France resulting from cuts in government funding to chambers of commerce, new forms of funding, such as private equity investment in EMLyon, are emerging in response to austerity. Yet the same dean's discourse is apparent. For instance, Tawhid Chtioui, dean at EMLyon, talks about rising in media rankings, multi-disciplinarity, CSR and societal impact (Hazlehurst, 2019). In his case, this will be achieved through acquiring new institutes and inviting faculty members, students and alumni to invest in EMLyon.

As another illustration of learning from the past, during the early days of the formation of GISA (Graduate School of Industrial Administration), now Tepper School of Business at Carnegie Mellon University, the first dean of the school brought with him the department of economics and a group of well-known organizational theorists and operations researchers. It is still a moot point in business schools whether to include economists as faculty members. He also led the first computer simulations for experiential learning, including Wall Street trading firms' software. More recently, in 2020, when Robert Dammon stepped down as dean at Tepper School of Business after nine years, he was thanked for being a 'thoughtful, encouraging, and analytical' administrator and for leaving 'a lasting legacy in shaping the school's future' (Carnegie Mellon University, 2020a).

Isabelle Bajeux-Besnainou, a French-born professor of finance who was previously a dean at McGill University in Montréal, now leads this private, well-endowed business school that also offers undergraduate degrees. This indicates greater diversity in the appointment of foreign-born and women deans. Her first message during the COVID-19 pandemic focused on community and the school's historical roots, its 'legacy in management science and our highly interdisciplinary culture'. At the time of her appointment, Bajeux-Besnainou talked about how the school's community might 'grow, thrive, and create monumental change that can impact the world' (Carnegie Mellon University, 2020b). She explains her career move:

> I decided to make the transition to become dean … and to bring my experience as a professor and my passion for building a culture that is focused on students, research, and community here… it was initially somewhat by chance, but became more and more intentional on my side.

As a self-confessed introvert, she emphasizes empathy, communication, courage, optimism and passion, innovation, growing, thriving and managing change in uncertainty to make an impact (Vlad, 2021). Importantly, Bajeux-Besnainou stresses that the dean's team is vital and that deans should surround themselves with smart people. She reiterates her belief that uncertainties provide invaluable opportunities for innovation.

Multiple Perspectives on the Business School Deanship

Figure 2.8 presents a view of the business school dean operating at the centre of multiple constituencies (internally and externally), demonstrating the complexity and challenging nature of the role.

Individual Perspectives and Models of the Deanship

Typically, deans need to reconcile competing, such as differentiating the business school brand identity while integrating institutionally to break down silos and building bridges with organizations, funding bodies and other key stakeholders. Business school deans are often conflicted and stressed as they must simultaneously comply with regulations, control budgets, improve quality and inspire innovations and future leadership. This entails storytelling and negotiating as impactful role models. Increasingly, the dean's ability to generate financial surpluses is a key metric for success.

Davies and Thomas (2010) asked 'what do deans do?' They explored motivations, preparation for the position, ambitions and behaviours in the role, including dilemmas and triggers for deans' departures as well as life post deanship. Berliner (2017), in the United States, considered the changes in his role as

SOCIETAL CONTEXT: politics; economics; technology; grand challenges – UN's sustainable development goals, climate emergency; cost of living; inequalities; local communities; culture wars.

B-SCHOOL INDUSTRY: history; models, paradigms; journal rankings; publishers; impact agenda (BSIS, PRME, RRBM); accreditation agencies; professional bodies; scholarly associations; editors; media rankings; executive search consultants; issues of legitimacy, purpose, impact, rigour, relevance.

NATIONAL CONTEXT: higher education regulations; government funding; research evaluation policy; media rankings of national b-schools; student/staff satisfaction measures; quality assurance; employment law; demographics of students/faculty members.

PARENT UNIVERSITY: location(s); strategy; mission; vision; values; brand strength; popularity; systems; expectations of a financial surplus from a b-school; STEM priorities; power, politics; internal processes.

B-SCHOOL: type; funding; history; purpose; strategy; mission; vision; values; policies; internal processes and data; culture; competitive positioning; ranking; internal/external reputations; size; strength of sub-brand; resources; capabilities; reserves; revenues; surplus; location(s).

B-SCHOOL DEAN: rhetoric and realities; job descriptions; line manager; academic discipline; research impact and citations; traits; behaviours; background; reputation; competences; priorities; expectations; predecessor; well-being; term of office; contractual status; mandate; fit with the b-school/university; experience on boards; career stage; track record; autonomy; energy; teams; support; achievements; incentives; reward systems; digital platforms; communications; decision-making; attitude to risk, change and continuity; ability to influence and implement strategy.

Relationships with the central university / owner; governance; advisory board; donors, sponsors; decolonising the curriculum; culture; structure; workforce; students; unions; employers; partners; alumni; portfolio; orientation; rankings; accreditations; public relations experts; recruitment agents.

Learning culture; relative size and reputation of the b-school in the university, synergies, tensions; local, regional ecosystems, university-government-industry-media-citizen links. austerity/prosperity; national associations; visa regime; post-study opportunities; research funders; industrial strategy; forms of capitalism; philanthropy; limits on student numbers and fees; political support for STEM and non-STEM disciplines.

COMPETITORS/COLLABORATORS: strategic groups, local, global b-schools; publishers; edtech; App developers; big five tech giants - Apple, Amazon, Google (Alphabet), Meta, Microsoft; management consultants; private equity investors.

Global crises, extreme events: recessions, public health, environment, poverty, humanitarian, geopolitical conflicts, fake news, culture wars, activism.

Figure 2.8 Influences on business school leadership.
Source: Authors.

dean separated by 25 years. He highlights the increased pace and difficulties in achieving work-life balance in contemporary business schools. Davies (2012) illustrates learning experiences for new deans on the ABS/EFMD international deans' programme, while Cremer (2018) discusses lessons from EFMD's strategic leadership programme and re-iterates the value of deans reflecting on real-life cases with peers and what they might have done differently.

In his *Global Focus* article, the influential Irish management thinker Charles Handy (2015) asks a critical question: 'Are business schools becoming just too expensive to survive as they are today?' He argues for greater attention to manager development, different types of faculty and reward systems, and reframing business schools as think tanks. As a salutary warning to deans, Handy contends that business schools will decline without substantive reforms. The growing research impact agenda is changing human resource management practices in business schools (Lejeune et al., 2015). A concern with impact is stimulating outward-looking and cross-disciplinary behaviours. It is resulting in the creation of new support roles and IT impact tracker systems, enhanced brands, but also adding to faculty workloads. Francis' (2019) article on leadership development at Bayer AG is useful in offering insights into what business schools might offer in executive education and what business school deans might learn personally from the organizations they serve. She comments on the company's shift to a paradigm of humble, inclusive, resilient, mindful and reflexive team leadership that recognizes wider organizational contributions in challenging contexts. How deans communicate during crises is one challenge which can influence success in their tenures. Bieger and Schmid (2019) provide examples of crises deans face and recommendations for anticipating and dealing with them when appropriate.

Thomas and Thomas (2011) illustrate an interactionist model (see Figure 2.9) of business school leadership based on deans' different leadership styles, characteristics, faculty needs and the context. They liken certain deans to partners in professional service firms. Business school leadership is portrayed as balancing attention to strategy, academic and economic models, corporate and scholarly engagement, overcoming resistance and generating key resources. Fragueiro and Thomas (2011) adopt contextual and processual approaches in explaining their own experiences as deans in South America, the USA, UK and Asia in enacting four key strategic leadership processes of environmental scanning, issue diagnosis, issue legitimization and power mobilization.

The dean's role is particularly complex because of the barrage of criticisms about business schools and questions about the legitimacy of business studies as an academic discipline. Aside from identity issues, deans must also deal with competitive positioning as well as the idiosyncrasies of managing a professional

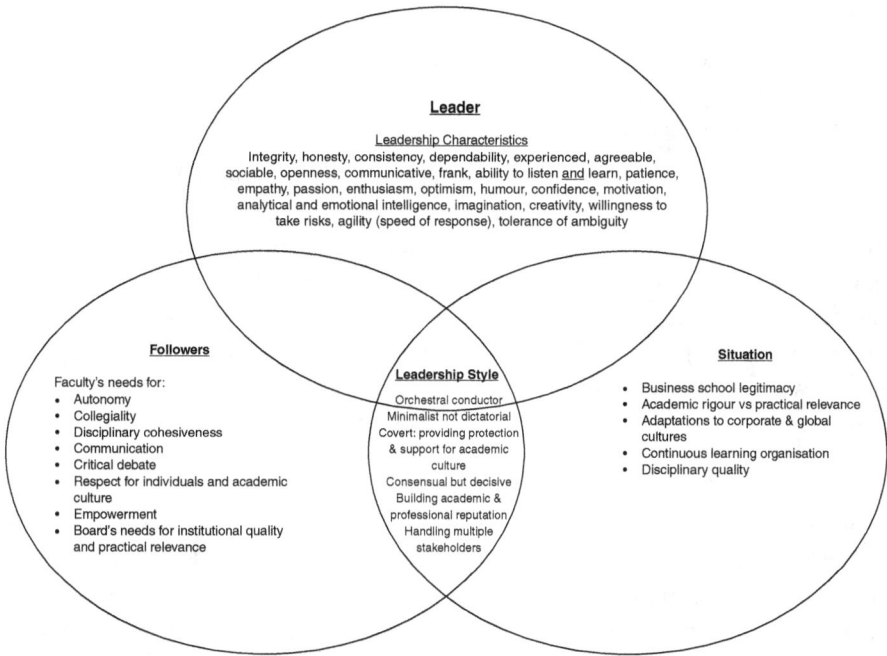

Figure 2.9 Interactionist business school leader(ship) characteristics framework.
Source: Thomas and Thomas (2011, p.536).

school, understanding culture, systems, people and processes to execute strategy successfully. The role requires the dean to establish a clear sense of purpose and values to position the business school's offerings in the market. Moreover, like partners in professional service firms, deans must attend closely to the bottom line while working in a knowledge intensive organization.

Thomas and Thomas (2011) recommend a leadership style based on building consensus and covert leadership (Mintzberg, 1998), like an orchestra conductor, rather than a dictatorial approach. In times of austerity, however, and in the increasingly marketized academy where academics feel disenfranchised and assessed only on the basis of performance metrics, the interactionist model of leadership that Thomas and Thomas advocate may be harder to achieve. Nevertheless, experience and capabilities in learning, communicating (especially listening patiently and with good humour), emotional and analytical intelligence, effective communications, self-confidence, consistency, dependability, enthusiasm, honesty, motivation, optimism, sociability, responsiveness, openness, imagination and willingness to take risks while allowing for faculty to feel respected and to exercise autonomy, collegiality and critical debate are listed as desirable attributes. Overall, Thomas and Thomas conclude that 'the leadership role of the dean may be narrowed down to … environmental scanning, issue diagnosis, issue legitimisation and power mobilisation' and '[a] dean thus must create a style of strong, stable, supportive and consistent leadership while recognising the pressures and stresses' (ibid).

Accounts of how individuals became successful deans often refer to luck, with others recognizing their ability to lead and manage change, and being able to engage conversationally with a broad range of constituents. Typically, deans view themselves as stewards of collective energy, consulting and communicating meaningfully, authentically and regularly to make decisions, gain goodwill and act as an integrator within a learning community (Rys, 2020). Being able to deal with crises and demonstrating inclusive leadership are also important. Business school deans must embrace systems and relationships that support the school's mission. Followership is, of course, intrinsic to good leadership. Bryman and Lilley (2009), who were successive business school deans, questioned leadership scholars about what they considered to be effective higher education leadership. The researchers responded that context, trust, honesty and personal integrity are imperative. They felt that effective deans make time to talk with people, taking an interest in and supporting academics to achieve their goals. The leadership scholars wanted to be consulted on decisions and they appreciated deans with transparent values and clear goals. They wanted leaders who provided them with autonomy and time, who promoted collegiality and collaborations. The leadership scholars disliked laissez-faire leadership styles, generic competency frameworks, and higher education leaders who condone unprofessional behaviours. They recognized that university leaders are 'herding academic cats' who will question leaders. One interviewee commented that all leaders need to 'deal with structural issues, …cultural issues, … personnel issues, [with] … a very clear vision of where their organization is going and … some sort of sense of how they're going to get it there' (ibid).

University Constraints

Given that the university-based dean occupies a middle position in the governance hierarchy, constructive relationships between the business school dean and central university are imperative to make progress. When reflecting on contingencies in the parent university, Alajoutsijärvi and Kettunen (2016) emphasized the importance of matching a dean's worldview to a university's context for his/her survival and success. They argue that there is no one-size-fits-all approach. Deans need to consider the evolution of the three types of traditional research, academic capitalist and corporate universities in terms of their priorities.

Davies and Thomas (2010) discussed how business school deans emerge and grow, stressing the importance of social capital, consultancy, team building skills, differentiation strategy and dean-business school fit. In their empirical study, psychometric preferences of deans indicated Jungian extroversion, tough mindedness, seeing patterns and making connections, strategic thinking, and a tendency to bring issues to closure. They recommend improved dialogue between business school deans and university heads as deans must maintain the confidence of the university president/vice-chancellor.

The real challenge for deans, however, is that '[a]s the economic viability of some universities has become dire, some university academics feel the pursuit of scholarship is being sacrificed to the exigencies of the marketplace' (Thomas et al., 2013a, 2013b).

> European critics would argue that accreditation and rankings are forcing business school deans to focus on the wrong things: that is, image management at the expense of concentrating on, for example, narrowing the gap between theory and practice and providing sound advice to professional managers.
>
> (ibid)

National Context

National contingencies and stakeholders influence all business schools, including world-class global institutions. Deans must not only exhibit sensitivities to university and business school cultures, but they are subject to national higher education, immigration and industrial policies, as well as consumer and employment law. There is more staff casualization in Australia than in the UK, for instance (Bareham, 2004). Deans in China must be skilled in developing strong relationships with government agencies (Zhang et al., 2020). Alajoutsijärvi and his colleagues (2018) detail a failed accreditation attempt in an underdog business school in Finland and its impact on the dean's decision to step down. Based on their work on British and French business schools, Thomas and colleagues (2014a, 2014b) reflect on convergence and divergence dynamics and Stokes et al. (2017) consider private higher education operators in the UK. Juusola and Alajoutsijärvi (2019) offer useful insights into business school bubbles in the Middle East in the context of Dubai.

Howard Thomas and his colleagues (2013a, 2013b) consider the identity, legitimacy and status of university-based business schools and the evolution and growth of new business school models in the United States, Europe and Asia from historical and systematic perspectives. They reflect on changes in roles, curricula, pedagogies, technology, delineating organizations and debates about management as a profession.

In defining the characteristics of the European model of management education for EFMD's 40th anniversary, Thomas (2012) asserted that management education originated in Europe and that EFMD has been highly influential in shaping the identity, positioning and legitimacy of European management schools which now feature strongly in the FT's top 100 schools. European business schools emulated early 'trade school' models from the United States and since the 1960s they adopted more scientific approaches based on the social sciences, graduate and doctoral programmes. Thomas argues that distinctive features of European business schools have been reflections on action and project-based learning and diversity in different European contexts. European schools benefit from internationalization within the large European trade bloc. The rise of internationally ranked national business school champions in Europe (such as Copenhagen Business School) relies on quite different models from those developed in the United States which have substantial philanthropic endowments. Thomas explains that European business schools have benefited from cross-border trading and international relations expertise, influential European-based MNCs, and strong links with the government and public sector organizations. There is also a strong bias towards socially responsible capitalism and centrist models within the European Higher Education Area. Furthermore, Thomas argues that while European business schools may focus less on rigorous quantitative analysis than in the United States, they facilitate more relevant research and soft skills with critical, balanced and diverse perspectives.

Business School Industry Sector Influences

AACSB (in 1917) and the Academy of Management (in 1936) were founded in the United States in the first half of the 20th century. The Ford Foundation helped to stimulate post-war recovery through supporting management education in Europe during the 1950s–70s (for example, it helped to sponsor and develop the European Institute for Advanced Studies in Management (EIASM) in Brussels, Belgium). In the United States, the Carnegie Foundation report (Pierson, 1959) encouraged liberal arts in undergraduate degrees and the Gordon-Howell (Ford Foundation) report on graduate business studies influenced a dominant research-based analytic model and the rigour-relevance debate in the context of the Cold War (McLaren, 2019). With the foundation of EFMD in the early 1970s, followed by the Association of MBAs, European business school deans were able to influence accreditations beyond the Americanization of management education. Then, at the end of the 1980s, both the *Business Week* and the *US News and World* Business School rankings clearly highlighted the successes of US business schools. The creation of the *Financial Times* rankings in 1999 provided a counterbalance to showcase excellent management education in Europe. At the same time as an increasing interest in business school accreditations and rankings, the Bologna Declaration created the European Higher Education Area which harmonized degree programmes. Meanwhile, Beyond Grey Pinstripes rankings and PRME initiatives in the 21st century, along with the 2008 global financial crisis, were focusing deans' minds on sustainability issues. Mintzberg had questioned the value of pre-experience MBAs in the United States. Austerity in the recession following the global financial crisis resulted in business school mergers, for example, in France following government and chambers of commerce funding cuts, and even in Nordic countries we have seen new models of business schools emerge following mergers that have been unsettling for academics, e.g., at Aalto in Finland (Nordbäck et al., 2021).

The historical evolution of business school industry norms strongly influences how the business school deanship is enacted. Alajoutsijärvi and his co-authors (2018) chart the historical developments of business schools as academic and professional institutions and the transitions in ethos and practices. There are constant debates in the sector about the legitimacy and identity of business schools as well as contradictions and threats for deans to grapple with. Periods of scientization, politicization and corporatization, as well as legitimacy paradoxes, present considerable challenges for business school leaders. Tourish (2020) contends that the field of management studies is in crisis, unintelligible outside its echo chamber. He recommends approaches that communicate a deeper sense of purpose.

Peters and his co-authors (2018) make a clear case that, in various strategic groups, business schools must re-evaluate and innovate funding models. Deans must examine value chains for different offerings in the context of competition, disruption (business school alliances, mergers, failures) and technology-enabled learning for survival and growth. D'Alessio and Avolio (2009) argue that funding and faculty productivity are key challenges for many deans. Full-time professors with high salaries and low teaching loads who are not engaged with the school can present a difficult situation for business school leaders. Their article presents six models for financing business schools (in essence, quasi strategic groups): a business school fully financed by the parent university, no own brand; business schools partially financed by a host university; schools on a separate site from the parent university with some university financing; a self-financing business school within a university; standalone business schools; and independent business schools that create universities (e.g., IE University). There is scope in the literature to explore competitive advantage among business school competitors and collaborators as we see growing evidence of private equity investment in business schools (e.g., EMLyon) and partnerships with publishers and tech giants.

Societal Issues and Demands

The rise of social media and digital apps facilitated online learning in the second decade of the 21st century with Coursera and edX offering different models of delivering management education. Business school deans are visible on Facebook, LinkedIn, TEDx, TikTok, Twitter, YouTube and podcasts which can support their brand as thought leaders and influencers. An example of this is Nohria's 2011 TEDx talk on practising moral humility. However, in doing so, they risk making non -'woke' comments.

The UN's Sustainable Development Goals (SDGs) since 2015 have influenced how business schools position their socially responsible behaviours. At the same time, there has been a growing preoccupation with journal rankings and research impact. Digital learning accelerated during the pandemic while international flows of students decelerated abruptly. If we project forward, clearly there is a climate emergency, issues of ageing populations in the West and China, the gig economy, growing inequalities and the unsustainable costs of management education to tackle, amongst other pressing issues. Business schools have been a phenomenal success in terms of popularity and financially, but there are indications that the golden age has passed. Arguably, the 21st century is Asian, the MBA is no longer a golden passport (McDonald, 2017), and calls for the sector to 'disrupt or be disrupted' (Thomas et al., 2014b; GMAC, 2015) have in part been addressed by the COVID-19 pandemic which has accelerated changes and exposed inertia in business schools with opportunities for a better new normal (Brammer et al., 2020). It is timely in the context of accelerated inequalities, public health, economic and environmental crises and crises of confidence in leaders to reflect on insights into business school leadership and how slow business schools have been to practise what they profess about sustainability, ESG, CSR and other areas of responsible business (Jack, 2021).

E.O. Wilson stated humanity's real problem is that 'we have paleolithic emotions; medieval institutions; and godlike technology...it is terrifically dangerous, and it is now approaching a point of crisis overall' (Harvard Magazine, 2009). He suggested that the world needs to 'be run by synthesizers, people able to put together the right information at the right time, think critically about it, and make important choices wisely' (Wilson, 1998).

In extending this problem to the business school deanship following the outbreak of COVID-19, we argue that emotional intelligence, social relationships and well-being really matter. Yet heads of universities increasingly expect business school deans to enhance financial surpluses, technical solutions and reputations. At the same time, deans are focusing on compliance while in denial about threats to business school models and society more broadly. They are insufficiently courageous and impactful in stepping up to address a crisis of leadership in society and communicate a higher sense of purpose. Meanwhile, socially responsible management education and impact initiatives are supporting endeavours to change traditional paradigms and reduce inequities in the current context of calls for greater humanity (Dutta and LeClair, 2021) in the business schools that deans lead.

While historically deans may have emerged as 'first among equals' from inside the academic ranks, some deans are appointed with career tracks in administration, corporations and government (Biemann and Datta, 2014). Kambil and Budnik (2013) argued that incoming deans typically experience challenging transitions and that previous experiences in academia and industry are often inadequate preparation for the requirements to be a strategist, catalyst, steward and operator. Williams (2009) considered the value of appointing successive deans from industry and then from the academy. He recommends research to assess the positive and negative impacts of deans with mainly business backgrounds compared with purely academic deans.

It is interesting that, in his autobiography, the Nobel laureate Herbert Simon concluded that 'in most universities of even modest distinction, a dean cannot be appointed without strong support from the faculty of the college' (Simon, 1991). Over four decades later, the appointment of executive deans of major business schools often depends on executive search firms with little, if any, input from the rank and file of business school faculty members, except perhaps a few questions during a prospective dean's presentation.

For Lorange (2000), who founded and later sold his own business school, the central issue is not where deans are sourced but how do deans gain enough power, authority, influence and resources to lead, define and implement a strategy that sticks? He states that

> [T]he key to creating value in a business school is keeping the 'dynamism' in dynamic balance. But the forces can easily go out of balance…It is all too easy, for instance, for a business school to proceed by letting the bottom-up entrepreneurial forces get 'free play', with the dean or president playing the role of a 'non-existent' figurehead.

Aside from concerns about whether deans should be hired from academia or industry, McTiernan and Flynn (2011) advocated greater equity, diversity and inclusion in deanship, including the appointment of women deans. Mohrfeld (2020) found that women deans' initial paths were typically incidental and resulted from others having encouraged them to consider taking on the role. Women deans reported that they had little formal preparation for deanship and that their development was largely self-directed. Nevertheless, women business school deans said that they found the job rewarding as it enabled them to exercise broader influence.

Once appointed, what do deans do? At one time, deanship might have been regarded as a relatively comfortable pre-retirement internal appointment. In contemporary business schools, however, financial performance can largely make or break a dean's tenure. As McTiernan and Flynn (2011) observe, '[i]n terms of priorities, once in the dean's office, institutional reputation, accreditation, faculty, and finances dominate'. They suggest that this requires high social and emotional intelligence, shared governance, effective mediation, listening and negotiation skills. The authors stress the dean's ability to be creative, entrepreneurial, to delegate, by motivating others and gaining trust through consensus and collaborations with multiple internal and external stakeholders. Bareham (2004) sees deans' roles as implementing strategy and developing internal/external relationships. Importantly, he underscores the view that deans' roles are about preserving the school's collective energy through decision-making and conflict resolution, reducing time and energy on valueless activity, building credibility and trust, and managing tensions between participative collegiality and performance improvement.

Based on his analysis of ten successive business school deans, Williams[1] lists 14 key dilemmas and conflicting forces facing business school deans. These include prioritizing within strategic dilemmas; acting as boundary spanners in overseeing relationships with external stakeholders; culture change and continuity. Lorange (2000) further advises deans, irrespective of their backgrounds, to focus on people, partners, processes and projects. These are linked to three strategic choices to create value based on mass production with high student numbers; networks and exclusive clubs; and solving unique problems.

Metaphors and Identity Transitions

A common theme in the literature on the business school dean's role relates to the university-based dean, especially as a middle manager. Over two decades ago, Gallos (2002) captured the network centrality of the deanship which can be both exhilarating and enervating. She wrote based on her own experiences that '[d]eans are, in essence, classic middle managers: They have enormous responsibilities, little positional power, insufficient resources, and limited authority' grappling with demands from '[i]nside and outside' as an '[e]ducator and executive'. We suspect that her characterization of university-based business school deans in particular persists:

> Long hours, the juggling, the disappointments, the need to satisfice more than satisfy, the pressures, frustrations, countless meetings, dropped balls, painful trade-offs, the downsides of confidentiality, the absence of appropriate and sympathetic ears, the new challenges, the recurring problems, and the endless complaints and requests are powerful daily forces in a dean's life.

Gallos uses the metaphors of a vice and a sandwich as deans experience the 'daily pressures of a life spent sandwiched between colliding cultures, local and global concerns, and internal and external expectations' (ibid).

Fragueiro and Thomas (2011) also depict deans as 'the meat in the sandwich between the central administration and the school staff, students and faculty'. Consequently, they contend that deans should be attentive listeners, 'straightforward, approachable, honest, direct and diplomatic' with effective negotiating skills and a good sense of humour. Deans need to develop competences as aggregators and integrators, facilitating entrepreneurship, the vision, communications. Political skills to deliver results closely linked to organizational context and timeframes are vital for the success of deans as boundary spanners if they are to avoid being 'stuck in the middle'.

Gjerde and Alvesson (2020) extended the metaphor of the dean as a defensive middle manager to the notion of 'an umbrella carrier ... protecting subordinates from what is seen as unnecessary and/or damaging initiatives and information from top management above, in order to allow for good professional work to take place below'. As critical management scholars, they describe how deans act to resist top-down approaches to avoid staff overload.

Likewise, Davies (2016) labelled university-based deans as hybrid upper middle managers. Delbecq (1996) viscerally conveyed his intense experiences and sheer exhaustion as he stepped down: 'I spent much of each workday as dean advocating, buffering, and dealing with problems over which I had limited control.' Roper and Kennedy (2010) view deans as trapped between a rock and a hard place. By adopting different human resource, structural, political and symbolic frames of rituals, sagas and gossip, deans can navigate within this dynamic context.

Dawson (2008), former Director of Cambridge University's Judge Business School, talks about her experiences as dean in bridging relationships between different constituencies. She frames the business school as a 'tri-fold hybrid organization' and her role as dean of aligning public sector management, professional service partnership and commercial activities. A key challenge for the dean is 'to realize a strategic plan for growth in revenues, reputation, and scale in such a way that growth is never at the expense of quality', advancing knowledge and enabling leadership using 'creative and constructive solutions'.

De Onzoño and Carmona (2016) use the metaphor of an 'academic triathlon' for business school academics who engage with research, teaching and external stakeholders such as organizations and the professions as an alternative to self-interested 'methodolatry' (Bennis and O'Toole, 2005). This analogy applied to business school deans would make them at least hexathletes as they engage in games of internal politics in the business school and university, rankings games (Corley and Gioia, 2000), alumni, corporate, civic, public, corporate engagement, media relations, staff and student satisfaction scores, and importantly financial and quality targets. Analogies of the dean as coach or manager of a sports team, a player manager or orchestral conductor, or as a covert leader (Mintzberg, 1998) managing fellow professionals, might be more appealing in an academic culture than the idea of the dean as a (mini) CEO. The relatively low research productivity and citation impacts of publications by deans in many non-elite business schools, however, points to the challenges faced by deans without outstanding research records or current publications or funding in exhorting others to improve their research productivity when the deans themselves are not role models. This may be less of an issue in teaching-only business schools, but the drive to enhance reputations through research in top tier journals means that deans are conflicted between short-term financial surpluses generated by tuition fees and providing workload allocations and time for research.

Key Challenges

Deans' work can also be relentless, often with significant accountabilities for teaching quality and research productivity, whilst being evaluated for performance metrics beyond their control, which can result in burnout (Gallos, 2002). They experience considerable role ambiguity, conflict and work-related stress (Wolverton and Gmelch, 2002).

Writers such as Parker (2021a) offer multiple stakeholder ecosystem models as alternatives to traditional business schools that emphasize shareholder capitalism. His so-called 'School for Organizing' poses interesting challenges for incumbent and aspiring business school deans. For example, he suggests curricula that include data on carbon reductions to be included in every module, localization as a counterpoint to globalization, with teaching cases based on business, government and civil society organizations with no more than half on the global north. Parker also believes that teaching and research should be linked with other disciplines, and that ethical business practices and politics should be discussed widely in the curriculum. He advocates that funded business school research should be directed towards public sector and other third sector organizations that are less researched than business organizations. Additionally, he calls for local citizens and employers to sit on business school advisory boards, and for universities to stop treating business schools as cash cows and to respect them as social science-based management schools.

Metrics

A clear focus on metrics (Thomas, 2007) might have reduced ambiguity in the role of business school leader. The listing of positive critical achievements in publications such as *Poets&Quants* when deans step down indicates typical expectations of successful business school deans. For example, it was reported that Scott DeRue as Dean of Michigan Ross launched an online MBA and major renovations of executive education facilities, secured a $50m gift, promoted experiential learning (including leading students on major climbing trips) and led the way in the business school sector by acting immediately on diversity and inclusion issues following George Floyd's death (Ethier, 2021).

Robert Bruner, Dean for 10 years at UVA Darden School of Business, emphasized that good deans' values should fit with the mission of the school they lead. He suggested that business school deans ought to demonstrate 'readiness, temperament, and purpose' as well as 'general management experience … high self-confidence, resilience to failure, humility, and a bias for action' (Bruner, 2017). Others might argue today for a focus on achieving a range of performance metrics based more on finances, despite knowing that a balanced scorecard approach (Thomas, 2007) is what business school professors actually teach.

According to a 2020–21 AACSB survey, 12 activities which take most of the dean's time include:

1. Working with central administration
2. Strategic planning

3. Academic and programmatic development

4. Accreditation management

5. Fundraising

6. Engaging with the business community

7. Faculty development

8. Communications (public relations, marketing, etc.)

9. Budget planning

10. Faculty recruitment and retention

11. Student recruitment and retention

12. Risk/crisis management.

According to Eurostat (2020) data, within the EU-27 the most frequently awarded degree in 2018 was management and administration. Importantly, 22% of all students in tertiary education in 2018 were studying business, administration or law and 24.6% of all tertiary students graduated in business, administration or law with 1.4 times more female than male graduates. This included 191,000 undergraduates graduating and 120,000 with a master's degree. There were especially high levels of graduates in these subjects in Luxembourg (42.5%), Cyprus (39%) and France (34.3%). These data indicate that deans of schools of business (of management schools and deans of faculties of business and law) are responsible for a significant proportion of higher education. On the one hand, this suggests that deans have considerable clout. On the other hand, Spender (2016) argues that governance problems of business schools being treated like businesses 'present the university and the whole educational apparatus with major "systemic" risks'.

Undoubtedly, over the last half century since EFMD was founded, business and management studies have been a phenomenal success in the higher education sector in terms of popularity and branding. While many business school mission statements claim to produce future leaders who make a difference in the world, business school leaders are increasingly grappling with questions about the purpose, legitimacy, affordability and impact of business and business schools in society. We know little, however, about what deans do and how it feels to enact the role.

Deanship: Defining Purpose, Legitimacy and Impact

Some insights on deanship offer a prescriptive approach (e.g., AACSB's five questions [Beck-Dudley and Bryant, 2020]) with normative advice on 'how to be a dean' (Aspatore Books, 2006, 2008), usually in an elite North American context (Slaughter, 2015). Dhir's (2008) edited collection of business school deans' perspectives highlights preoccupations with developing faculty, delivering an appropriate curriculum, assuring high quality teaching, stakeholder engagement and focusing on rankings. What the business school dean does clearly varies in parts of the world where there are different forms of capitalism, regulation and government funding. These shape the purpose of the business school in a particular culture and context.

Over time, the role of business school dean has become more professionalized and executive. 'Mission: Impossible'-type job descriptions in university-based business schools and lack of leadership development can result in deans becoming overwhelmed, feckless and burned out in the role unless they build solid teams and wider relationships to enact strategic leadership successfully while significantly contributing to the bottom line. We consider the deanship from historical, contextual, processual and relational perspectives.

The idea that the deanship is a calling, just as Hoffman (2021) argues that management should be a calling, is appealing. Jim March, the highly respected sociologist who served at one time as a professor of higher education, commented that '[l]eadership involves plumbing as well as poetry (Augier, 2004)'. Applied to business school deanship, this may translate into a concern for basic infrastructure and inspiring words. Jim March also emphasized the importance of joy, 'having a sense of humor; having a playful enthusiasm that transforms acts of leadership and education into acts of pleasure' (ibid). The tyranny of metrics is crowding out a sense of joy nowadays. As deanship becomes more of an executive role in the neoliberal university, however, a professional cadre of deans is emerging for whom deanship is a permanent career move. Our research suggests that some deans are unable to return to the ranks because they are no longer research-active and they may not wish to rise in the university hierarchy because there are few financial incentives and they would lose contact with deans' clubs and lack responsibility for a large budget.

A key issue for deans is that faculty members would like to see them as first among equals with a deliberative approach who buffer them from organizational 'noise' that distracts them from their research. In reality, central university administrators view the dean as a strategic business unit leader whose primary role is to meet financial surplus targets. Hence, there is a disconnect between expectations of academic freedom in the business school and central compliance with university policies. Yet, deans' advisory board members and external stakeholders might assume that as leaders of academic units deans would be able to exercise high levels of discretion and thus have significant power to influence society, to implement fair practices to serve business and society and to make positive environmental impacts.

There are opportunities for business school deans to behave as 'tempered radicals' (Meyerson, 2008) successfully integrated as organizational insiders while operating on fault lines and representing ideas that are at odds with dominant cultures. We argue that deans as scholars-CEOs-academic entrepreneurs, should be experimenting as change agents (Heifetz, 2019). March echoes this sentiment: 'In a world in which most of the pressure is for efficiency and rationality, an administrator has to help sustain experimentation. In a world of craziness, an administrator has to sustain order (Augier, 2004).' Business school deans should be having difficult conversations and turning threats into opportunities rather than playing safe all the time. At the same time, they need trusted confidants and support to help them when they feel vulnerable in environments where others expect a sense of psychological safety (Edmondson and Lei, 2014) from them, which the deans themselves do not feel. Elangovan and Hoffman (2021) argue that a fixation with A-rated journals, where theorizing is imperative, is destroying the essence of education.

Mullins (2020) listed the most followed deans on LinkedIn and contended that the dean's personal brand is an important asset. An alternative approach is management by algorithms and metrics focused on journal fetishism, sociotechnical imbalances and over-engineering the business school. Deans must consider trends (Marr, 2022) for educators to be facilitators rather than deliverers of content, using personalized, self-directed and self-paced learning and collaborative learning through projects and bite-sized and immersive learning.

The dean must navigate tensions between the rhetoric of branding and job descriptions with the realities of generating funds and maintaining quality. Deans must also consult on and communicate a shared sense of purpose while recognizing diversity and pluralism in academic and professional cultures and narrow performance metrics of surpluses, A-rated journals and rankings. At the same time, incumbents must respect the past, being mindful of current challenges with multiple local and international stakeholders and the future sustainability of traditional business school models as well as their own career prospects.

In times of austerity, academics feel disenfranchised and assessed purely on the basis of performance metrics; the interactionist model of leadership that Thomas and Thomas (2011) advocate may be harder, but not impossible, to achieve. The performance of university-based business school deans in marketized higher education systems is based on an increasingly narrow range of metrics. These are usually related to financial performance (typically, surpluses generated for the institution) and various forms of reputational capital such as branding, quality assurance, accreditations, rankings, student satisfaction ratings, publications in A-rated journals and, sometimes, measures of societal impact. This means that the dean is constantly balancing decisions about cash and quality, supporting learning and employee and student satisfaction while raising standards and measuring performance. While inspiring and influencing others as a role model and overseeing a portfolio of management education and research in a pluralistic and complex context, deans are not only managing the business school but multi-stakeholder and multi-level relationships.

Kaplan (2018) argued that deans 'need the courage to sacrifice some sacred cows', which is difficult as they balance multiple viewpoints to build coalitions. During the COVID-19 pandemic, Sarah Kaplan (2020) claimed that business schools have made impoverished responses to crises within society such as social inclusion and inequalities, the damaging effects of climate change and the effects of artificial intelligence (AI) on employment. She called for them to step up and go beyond making modest incremental changes. Tufano (2020), former Dean of Saïd Business School, University of Oxford, also argued for a bolder approach, with business schools acting as a force for good for multiple stakeholders by taking the lead in addressing the climate crisis and social changes. He stated that 'the traditional business school model is looking dated' and calls for bolder leadership to deal with intractable systemic challenges.

Cornuel (2008) has written about historical resource limitations and argued for diversified sources of funding to achieve significant change in European business school models. More recently, Parker (2020) asserts that '[i]t is as yet unclear what will finance the forms of business education that must underpin the next economy'. This means that deans direct much of their time and energy on meeting financial surpluses set by the central university, branding, journal fetishism and a narrow range of metrics such as student satisfaction ratings, media rankings and accreditation criteria. Current challenges for UK business schools (where 20% of postgraduates and 17% of undergraduates study) include competition from the international and private sector, especially low-cost, high-quality overseas providers, comparatively lower research funding and siloed behaviours in universities (The British Academy, 2021).

The popularity of business schools underscores the importance of business school leadership in sustaining relevant management education. Parker (2021b) suggests that 'in 95% of these business schools, 95% of the time, future citizens of our warming planet are being taught about digital marketing, data analytics, capital markets, brand strategy, strategic HRM and innovation with no reference to political economy or the planetary boundaries of global capitalism'. While Parker may be overstating his case this means that there is definitely considerable scope for deans to address 'planet and people' agendas and to facilitate more socially responsible, inclusive and impactful leadership in different forms of business organizations and wider society.

It is apparent that, because of resource constraints, business school deans are not walking the talk in effectively implementing responsible management education (Maloni et al., 2021). Despite the *Times Higher Education* university impact rankings, there is widespread evidence of business school deans failing to embed the UN's sustainable development goals within their own operations, for example, decent work conditions and gender and ethnic equality for business school faculty. Deans of UK business schools, for instance, are facing persistent workforce inequalities, particularly amongst women academics from ethnic minority backgrounds, with women representing only 26% of professors and 2% of professors identifying as black (Śliwa et al., 2021).

In the context of the third decade of the second millennium, like university presidents, business school deans must be alert to addressing, sympathetically and carefully, issues of free speech, academic freedom and culture wars and mediate, when necessary, with social media interventions. These issues can rapidly escalate to polarize students and faculty on topics such as critical race theory, transgender rights (*The Economist*, 2021), multiculturalism and green narratives. From one perspective, it might seem that business school deans are beleaguered by successive and recurrent crises (Davies, 2016) within marketized university systems and managerialist imperatives (Locke and Spender, 2011). There is a real threat of a dean being derailed by events that they feel are beyond their control. For example, one popular dean stepped down when an interim university president alleged that he had failed to deal with harassment and discrimination claims (Ellis, 2019). In other universities, central university administrators have diluted the treatment of critical management studies (Parker, 2020) and industrial relations in business schools. Harley (Harley and Fleming, 2021) talks about the need to confront the crisis of confidence in management studies with senior leaders and scholars in business schools by stepping up to the plate and acting as better role models (Thomas and Hedrick-Wong, 2019).

Yet this succession of crises in society that highlight issues of the legitimacy and impact in business schools means that deans have the incentive to make significant contributions during their tenures to promoting and achieving 'higher aims' (Khurana, 2007) of societal impact rather than behaving as 'hired hands' or 'hired guns'. Internally, deans can lower the walls of a business school to collaborate with other parts of the university for societal impact (Currie et al., 2016). They can nurture the next generation of scholars and students and have a positive influence in society more broadly. Deans are in powerful positions to facilitate curriculum development and impactful research to mitigate crises in climate change, democracy, inequities, leadership, public health and other grand challenges. They can also champion different forms of organizing beyond merely focusing on shareholder capitalism and profit maximization (Parker, 2021a, 2021b) by supporting forms of organizing which are frequently overlooked in business schools, such as micro-firms, co-operatives and social enterprises.

There is a risk, however, of deans becoming puppets and bankers to heads of universities, playing safe by complying with central administration requirements, and focusing narrowly on business school metrics in a mature industry rather than experimenting with new social imaginaries that are culturally relevant. It is interesting that when UK business school deans were asked what public good means, 'very few responses were either anchored in scholarly work or drew on formally stated conceptions of public good' (CABS, 2021). This might suggest that some business schools have indeed 'lost their way' (Bennis and O'Toole, 2005) by prioritizing 'profits, productivity, and shareholder well-being' over 'improving the well-being of all organizational stakeholders' and social matters (Pfeffer, 2009).

The increasing loss of tenured professors and greater use of contingent faculty in many business schools and organizations is resulting in the gig academy (Kezar et al., 2019). This reflects neoliberal policies and academic capitalism alongside a lost sense of community. Management by algorithm, platform working to deliver online learning and centralized systems are alienating isolated students, employees and other key constituencies of business schools. The counterbalance in some institutions (e.g., University College London) is shifting towards the 'hyper-personalization' of the employee experience (Pir, 2020) in addition to personalizing the student experience (Yazdani, 2016).

In terms of the talent pipeline, the best scholars may not be stepping up to business school leadership positions for several reasons. In a US study of over 4,000 professors in nearly 40% of top 100 business schools, Dyer and his co-authors (2021) found that university leaders typically seek to appoint associate deans from a talent pool of research high performers. The latter, however, are often reluctant to take on these well-paid leadership positions. The authors propose that this is because '[r]esearch faculty rarely possess "slack" resources sitting on the sidelines that allow them to take on new responsibilities without sacrificing some other task or work.' Highly published faculty members 'are generally aware of the relative personal returns to service assignments versus research productivity' and prioritize the time they spend on research rather than on administrative activities. In some universities, research stars may be 'protected' from administrative and teaching duties so that they can concentrate on enhancing a business school's research rankings. This predicament illustrates the 'firm-specific human capital dilemma' in the academy. Surprisingly, in the US study associate deans with lower research productivity were paid a salary higher than high performing scholars who became associate deans. This raises questions about the pipeline for the business school deanship.

If leadership is essentially relational and learning is a social, dehumanized, automated process, with remote deans and overloaded instructors on precarious employment contracts, this does not support a sense of community or meaningful staff and student engagement and satisfaction. If deans over-engineer their approach to leading and managing people remotely through a dashboard of metrics for optimal efficiencies, with armies of adjuncts and teaching assistants, while focusing on student numbers and rankings for prestige using a corporate logic (Donoghue, 2008), inevitably they will experience tensions. A model of a contingent, part-time and outsourced workforce, weak unions, and a few highly paid research professors is already well established in some triple accredited business schools. The Open University Business School in the UK has always relied on a very large proportion of associate lecturers rather than full-time employed faculty. The model of flying in faculty in the executive education arena at Duke's Fuqua University is at the high end of pay. These approaches to flexible working are clearly mirrored in changing employment laws and in the workforce more widely and can be mutually beneficial for business schools and employees. On the other hand, they can result in a form of academic apartheid, with limited career prospects for some teaching-only faculty (Bamber et al., 2017) and in-work poverty for academics (Kezar et al., 2019). Faculty segregation in business schools results in the gendered reproduction of knowledge (Davies et al., 2020), where under-represented groups in the workforce are overloaded with teaching (synchronous, asynchronous, just-in-time) without opportunities to undertake personal scholarship. Managerialism in business schools has resulted in higher levels of burnout and turnover as a result of a 'metrics culture', increased workloads, less workplace support and academic freedom. McCarthy and Dragouni (2021) suggest this can be mitigated by a more collegial and engaged working culture with greater recognition and autonomy in academic communities to improve psychosocial and organizational well-being.

In the context of Industry 5.0 and a climate emergency, the socio-technical challenges of humanizing and automating work while enhancing the employee and student experience are important considerations for deans. There is a real risk of business school deans becoming chief compliance officers at the behest of a university president/vice-chancellor, managing faculty by a dashboard of metrics. Meanwhile, as the planet burns, members of the business school are busy platform working and (trying) to publish in top tier management journals that, paradoxically, neglect the major challenges confronting humanity (Harley, 2019). Certainly, deans are increasingly aware that they must be mindful about their own and others' mental health and well-being (Edwards et al., 2021) in a culture of increasing workloads and performance management.

Tenures and Career Trajectories

If learning for business school deans is primarily on the job (Thomas and Thomas, 2011), it may feel like learning to ride a bike in public, a difficult balancing act. In public sector, full-service business schools in comprehensive universities there is a pluralism of disciplines within the school and multiple demands in the organization as a whole. From their share of deans' experiences in a range of different types of business school, Fragueiro and Thomas (2011) describe the strategic leadership processes that deans should undertake as: 'the set of decisions, actions and events produced by the whole set of key people in providing direction, influencing big strategic choices and implementing them, in order to achieve the organizational mission over time'. While this may be an approach taken in any type of organization, the nature of academic culture means that despite business schools being managed more like businesses they are really more like professional service firms and need consensual forms of leadership. In Chapter 4, we ask more formally about consensual approaches and particularly how we can 'strengthen and professionalize business schools' leadership?' (Thomas and Thomas, 2011).

Despite business schools developing leaders(hip), deans themselves tend to lack formal training. Amann (2021) is concerned about insufficient attention to the business school leadership pipeline and lack of leadership development for deans. Bareham (2004) found in his study on Australian and UK business school deans that only one dean had any specific training for the role.

Learning and attrition over time are explained in the four seasons model of deanships (Gmelch et al., 2012). Gmelch and his co-authors suggest that deans move through four seasons of 'getting started' during the first three years (springtime), 'hitting your stride' (summer, four to seven years), 'keeping the fire alive' (autumn, after eight years) and the winter of 'ending an era' and moving to a life after a deanship.

Thomas and Thomas (2011) note that deans primarily learn on the job and emphasize the need for deans to develop their communication and personal skills. They recommend further research on business school leaders' roles, characteristics and training in change and leadership drawing on in-depth case studies. Furthermore, Davies (2015) states that we need to (1) understand better how deans and business schools can contribute to the wider university; (2) promote peer-to-peer support mechanisms; (3) demonstrate evidence-based leadership development for deans as visible boundary spanners, intermediaries and ambassadors; (4) enhance career management support; and (5) support the business school leadership pipeline.

In order to encourage more women to apply to be business school deans, Mohrfeld recommended promoting opportunities and the benefits of being an academic leader to raise awareness amongst early career women faculty members with institutional support as well as specific leadership development.

The dark side of the deanship is evident in several commentaries by business school insiders. Twenty years ago, Bedeian (2002) warned incumbent deans of the 'dean's disease', where sycophantic followers boost a dean's ego in a culture of insularity that lacks integrity. He also cautioned deans who might have intended to return to the ranks that 'there seems to be a point in every dean's tenure where, if he [or she] does not move up, returning to a faculty appointment is no longer a viable option'. As deans are experiencing 'a growing audit culture, reduced resources, more directive management, and more emphasis on performance indicators', Bareham (2004) states that even those who were active researchers or teachers when they became deans usually cannot continue these activities. Several UK management scholars (see Brown et al., 2021) examined business school deans' self-authoring as hard-working, research credible and scrupulously moral professionals in attempts to mitigate threats to their fragile identities. Despite this, the authors noted the potential for deans to experience losses in equanimity (peace of mind) integrity and researcher identity.

Moules (2020) highlighted the rapid turnover of deans, the AACSB findings amongst its members that in 2017–18 the average tenure for business school deans was 5.9 years, and that 25.8% of business schools were led by women. He suggests that qualified individuals do not wish to take on such a broad role with its conflicting demands. Consequently, deans are being sourced from more varied backgrounds and from other university departments, such as social sciences.

In practice, an eight-year deanship may be unrealistic in spite of four-year renewable tenures in some cases. Several commentators have highlighted the short tenures and high turnover of business school deans. For instance, Starkey and Tiratsoo (2007) contrast traditional and contemporary tenures:

> Forty years ago running a business school was something that a senior professor might well take on as a matter of duty shortly before retirement. Nowadays deans almost constitute a profession in their own right … Turnover is fast, with many moving on after little more than a handful of years.

An article in *The Economist* in 2006 illustrated the precarious nature of deans' tenures:

> the average tenure [of a business school dean] is three to five years. Now a dean is expected also to be a full-time fund-raiser, the project manager of a significant on-campus property development ... and (crucially) the guardian of the school's position in the all-important league tables ... [which] has put deans into the same league as sports' coaches... The new breed of dean is ... a sort of freelance professional who shops around a bit like a sports coach.

Table 2.1 illustrates individuals who have held multiple successive deanships in transnational careers.

It is interesting that Chris Earley held five deanships in the USA and Asia. Howard Thomas has been a dean in America, Australia, Europe and Asia, with relatively long stints in each. Contrary to discussions about high turnovers and short tenures of deans, there are some very long tenured business school deans (see Table 2.2).

Table 2.1 Individuals with multiple international deanships

Chris Earley (five deanships)

NUS Business School, Singapore (three years); University of Connecticut School of Business, USA (almost four years); Krannert School of Management at Purdue University, USA (almost three years); Tasmanian School of Business and Economics, Australia (five years); University of Technology Sydney, Australia (two years to date).

Geoff Garrett (four deanships)

University of Sydney Business School (one year); UNSW Business School (one year); Wharton (six years); USC Marshall School of Business (since 2020).

Dipak Jain (three deanships)

Kellogg School of Management, USA (eight years); INSEAD, France (two years); Sasin School of Management, Thailand (five years); President (European) CEIBS, China (current).

Howard Thomas (three deanships)

Dean of Lee Kong Chian School of Business, Singapore (six years); Warwick Business School, UK (ten years); University of Illinois at Urbana-Champaign, USA (nine–ten years).

Table 2.2 Long-serving deans

Dezsö Horváth, York University's Schulich School of Business, Canada – 32 years (retired in seventh term).

Toemsakdi Krishnamra, Sasin School of Management, Thailand – 32 years.

Don Jacobs, Kellogg School of Management, USA – 26 years.

John Kraft, University of Florida Warrington College of Business – 26 years.

Roger Mansfield, Cardiff University, Wales; Paul Danos, Tuck School of Business, USA – 20 years.

Joseph DiAngelo, Haub School of Business, USA – 20 years to date following 12 years as dean previously.

Some individuals may use the deanship to gain a professorship and then return to a substantive post of professor after a few years. While the deanship may leverage a professorship, the individual must generate scholarship post-deanship unless they take on another administrative role.

The list of reasons (Table 2.3) for deans departing earlier than expected is an important reminder of the need for good governance, ethical behaviour and the dean acting as a role model. These range from gross misconduct, fraud and loss of confidence to failure to act in discrimination claims and not making sufficient surplus for the university to instances when no reasons are given for a dean stepping back to a tenured role with immediate effect. Declining rankings is also a trigger for deans to exit (Fee et al., 2005).

Some deans follow predictable career paths (Moore et al., 1983) from PhD student to lecturer, professor, head of department/centre, associate dean to dean and subsequently university president/vice-chancellor in a sector where many academics are not interested in taking on leadership positions. Others return to their previous roles after one stint in the position or repeat the role in the same or different university. Indeed, categories of transnational and interim deans are now emerging as the business school sector matures. Universities increasingly rely on executive search firms to carry out global searches for talent, encouraging candidates to apply for the role who may have not considered the deanship as a career option before they were approached.

An understanding of the differences between business school deans' intended and actual exit strategies can help individuals to prepare for leadership transitions. Table 2.4 indicates the choices for postholders following a business school deanship.

Table 2.3 Reasons given for deans stepping down earlier than expected

(1) Loss of confidence by the board

The chairman of the board of Copenhagen Business School in Denmark stated of Johan Roos that 'the president has lost his esteem at CBS' (Bradshaw, 2011).

(2) Governance, lack of due process, gross misconduct

Overseas joint venture proposal for a new university and hospital in Kuwait was not disclosed by the vice-chancellor and dean of school of management at Swansea University who were both fired (Barry, 2019).

(3) Unethical past conduct

Tony Antoniou at Durham Business School in the UK was dismissed for plagiarizing his PhD (Tahir, 2008).

(4) Falsifying information for MBA rankings

The Dean of Fox School of Business, Temple University, USA was fired (Byrne, 2018b) for refusing to step down after knowingly falsifying information about GMAT completions of incoming students to US News over several years to gain No. 1 ranking for its online MBA programme.

(5) Sexual harassment by faculty and students proven in court

At Columbia Business School in the USA, a junior female professor harassed by a male senior professor and mentor was awarded a $1.25m payout. A current female MBA student and her female peers were sexually assaulted by male students at school social events (Allen, 2018). Subsequently, Glenn Hubbard stated he would step down from the deanship at the end of the year.

(6) Falling out with faculty, bullying culture

Paul Bates, a businessman without a degree who was Dean of DeGroote School of Business, McMaster University, Canada, resigned and moved into another position in the University after a report that stated that there was a culture of 'bullying, harassment, mean-spirited sarcasm, intimidation and disrespect' (Maclean's, 2020). There was a history of in-fighting which continued after Bates' departure.

(Continued)

Table 2.3 (Continued) Reasons given for deans stepping down earlier than expected

(7) Discrimination claims against the dean

Garth Saloner at Stanford Graduate School of Business in the USA stepped down from the deanship after allegations from his partner's husband, who was a former member of the faculty, of discrimination. This was subsequently not upheld in court (Streitfeld, 2017).

(8) School not being listed in MBA rankings

Linda Livingstone at GWU Business School left after three years to become a university president as the School lost its place in the US News full-time MBA rankings (Byrne, 2017).

(9) Larger than expected expenditure, new university president

Doug Guthrie at GWU Business School returned to his tenured position after his new boss found the School's expenditure to invest in new programmes unacceptable (Anderson, 2013).

(10) Ousted for failing to respond to complaints

An interim president at the University of Southern California removed the popular dean James Ellis over allegations of his failure to act on complaints to the University's Office of Equity and Diversity (Valbrun, 2019).

(11) Disagreements over programme closure, student and alumni petitions

Anne Massey stepped down after less than six months in her deanship at WI School of Business, University of WI-Madison, USA, when there was a backlash about her decision to close the two- year full-time MBA immediately, although she subsequently rescinded the decision (Ethier, 2017).

(12) No reason given

Two years after controversially merging three schools internally in Cornell University, Dutta stepped down immediately and returned to his tenured position with no explanation given (Byrne, 2018a).

Table 2.4 Post-business school deanship trajectories

- Return to a faculty position

- Deanship renewal

- Accepting a new deanship in a different institution

- Provost or Vice President for Academic Affairs

- University president/vice-chancellor role

- Other administrative positions

- Opportunities outside the university – industry, private, non-profit sector

- Retirement, bridge employment, emeritus, interim deanship.

Trends in Management Education and the Future of Work

Business school deans need to understand the changing and dynamic conditions in which they operate. These include subscription models; flexible, modular and bite-sized certificate programmes that add up to degrees taken over working careers; affordability and democratization of education; and micro-credentials in individuals' portfolios. Coursera, for instance, offers entry-level professional certificates with organizations such as IBM, Meta and Google.

The futurist Bernard Marr (2022) observes: 'The traditional method of delivering lectures isn't the best use of anyone's time… in-classroom time could be spent discussing that content and relating it to real-world contexts.' Management educators need to facilitate student learning using digitized, self-directed, self-paced and personalized learning (using artificial intelligence) with project-based collaborations, bite-sized and immersive experiences. There are significant trends in life-long learning (IEDP, 2022) away from traditional one-size-fits-all educational models that focus mainly on investing in 18–24 year-olds. This can be enabled by connecting business schools with businesses and technology partners for responsive, flexible, demand-led solutions, agile and innovative ways of working aligned to changing end user and client needs. Deans must also be mindful of the changing nature of work, as indicated in Table 2.5.

Prospects for the Business School Deanship

Hotchkiss (1920) defined five essential qualities of a university-based business school that persist today. This included orientations to public interest,

Table 2.5 Future jobs

Increased remote working, rapidly digitalized working processes, technology integration, cloud computing, big data, greater use of contractors for specialized tasks, and concern for productivity and worker well-being.

Greater employer demands for critical thinking and analysis, problem-solving, self-management, and active learning skills, flexibility, resilience, and stress tolerance.

Jobs displaced and emerging as labour shifts between humans and machines using algorithms. Internal redeployment of workers displaced by technological automation and augmentation.

The COVID-19 crisis, economic downturn, and greater use of technology exacerbating existing inequalities, especially for low wage, younger and women workers.

Employers are recognizing the need to invest in human capital development to upskill and reskill employees with online learning to improve digital skills and employees' growing interest in personal development courses.

Reskilling and upskilling at-risk or displaced workers. Public sector incentives for investments in tomorrow's jobs; stronger safety nets for job transitions; and improved education and training systems.

Changing locations for workers and value chains. The need to create a sense of community, connection and belonging among employees using digital tools.

Corporate investment to improve metrics of human and social capital by adopting environmental, social and governance metrics with renewed measures of human capital accounting; the need for industry and public-private collaborations for cost-effectiveness and wider social benefits.

Source: World Economic Forum (2020).

connections within higher education systems, systematic analysis of real-world organizational phenomena, professional business training and a vision to pre-pare students for the future of work based on good business rather than just graduates' private benefits. Current debates about a business school model for the public good (Kitchener and Delbridge, 2020) and integrating the liberal arts (Harney and Thomas, 2020) and other disciplines represent constant themes. Spicer et al. (2021) suggest that today's deans can be inspired by some of the earlier models of management education. They argue that there is 'hope for a plurality of futures beyond the "neo-liberal" business school'; for instance, 'some non-elite business schools might find hope in seeing themselves as engines of social mobility'.

In looking to the future, Ewan Ferlie (Davies et al., 2021) suggests a research agenda on business school leadership that includes diversity in roles, teams and models. Howard Thomas (Thomas and Hedrick-Wong, 2019) calls for deans to be more courageous in supporting communities in digital environments, social inclusion, reskilling and lifelong learning and sustainable capitalism with greater appreciation of alternative models of leadership and business schools in addition to localism. Importantly, Thomas and his colleagues (2021) promote human(e), socially responsible and business school leadership engaged with multiple stakeholders.

Conclusion

Chapter 2 has offered insights into norms expected of the business school deanship by comparing job titles and descriptions in different countries, institutional contexts and cultures. It highlighted historical shifts from collegial models of deans as management educators to their roles as (scholar-)executives in managerialist (Locke and Spender, 2011) and marketized systems. An understanding of different business school sector, national, university, business school and individual perspectives as well as metaphors of deans' identities, and transitions pre-, during and post tenure help us to understand deans' concerns for reputations, revenues and performativity.

We illustrated how various types of deans gain and sustain legitimacy and impact. They negotiate local autonomy and integrate the business school in the parent university while differentiating the sub-brand and mixing management scholars and practitioners. Deans can be distracted from value-added contributions by many time-consuming activities while grappling with centralization, compliance and social and technical tensions. Increasingly, business school deans are having to deal with culture wars, grand challenges, a casualized workforce, IT platforms and edtech companies which are disrupting established paradigms. Vignettes of deans' achievements, their reflections on leadership, and media reports of deans' comings and goings help us to understand opportunities and threats to legitimacy and impact in the role. Examples of serial and long-serving deans and those who suddenly step down from the position provide valuable lessons about legacies, career trajectories and job precarity.

Moreover, the COVID-19 pandemic has rapidly accelerated much needed changes in business schools delivering online and hybrid management education. Successive and simultaneous crises have exacerbated inequalities, emphasizing the need for business schools to democratize higher education with greater affordability and accessibility. There are significant opportunities for business school deans to support national productivity and well-being agendas in reskilling and upskilling workers and to facilitate the positive impact of business and management studies in society to generate future leaders through connections and collaborations. They must also be mindful about their own personal self-care and employability post-deanship in a typically mid-level position that can be overwhelming, exhausting and precarious.

Yet there are strict regulatory and institutional constraints on business school deans' autonomy, authority and ability to resist conservative forces. Governments globally are prioritizing STEM disciplines, executive search firms are struggling with tapping the pipeline for business school deans (Amann, 2021), and, at an individual level, deans are interacting with multiple stakeholders (Thomas and Thomas, 2011) with new forms of remote and hybrid working. New geo-political and economic realities, tech titans and questions about integrity and inclusivity in public life are affecting business school deanships. There are pressing needs for business school deans to enable community building and well-being alongside digitized working and technological integration. Lifelong jobs are disappearing as the need for interactive, experiential, immersive and lifelong learning is growing. These transformations in the future of work have implications for what business school deans do and should do. To sustain high-quality and relevant management education in professional schools as well as the viability of their own organizations and careers against a backdrop of culture wars and deglobalization (Paul and Dhir, 2021), we argue that business school deans must engage in constant dialogue.

We hope that vignettes of critical incidents presented in Chapter 3 complement rhetoric found in the job descriptions and public accounts we have discussed in this chapter.

Note

1 Williams, A.P. (2009) Leadership at the top: Some insights from a longitudinal case study of a UK business school. *Educational Management Administration & Leadership*, 37 (1) pp.127–145.

References

AACSB (2021) *Deans survey participant report 2020–21*. Available at: https://www.aacsb.edu/-/media/publications/research-reports/deans_survey_2021_report.pdf?rev=401c3d1a8f914e6db3928015dfe607ce&hash=6C57F04C2ADECF10B7230ACEC785BCB2

Alajoutsijärvi, K. and K. Kettunen (2016) The "dean's squeeze" revisited: A contextual approach. *Journal of Management Development*, 35(3) pp.326–340.

Alajoutsijärvi, K., K. Kettunen and S. Sohlo (2018) Shaking the status quo: Business accreditation and positional competition. *Academy of Management Learning & Education*, 17(2) pp.203–225.

Allen, N. (2018) The biggest b-school scandals of 2018. *Poets & Quants*, December 31.

Amann, W. (2021) *Building a leadership pipeline for deans in business schools*. Little Rock, AR: walnutpublication.com.

Anderson, N. (2013) GWU business school dean is praised, then fired. *Washington Post*, September 13.

Antunes, D. and H. Thomas (2007) The competitive (dis) advantages of European business schools. *Long Range Planning*, 40(3) pp.382–404.

Aspatore Books (2006) *Business school leadership strategies: Top deans on creating a strategic vision, planning for the future, and developing leadership in education*. New York: Thomson Reuters/Aspatore.

Aspatore Books (2008) *Business school management: Top educational leaders on creating a strong school reputation, offering competitive programs, and thriving in the educational marketplace*. New York: Thomson Reuters/Aspatore.

Augier, M. (2004). James March on education, leadership, and Don Quixote: Introduction and interview. *Academy of Management Learning & Education*, 3(2) pp.169–177.

Bamber, M., J. Allen-Collinson and J. McCormack, (2017) Occupational limbo, transitional liminality and permanent liminality: New conceptual distinctions. *Human Relations*, 70(12) pp.1514–1537.

Bareham, J.R. (2004) *The leadership and management of business schools*. Occasional/working paper series BBS03-2, 3(2) pp.1–32. Brighton: Brighton Business School.

Barry, S. (2019) Swansea University sack vice chancellor and dean of management school for gross misconduct. *BBC Online*, July 30.

Beck-Dudley, C. and S. Bryant (2020) *So you want to be a dean? Ask yourself these 5 questions*. Tampa FL: AACSB International, January 17.

Bedeian, A.G. (2002) The dean's disease: How the darker side of power manifests itself in the office of dean. *Academy of Management Learning & Education*, 1(2) pp.164–173.

Bennis, W.G. and J. O'Toole (2005) How business schools have lost their way. *Harvard Business Review*, 83(5) pp.96–104.

Berliner, H. (2017) Dean déjà vu. *Global Focus*, 2(11) pp.30–34.

Bieger, T. and U. Schmid (2019) Take control-seven steps for crisis communications in business schools. *Global Focus*, 3(13) pp.12–17.

Biemann, T. and D.K. Datta (2014) Analyzing sequence data: Optimal matching in management research. *Organizational Research Methods*, 17(1) pp.51–76.

Blagg, D. (2019) *The school that Donham built.* Boston, MA: Harvard Business School. September 4. Retrieved from: https://www.alumni.hbs.edu/stories/Pages/story-bulletin.aspx?num=7091

Bradshaw, D. (2011) Copenhagen Business School fires Johan Roos. *Financial Times*, March 28.

Brammer, S., L. Branicki and M.K. Linnenluecke (2020) COVID-19, societalization, and the future of business in society. *Academy of Management Perspectives*, 34(4) pp.493–507.

Brown, A.D., M.A. Lewis and N. Oliver (2021). Identity work, loss and preferred identities: A study of UK business school deans. *Organization Studies*, 42(6) pp.823–844.

Bruner, R.F (2017) The 3 qualities that make a good dean. *The Chronicle of Higher Education*, January 15.

Bryman, A. and S. Lilley (2009) Leadership researchers on leadership in higher education. *Leadership*, 5(3) pp.331–346.

Byrne, J.A. (2017) GW dean departs after MBA ranking mishap. *Poets & Quants*, April 18.

Byrne, J.A. (2018a) Cornell b-school dean abruptly resigns. *Poets & Quants*, January 31.

Byrne, J.A. (2018b) Temple dean sacked over ranking scandal. *Poets & Quants*, July 9.

CABS (2021) *Business schools and the public good.* London: Chartered Association of Business Schools.

Carnegie Mellon University (2020a) 9th Dean of the Tepper School of Business. Robert M. Dammon 2011–2020. Available at: https://www.cmu.edu/tepper/why-tepper/our-leadership/deans-office/dean-dammon.html. Accessed 6 June 6 2021.

Carnegie Mellon University (2020b) Hello and bonjour: A message from Isabelle Bajeux-Besnainou, the new dean of the Tepper School of Business. Available at: https://www.cmu.edu/tepper/news/stories/2020/october/dean-isabelle-bajeux-besnainou.html

Corley, K. and D. Gioia (2000) The rankings game: Managing business school reputation. *Corporate Reputation Review*, 3(4) pp.319–333.

Cornuel, E. (2008) University challenge. *Global Focus*. Available at: https://www.globalfocusmagazine.com/university-challenge/

Coursera. Available at: https://www.coursera.org/certificates/launch-your-career

Cremer, R.D. (2018) Stepping into the role of the dean. *Global Focus*, 3(12) pp.10–14.

Currie, G., J. Davies and E. Ferlie (2016) A call for university-based business schools to "lower their walls:" Collaborating with other academic departments in pursuit of social value. *Academy of Management Learning & Education*, 15(4) pp.742–755.

D'Alessio, F.A. and B. Avolio (2009) Business schools and resources constraints: A task for deans or magicians? *Research in Higher Education Journal*. Available at: http://www.aabri.com/manuscripts/11912.pdf

Davies, J. (2012) Inciting exciting insights. *Global Focus*, 6(3) pp.42–45.

Davies, J. (2015) *Reflections on the role of the business school dean*. London: Chartered Association of Business Schools. Available at: https://charteredabs.org/publications/reflections-on-the-role-of-the-business-school-dean/

Davies, J. (2016) Are business school deans doomed? The global financial crisis, Brexit and all that. *Journal of Management Development*, 35(7) pp.901–915.

Davies, J., E. Ferlie, H. McLaughlin and H. Thomas (2021) Examining business school leadership. *Global Focus*, 1(15) pp.66–73.

Davies, J. and H. Thomas (2010) What do deans do? *Global Focus*, 4(1) pp.44–47.

Davies, J., E. Yarrow and J. Syed (2020) The curious under-representation of women impact case leaders: Can we disengender inequality regimes? *Gender, Work & Organization*, 27(2) pp.129–148.

Dawson, S. (2008) Building a business school at the heart of Cambridge. In Aspatore, *Business school management. Top educational leaders on creating a strong school reputation, offering competitive programs, and thriving in the educational marketplace*. Boston, MA: Thomson Reuters/Aspatore, pp.157–174.

Delbecq, A.L. (1996) What's next after 10 years as dean? Reflections of a reemerging professor. In P.J. Frost and M.S. Taylor, *Rhythms of academic life: Personal accounts of careers in academia*. Thousand Oaks, CA: Sage, pp.437–442.

De Onzoño, S.I. and S. Carmona (2016) The academic triathlon–bridging the agora and academia. *Journal of Management Development*, 35(7) pp.854–865.

Dhir, K. (Ed.) (2008) *The dean's perspective*. Atlanta, GA: Decision Sciences Institute.

Donoghue, F. (2008) *The last professors: The corporate university and the fate of the humanities*. New York: Fordham University Press.

Durham Business School. Available at: https://www.durham.ac.uk/business/news-and-events/news/2022/03/the-business-school-says-farewell-to-professor-susan-hart-and-announces-new-interim-executive-dean/

Dutta, S. and D.R. LeClair (2021) *The world after COVID-19: Insights from 20 global business school deans and corporate leaders*. Washington DC: Global Business School Network.

Dyer, J., D. Kryscynski, C. Law and S. Morris (2021). Who should become a business school associate dean? Individual performance and taking on firm specific roles. *Academy of Management Journal*, 64(5) pp.1605–1624.

Edmondson, A.C. and Z. Lei (2014) Psychological safety: The history, renaissance, and future of an interpersonal construct. *Annual Review of Organizational Psychology and Organizational Behaviour*, *1*(1) pp.23–43.

Edwards, M.S., A.J. Martin and N.M. Ashkanasy (2021) Mental health and psychological well-being among management students and educators. *Journal of Management Education* 45(1) pp.3–18. Available at: https://doi.org/10.1177/1052562920978252

Elangovan, A.R. and A.J. Hoffman (2021) The pursuit of success in academia: Plato's ghost asks "What then?" *Journal of Management Inquiry*, *30*(1) pp.68–73.

Ellis, J. (2019) Op-Ed: James Ellis: Setting the record straight about my departure from USC. *Los Angeles Times*, June 30.

Erikson, E.H. (1950) *Childhood and society*. New York: Norton.

Ethier, M. (2017) Wisconsin dean resigns amid backlash. *Poets&Quants*, December 19.

Ethier, M. (2021) Michigan Ross Dean Scott DeRue to step down. *Poets&Quants*, April 9.

Eurostat (2020) *Tertiary education statistics*. Luxembourg: European Commission. Available at: https://ec.europa.eu/eurostat/statistics-explained/index.php?title=Tertiary_education_statistics#Fields_of_education

Fee, C.E., C.J. Hadlock and J.R. Pierce (2005) Business school rankings and business school deans: A study of nonprofit governance. *Financial Management*, *34*(1) pp.143–166.

Fenwick, I. (2020) Why did Sasin School of Management create the position of Chief Impact Officer? *EFMD Blog*, April 1. Available at: https://blog.efmdglobal.org/2020/04/28/why-did-sasin-school-of-management-create-the-position-of-chief-impact-officer/

Fragueiro, F. and H. Thomas (2011) *Strategic leadership in the business school: Keeping one step ahead*. Cambridge: Cambridge University Press.

Francis, S. (2019) Leadership development has to reflect modern contexts. *Global Focus*, *3*(13) pp.29–34.

Gallos, J.V. (2002) The dean's squeeze: The myths and realities of academic leadership in the middle. *Academy of Management Learning & Education*, *1*(2) pp.174–184.

Ghoshal, S. (1995) *The smell of the place*. Davos: World Economic Forum. Available at: https://www.youtube.com/watch?v=YgrD7yJwxAM

Ginsberg, B. (2011) *The fall of the faculty*. Oxford: Oxford University Press

Gjerde, S. and M. Alvesson (2020) Sandwiched: Exploring role and identity of middle managers in the genuine middle. *Human Relations*, *73*(1) pp.124–151.

GMAC (2015) *Disrupt or be disrupted: A blueprint for change in management education*. GMAC. San Francisco, CA: Jossey-Bass.

Gmelch, W.H., D. Hopkins and S. Damico (2012) *Seasons of a dean's life: Understanding the role and building leadership capacity.* Sterling, VA: Stylus Publishing, LLC.

Handy, C. (2015) The past is not the future, *Global Focus*. Available at: https://www.globalfocusmagazine.com/the-past-is-not-the-future/

Harley, B. (2019) Confronting the crisis of confidence in management studies: Why senior scholars need to stop setting a bad example. *Academy of Management Learning & Education, 18*(2) pp.286–297.

Harley, B. and P. Fleming (2021) Not even trying to change the world: Why do elite management journals ignore the major problems facing humanity? *The Journal of Applied Behavioral Science, 57*(2) pp.133–152.

Harney, S. and H. Thomas (2020) *The liberal arts and management education: A global agenda for change.* Cambridge: Cambridge University Press.

Harvard Magazine (2009) *An intellectual entente.* Boston, MA: Harvard Magazine, September 10. Available at: https://www.harvardmagazine.com/breaking-news/james-watson-edward-o-wilson-intellectual-entente

Hazlehurst, J. (2019) EMLyon's new dean: Here's how we will break into Europe's top 10. *Poets&Quants*, August 5.

Heifetz, R. (2019) *On leadership.* YouTube, April 6. Available at: https://www.youtube.com/watch?v=ioocNc-HvTs

Hoffman, A.J. (2021) *Management as a calling: Leading business, serving society.* Stanford, CA: Stanford University Press.

Hotchkiss, W.E. (1920) The basic elements and their proper balance in the curriculum of a collegiate business school. *Journal of Political Economy, 28*(2) pp.89–107.

IE Business School (2021) *IE University announces appointment of Lee Newman as Dean of IE business School.* Madrid: IE University, April 16. Retrieved from: https://www.ie.edu/business-school/news-and-events/whats-going-on/ie-university-announces-appointment-lee-newman-dean-ie-business-school/

IEDP (2022) *Executive summary. Lifelong learning and university-based business schools.* Available at: https://uniconexed.org/wp-content/uploads/2022/06/AACSB-IEDP-UNICON-LL-SWOT-Executive_Summary-FINAL.pdf

Jack, A. (2021) Business schools slow to practise what they teach on sustainability. *Financial Times*, February 3.

Jones, D.R., M. Visser, P. Stokes, A. Örtenblad, R. Deem, P. Rodgers and S.Y. Tarba (2020) The performative university: 'Targets', 'terror' and 'taking back freedom' in academia. *Management Learning, 51*(4) pp.363–377.

Juusola, K. and K. Alajoutsijärvi (2019) Revisiting Dubai's business school mania. *Academy of Management Learning & Education, 18*(3) pp.484–492.

Kambil, A. and S. Budnik (2013) *Taking the reins as a business school dean.* Westlake, TX: Deloitte University Press.

Kaplan, A. (2018) A school is "a building that has four walls… with tomorrow inside": Toward the reinvention of the business school. *Business Horizons, 61*(4) pp.599–608.

Kaplan, S. (2020) Deck chairs on the Titanic: The impoverished b-school response to a changing world. *Poets&Quants,* July 28.

Kets de Vries, M.F.R. (2021) *The CEO whisperer.* Cham: Palgrave Macmillan.

Kezar, A., T. DePaola and D.T. Scott (2019) *The gig academy: Mapping labor in the neoliberal university.* Baltimore, MD: Johns Hopkins University Press.

Khurana, R. (2002) *Searching for a corporate savior: The irrational quest for charismatic CEOs.* Princeton, NJ: Princeton University Press.

Khurana, R. (2007) *From higher aims to hired hands: The social transformation of American business schools and the unfulfilled promise of management as a profession.* Princeton, NJ: Princeton University Press.

Kitchener, M. and R. Delbridge (2020) Lessons from creating a business school for public good: Obliquity, waysetting and wayfinding in substantively rational change, *Academy of Management Learning & Education, 19*(3) pp.307–322.

Lejeune, C., J. Davies and K. Starkey (2015) The impact of the impact agenda. *Global Focus, 9*(2) pp.44–47.

Locke, R.R. and J.C. Spender (2011) *Confronting managerialism: How the business elite and their schools threw our lives out of balance.* London: Bloomsbury Publishing.

Lorange, P. (2000) Setting strategic direction in academic institutions: The case of the business school. *Higher Education Policy, 13*(4) pp.399–413.

Maclean's (2020) McMaster business dean resigns, December 20.

Maloni, M.J., T.B. Palmer, M. Cohen, D.M. Gligor, J.R. Grout and R. Myers (2021) Decoupling responsible management education: Do business schools walk their talk? *The International Journal of Management Education, 19*(1) p.100456

Marr, B. (2022) *Business trends in practice: The 25+ trends that are redefining organisations.* Chichester: John Wiley & Sons.

McCarthy, D. and M. Dragouni (2021) Managerialism in UK business schools: capturing the interactions between academic job characteristics, behaviour and the 'metrics' culture. *Studies in Higher Education, 46*(11): 2338–2354

McDonald, D. (2017) *The golden passport. Harvard Business School, the limits of capitalism, and the moral failure of the MBA elite.* New York: Harper Business.

McLaren, P.G. (2019) Stop blaming Gordon and Howell: Unpacking the complex history behind the research-based model of education. *Academy of Management Learning & Education, 18*(1) pp.43–58.

McTiernan, S. and P.M. Flynn (2011) "Perfect storm" on the horizon for women business school deans? *Academy of Management Learning & Education*, 10(2) pp.323–339.

Meyerson, D.E. (2008) *Rocking the boat: How tempered radicals effect change without making trouble*. Boston, MA: Harvard Business Review Press.

Mintzberg, H. (1998) Covert leadership: Notes on managing professionals. *Harvard Business Review*, 76 pp.140–148.

Mohrfeld, T.J. (2020) *Journey to academic leadership: Experiences of women business deans*. PhD thesis, Knoxville, TN: University of Tennessee. Available at: https://trace.tennessee.edu/utk_graddiss/5820

Moore, K.M., A.M. Salimbene, J.D. Marlier and S.M. Bragg (1983) The structure of presidents' and deans' careers. *The Journal of Higher Education*, 54(5) pp.500–515.

Moules, J. (2020) Business schools grapple with a high turnover of deans. *Financial Times*, March 2.

Mullins, S. (2020) Why the dean is the secret weapon to building a business school's brand. *EFMD Blog*, July 14. Available at: https://blog.efmdglobal.org/2020/07/14/-why-the-dean-is-the-secret-weapon-to-building-a-business-schools-brand/

Nohria, N. (2011) *Practising moral humility*. TEDxNewEngland, January 11. Available at: https://www.youtube.com/watch?v=NCHnK5ZK9iI

Nordbäck, E., M. Hakonen and J. Tienari (2021) Academic identities and sense of place: A collaborative autoethnography in the neoliberal university. *Management Learning*, April 3. Available at: https://doi.org/10.1177/13505076211006543

O'Donnell, E. (2020) Farewell Dean Geoffrey Garrett. *Wharton Stories*, June 29.

Parker, M. (2020) The critical business school and the university: A case study of resistance and co-optation. *Critical Sociology*, 47(7–8) pp.1111–1124.

Parker, M. (2021a) Against management: Auto-critique. *Organization*. Available at: https://doi.org/10.1177/13505084211020922

Parker, M. (2021b, November 15) Why are business schools killing our planet? *Primetime*. Available at: https://primetime.unprme.org/2021/11/15/why-are-business-schools-killing-our-planet/

Paul, J. and S. Dhir (2021) (Eds.) *Globalization, deglobalization, and new paradigms in business*. Cham: Palgrave Macmillan.

Peters, K., R. Smith and H. Thomas (2018) *Re-thinking the Business Models of Business Schools*. Bingley: Emerald Publishing

Pfeffer, J. (2009) Renaissance and renewal in management studies: Relevance regained. *European Management Review*, 6(3) pp.141–148.

Pierson, F.C. (1959) *The education of American businessmen*. New York: McGraw Hill.

Pir, S. (2020) Hyper-personalization: How organizations are rethinking the employee experience. *Forbes*, January 25.

Roper, S.S. and T.E. Kennedy (2010) *Peak performance for deans and chairs. Reframing higher education's middle*. Lanham, MD: Rowman & Littlefield Publishers.

Rys, R. (2020) A leader for this moment and beyond. *WHARTON Magazine*, Fall/Winter.

Sass, S.A. (1982) *The pragmatic imagination. A history of the Wharton School 1881–1981*. Philadelphia, PA: University of Pennsylvania Press.

Simon, H.A. (1967). The business school a problem in organizational design. *Journal of Management Studies*, 4(1) pp.1–16.

Simon, H.A. (1991) *Models of my life*. New York: Basic Books.

Slaughter, M. (2015) *How to be a dean*. YouTube, October 31. Available at: https://www.youtube.com/watch?v=vNSlr0zQ2s0

Śliwa, M., N. Beech, K. Mason, L. Gordon and A. Lenihan (2021) *Equality, diversity, inclusion and respect in UK business and management schools: Interim report March 2021*. London: British Academy of Management.

Spender, J.C. (2016) Universities, governance, and business schools. In J. Frost, F. Hattke and M. Reihlen (Eds.) *Multi-level governance in universities*. Dordrecht: Springer, pp.141–169.

Spicer, A., Z. Jaser and C. Wiertz (2021) The future of the business school: Finding hope in alternative pasts. *Academy of Management Learning & Education*, 20(3) pp.459–466.

Stanford Graduate School (2009). Available at: https://www.gsb.stanford.edu/experience/news-history/delivering-vision-message-dean.

Starkey, K. and N. Tiratsoo (2007) *The Business School and the bottom line*. Cambridge: Cambridge University Press.

Stokes, P., N. Moore, S.M. Smith, M.J. Larson and C. Brindley (2017) Organizational ambidexterity and the emerging-to-advanced economy nexus: Cases from private higher education operators in the United Kingdom. *Thunderbird International Business Review*, 59(3) pp.333–348.

Streitfeld, D. (2017) Harassment suit against a Stanford dean is rejected. *The New York Times*, August 2.

Symonds, M. (2009) *B-Schools in the hot seat*. Forbes.com, May 13.

Tahir, T. (2008) Dean dismissed for plagiarism. *Times Higher Education*, March 6.

The British Academy (2021) *Business and management provision in UK higher education*. London: The British Academy. Available at: https://www.thebritishacademy.ac.uk/documents/3289/Business-and-management-provision-in-UK-higher-education.pdf

The Economist (2006) Business-school deans. Light on their feet, April 27.

The Economist (2021) A backlash against gender ideology is starting in universities, June 5.

Thomas, H., (2007) Business school strategy and the metrics for success. *Journal of Management Development*, 6(1) pp.33–42.

Thomas, H. (2012) What is the European management school model? *Global Focus*, 6(1) pp.17–22.

Thomas, H. (lead editor) (2013, 2014) *Reflections on the role, impact and future of management education, EFMD Perspectives.* Volumes 1 and 2. *EFMD Annual Report 2013.*

Thomas, L., J. Billsberry, V. Ambrosini and H. Barton (2014a) Convergence and divergence dynamics in British and French business schools: How will the pressure for accreditation influence these dynamics? *British Journal of Management*, 25(2) pp.305–319.

Thomas, H., E. Cornuel and M. Wood (2021) Where do we go from here? *Global Focus* 15th anniversary issue. Available at: https://www.globalfocusmagazine.com/where-do-we-go-now/

Thomas, H. and Hedrick-Wong, Y. (2019) *Inclusive growth: The global challenges of social inequality and financial inclusion.* Bingley: Emerald Publishing.

Thomas, H., M. Lee, L. Thomas and A. Wilson (2014b) *Securing the future of management education: Competitive destruction or constructive innovation.* Volume 2. Bingley: Emerald Publishing.

Thomas, H., P. Lorange and J. Sheth (2013a) *The business school in the twenty-first century: Emergent challenges and new business models.* Cambridge: Cambridge University Press.

Thomas, H. and L. Thomas (2011) Perspectives on leadership in business schools. *Journal of Management Development*, 30(5) pp.526–540.

Thomas, H., L. Thomas and A. Wilson (2013b) *Promises fulfilled and unfulfilled in management education: Reflections on the role, impact and future of management education.* Bingley: Emerald Group Publishing.

Tourish, D. (2020) The triumph of nonsense in management studies. *Academy of Management Learning & Education*, 19(1) pp.99–109.

Tufano, P. (2020) A bolder vision for business schools. *Harvard Business Review*, March 11.

University of Pennsylvania (n.d.) *History of Wharton.* Pennsylvania, PA: The Wharton School. Available at: https://www.wharton.upenn.edu/history/

Valbrun, M. (2019) Revolt over dean's ouster. *Inside Higher Ed*, February 19.

Vlad, C. (2021) 12 Inspiring female b-school deans share leadership lessons. *Poets&Quants*, March 7.

Wharton (2020). Available at: https://www.wharton.upenn.edu/story/farewell-dean-geoffrey-garrett/

Wharton (n.d.) *About the dean.* Available at: https://www.wharton.upenn.edu/about-the-dean/

Wharton Magazine (2007) Wharton's leaders, July 2.

Williams, A.P. (2009) Leadership at the top: Some insights from a longitudinal case study of a UK business school. *Educational Management Administration & Leadership,* 37(1) pp.127–145.

Wilson, E.O. (1998) *Consilience: The unity of knowledge.* New York: Knopf.

Wolverton, M. and W.H. Gmelch (2002) *College deans: Leading from within.* Westport, CT: American Council on Education and Onyx Press.

World Economic Forum (2020) *The future of jobs report 2020.* Available at: https://www.weforum.org/reports/the-future-of-jobs-report-2020/

Yazdani, B. (2016) This time it's personal. *Global Focus, 2*(10) pp.28–31.

Zhang, X., X. Zheng and Y. Xi (2020) How governmental agencies legitimize organizations: A case study on Chinese business schools from 1977 to 2014. *Academy of Management Learning & Education, 19*(4) pp.521–540.

3
How Do Business School Deans Deal with Critical Incidents?

Introduction

In Chapter 3, we highlight a range of critical incidents that business school deans experience during their tenures. Significant events challenge a dean's sense of composure, identity, organizational legitimacy and the role of business schools and businesses in society. We suggest that it is useful to reflect on how deans deal effectively and ethically with critical incidents to gain and sustain legitimacy and impact (Pettigrew and Starkey, 2016). We consider four types of critical incidents (Bott and Tourish, 2016): rare unforeseen external events (e.g., terrorism); archetypal situations (e.g., annual budgeting); typical events (everyday encounters and routines); and internal shocks (e.g., fraud). These incidents have various levels of intensity, significance, frequency and outcomes. They may be categorized differently in a variety of historical contexts, countries, institutions and cultures.

We are interested in what principles guide deans' decisions and actions when tackling natural disasters, recessions, public health crises, political upheavals, rising cost of living and inflation, climate, energy and other crises like terrorism, corruption and mergers. Traditional promotion, appraisal and budget rounds and routine events such as annual planning committees can all represent critical incidents. Downsizing and financial cuts, constraints on their autonomy, well-being challenges and digital transformations can overwhelm deans.

Currently, business school leaders are operating in uncertain contexts of multiple, simultaneous and ongoing crises. We suggest that an appreciation of real-world and defining moments deans face provides a useful counterbalance to the rhetoric of glossy job descriptions and to sensational media reports (Ethier, 2021).

DOI: 10.4324/9781003178125-3

In this chapter, we use critical incident technique to draw inferences from interviews about deans' behaviours in different countries, institutional contexts and cultures when they are confronted with difficult choices in the role. This helps us to make sense of deans' reflections on their behaviours and the causes and consequences of defining moments, providing valuable learning opportunities. The different scenarios are also useful for deans to reflect on what they might have done differently in some seemingly impossible predicaments. Moreover, they are a reminder that a dean must act as a role model. While deans begin their new roles with optimism and enthusiasm, the endless meetings, emails and commitments to multiple stakeholders can represent a process of attrition. Business school deans must sustain clear priorities, build effective teams, adapt and use skills from their experiences as successful researchers, teachers, consultants and board members. A key question is how do deans practise the responsible and impactful leadership and management that business schools profess (Yarrow and Davies, 2022) while remaining on the front foot to achieve strategic goals and sustain their own careers?

We hope that readers can extrapolate from the range of critical incidents discussed in this chapter. On the one hand, we are dealing with major disruptions like climate emergency, cost of living crisis, deglobalization and digital and other inequalities following the COVID-19 pandemic. We are seeing university business schools being subsumed into large faculties when their cash cow status has been diminished and governments prioritize STEM (science, technology, engineering and mathematics) disciplines (e.g., in Australia [Hogan et al., 2022]). On the other hand, deans who are sufficiently courageous and embrace changes can position themselves and their schools to make influential choices. They can facilitate meaningful engagement across traditional disciplinary boundaries and sectors to address grand challenges (Currie et al., 2016). Such business school leaders can overcome critical incidents and drive innovations which facilitate the UN's sustainable development goals (UN, 2015). Prescient deans can leverage tricky circumstances to create opportunities by reducing inequalities (Zhang, 2021), creating public good (Kitchener and Delbridge, 2020), and generating 'transcendent goods' (Naudé, 2021). In this spirit, we also present critical incidents that result in inspiring innovations (AACSB, 2022) and excellence practices (EFMD, 2022) which extend well beyond merely 'shaking the status quo' (Alajoutsijärvi et al., 2018) of business school rankings and accreditations.

The Case of Warwick Business School

Before we discuss the four types of critical incidents business school deans talked about in a variety of countries, institutional contexts and business school cultures, we note that insights from Warwick University are mentioned throughout this chapter. These relate to a doctoral thesis completed by one co-author (Davies, 2014). They are also based on Howard Thomas's reflections on strategic leadership processes (Fragueiro and Thomas, 2011) from his experiences as Dean of Warwick Business School (WBS) for a decade. Thomas was hired to take the unit to the next level based on his strategic leadership competences and international experiences. Similarly, Thomas was hired as Dean of Lee Kong Chian School of Business at Singapore Management University to facilitate strategic changes which included building a cohesive and collectively strong school in a young university.

The forerunner of WBS was founded in 1967 as the School of Industrial and Business Studies (SIBS). This was when industrial relations as a research discipline was well supported and trade union membership was high. George Bain was instrumental in building this as a strong department although he had no previous general business school leadership experience beyond leading a nationally funded research centre.

Importantly, Dyson, Bain and Wensley were internally elected Chairmen [sic] of SIBS and Bain shaped a business model for the school. Thomas was the first externally appointed Dean of the newly named Warwick Business School that came into existence. Thomas facilitated significant changes to establish WBS as a world-class player (ibid). WBS was the first in the UK to achieve triple accreditation (AACSB, AMBA and EQUIS). During his 10 years at WBS, Thomas doubled the undergraduate programme, oversaw rapid growth in executive education and one-year master's programmes. He also revamped the school's business model and prioritized faculty and research growth in key areas. There was a clear strategic plan agreed by faculty and annual updates with regular verbal and written reports. Thomas enabled a clearly articulated organizational structure (involving deputy deans and associate deans) and negotiated a devolved budget approved by the vice-chancellor and registrar. Thomas also established a vibrant fundraising and alumni directorate in the school. He engaged actively with business school advisory board members. Thomas also set up peer review by deans that he initiated to gain feedback on particular aspects of the school.

In short, hiring Thomas was a signal by the relatively young university that the school would be transformed completely into a world-renowned business school with a dean who was originally from the UK and with extensive business school leadership experience in Australia and the United States, including at London Business School, AGSM and the University of Illinois at Urbana Champaign. This transnational career profile was unusual for a dean at the time. Even today, such breadth of business school experiences over prolonged periods on different continents is unusual for a business school dean.

Subsequent deans Taylor (2010–16) and Lockett (from 2016) grew the WBS brand further, with Taylor co-branding the business school with a new logo aligned to the university. During Lockett's deanship, WBS became the first UK business school to gain an Athena Swan award from the Equality Challenge Unit in 2014, and in 2018 the first to gain a silver Athena Swan Award for improving gender equality. In his second (non-renewable) term of office, Lockett revamped the doctoral programme to be highly selective and fully funded. Following considerable growth and success, WBS has continued its status as a university department in the Faculty of Social Sciences. These positive achievements contrast with tough situations that successive heads of the school experienced in its different manifestations.

Four Types of Critical Incidents

Rare External Events

Business school deans we interviewed talked about global and national external crises beyond their control which appear to be rare events. These included financial and economic crises, the COVID-19 pandemic and climate emergency. At a national level, deans were hit by changes in national government funding policy for higher education, national and local terrorist attacks, natural disasters and political decisions such as national border lockdowns and Brexit. In many cases, these predicaments led to innovative and empathetic responses. In one instance, however, a dean was burned out with work-related stress and resigned on medical advice at the end of his career. As we face successive, continuous and simultaneous economic, political, social, technological, climate and other crises, crisis management and leadership are clearly important competences for deans to deal with events that might appear to be more frequent than they were historically.

Financial and Economic Crises

Clearly, critical incidents such as the 2007–08 Global Financial Crisis (GFC) and the 2022 cost of living crisis also test business school deans' resolve. Despite the GFC and institutional constraints, Howard Thomas was very clear about the overarching strategic priorities for Warwick Business School (WBS). He focused on the dual goals of nurturing research excellence and practical relevance despite financial constraints:

> Towards the end of my tenure as Dean at WBS, there were tight central financial controls during the recession. Plans for building new Business School

facilities were stalled despite strong reserves. There was considerable procrastination in decisions to approve new and replacement appointments. A strategic departmental review took place at this time. The strategic objectives of WBS for 2008–15 were closely aligned to the university's strategy. Our ambitions were to be positioned in the top tier of European business schools through strong innovation, investment in academic and professional expertise, teaching, facilities, IT, and raising our international profile. The School's six strategic objectives for 2008–15 were to foster excellence in research, teaching and learning, raise our international profile, ensure service and practitioner relevance, our long-term future and build the WBS community.

(Fragueiro and Thomas, 2011)

Thomas ensured the careers service in the business school reached out to alumni who were affected by the financial crisis. He maintained a focus on competitive positioning that was underpinned financially by expansion in undergraduate numbers, new programmes and international partnerships.

It is interesting that during the early days of his Harvard Business School deanship following the GFC, Nitin Nohria (Pazzanese, 2020) introduced the FIELD (Field Immersion Experiences for Leadership Development) method to expose students to cases and live projects overseas. This initiative reduced reliance on historical case studies (e.g., on Enron [Harris, 2003] and the Icelandic banking industry that were circulated globally and explained unethical practices).

Business schools were heavily criticized during the 2008 GFC for encouraging managers to take huge financial risks based on shareholder value which disregarded responsible leadership (Podolny, 2009). The 2008 crisis indicated that academics need to be curious about what is really happening in organizations rather than focusing narrowly on obscure financial models (ibid). This insight is a major lesson for business school deans to heed as we navigate the effects of war in Ukraine and prospects of stagflation.

COVID-19 Pandemic

The global critical incident of the COVID-19 pandemic clearly tested many business school deans and resulted in some stepping down during what was a devastating time for many (Mavin and Yusupova, 2020). From March 2020, the COVID-19 pandemic forced business school leaders to minimize health and safety risks and make better use of educational technology (Davies et al., 2021). Peter Tufano (2020), former dean of Said Business School in Oxford University, argued that the pace of change in businesses is far faster than in business schools. The agility shown by business schools rapidly shifting to online learning (GBSN, 2020) during the COVID-19 pandemic illustrates changes to operating models that were long overdue.

There were opportunities to learn from deans of business schools who had experienced SARS outbreaks in 2002–04. During the pandemic, many staff resented requirements to teach in person and their research funds being sequestered for central contingencies. The public health crisis was a steep learning curve for many business school deans:

> The human and communications (especially listening) dimensions of the deanship are critical. At the outset of the pandemic, we had to deal with anxiety contagion, to contain the rumour mill about potential job losses as there was media speculation about this in the sector. I was impressed by the high levels of collegiality with staff working together for a common cause although there were some selfish behaviours.
>
> (Davies et al., 2021) [Heather McLaughlin]

COVID-19 pandemic lockdowns challenged deans' capacity to sustain constructive and multiple modes of communications, as Heather McLaughlin explained:

> We used multiple forms of two-way communication channels to reduce stress and support well-being such as drop-in sessions, exchanging good news stories, all faculty activities, webinars, weekly virtual coffee mornings, and Yammer. In internal discussions, we discussed resourcing for remote working, making efficiencies and streamlining courses to reduce workloads. In reflecting on returning to campus, we talked about how we would use space differently to create a sense of community in a context of reduced face-to-face communications.

During the pandemic recovery process, deans continue to face challenges about remote working and inequalities with digital divides and lost opportunities for corridor conversations and water cooler moments. Howard Thomas stresses the value of social space to build a sense of community which the COVID-19 pandemic has disrupted for many and remains a challenge still: 'Before the pandemic, I valued staff lounges where members of the business school, including doctoral students, could meet serendipitously and share ideas.'

During the pandemic, academic leaders (Kruse, 2020) struggled with limited authority to deal with people humanely as many decisions were centralized. Yet during this difficult time, at University College London, Nora Colton became founding Director of the new start-up Global Business School for Health based in the Faculty of Population Health Sciences. The public health crisis demonstrated the importance of healthcare management and leadership in global healthcare systems, extreme workforce shortages and burnout, as well as great advances in managing vaccination discovery and roll out with public and private sector partnerships.

> I am very aware how high-quality healthcare improves life outcomes and for business and health to be integrated. We cannot take the health sector for

granted and developing healthcare managers and leaders, especially women in senior roles, is critical for improving healthcare systems.

(Symonds, 2021) [Nora Colton, GBSH, UCL]

Climate Emergency

While one-off and episodic critical incidents in the external environment can unite business school stakeholders behind a dean's mandate, chronic wicked problems such as the climate emergency can make the deanship seem impossible. As Bill Gates warned in 2020, 'COVID-19 is awful. Climate change could be worse' (GatesNotes, 2020). Indeed, two years beforehand Al Gore stated that 'the climate crisis is a public health crisis' (Twitter, 2018). The problem is that climate change tends to be gradual and cumulative over many years with apparently unrelated events bolstering each other. Yet climate change (along with war in Ukraine) is also significantly impacting businesses and creating opportunities for phenomenal shifts in business and educational models.

Per Holten-Andersen, former President of Copenhagen Business School (CBS) and Rector of the Royal Veterinary and Agricultural University and forestry expert, is very preoccupied with the challenge of climate emergency. For him, this represents a global crisis which business school deans cannot ignore. Holten-Andersen talked about the necessity of engaging in tough debates about socially responsible values and climate change which is causing anxiety amongst students. As a business school leader, he was exercised about how a culture of socially responsible leadership and values-based capitalism with a conscience could be established within CBS:

> I have a strong belief in Pareto optimality, that is not benefiting personally at another's expense. Business schools must produce socially responsible leaders and behave responsibly themselves. We must educate people about values-based capitalism with a conscience. We cannot continue to destroy the planet at the pace we currently are doing.

National Government Funding Cuts

Business school deans must be alert to national changes in central and local government policy, legislation and regulation in managing a school's portfolio and risks. During the 1980s, George Bain, who led the School of Industrial and Business Studies (SIBS, now Warwick Business School), was faced with significant central government funding cuts. As an experienced industrial relations mediator and arbitrator with effective political skills in higher education, Bain recruited Jenny Hocking from the central administration to manage the school and liaise with colleagues in the centre. He also established a close partnership with the University's Registrar, Mike Shattock. Bain telephoned Shattock regularly early in the morning (YouTube, 2011a) before everyone else arrived on campus to discuss the school's progress. This example of constructive collaboration between the school and central university shows how deans can act as effective boundary spanners. It also illustrates adversity and necessity as the mother of invention and the importance of diversifying income streams, as Bain explains:

> Mike Shattock, a legendary registrar (one of the most senior administrative positions) at Warwick and closely involved in my appointment, is an inspiring example of responding creatively to government cuts. During the university cuts made by Prime Minister Margaret Thatcher in the 1980s, Shattock worked successfully with me when I chaired what was then called the School of Industrial and Business Studies based on a 'save half, make half policy'.
>
> (Clark, 1998)

Andrew Pettigrew noted: 'George would clear his desk of business school paperwork before everyone arrived in the mornings. That left him with time to call the registrar to negotiate deals and to get on with university politics the rest of the day (Pettigrew and Starkey, 2016).'

It is a challenge for deans of university-based business schools to integrate the business school within the rest of the university while differentiating the position of the business school brand amongst competition in the business school sector. Working with the grain of the academic institution and in partnership with central university administrators for mutual synergies during crises and everyday represents a tightrope for business school deans who want to sustain a degree of local autonomy.

Terrorist Attacks

Other emotionally challenging times for deans included national and local acts of terrorism which threatened health and safety and well-being following the 9/11 attacks in 2001 and the Boston marathon bombing in 2013. Dipak Jain talked about his experiences at Kellogg School of Management: 'I started my deanship on 9/11. We showed empathy by giving students breaks and supporting them. After 9/11, job offers were rescinded to some of our recent graduates. We asked our alumni to help.' He argues that moral rather than emotional intelligence or IQ matters most in the business school deanship. Moral intelligence (Lennick and Keil, 2005) is about the mental capacity to apply universal human principles to goals and actions with values of integrity, responsibility, forgiveness and compassion.

As Kets de Vries (2021) argues, leadership is a moral act. Effective leaders are capable of bringing people together to develop others and make them stronger. This depends, however, on value-driven leadership that establishes a clear moral tone. Kets de Vries talks about risks of 'rot at the top'. He argues that true leadership is about tackling tough problems to benefit future generations rather than being based on short-term populism and self-centredness. Jain highlights his ethos that 'we all eat the same grains' and should help each other. This approach underpinned Jain's behaviours in difficult situations such as during the 9/11 terrorist attacks and recession: 'As a leader, you must also be very grounded and humble. I treat my students like my own family, as if they were my own son or daughter. You must show empathy and compassion.'

In another example of deaths resulting from terrorism, Ken Freeman was very grateful for the central university's expertise at a distressing time following city bomb attacks: 'The Boston University communications team has a crisis communications plan. They were amazing during the Boston marathon bombing.'

Both these incidents indicate deans not acting alone and taking the time to appreciate the impact of wider tragic events on the community they serve in the business school and more widely. Both deans were willing to ask for help and to help others who were affected by the atrocities.

Natural Disasters

The Indian Ocean earthquake and tsunami in 2004 which Dipak Jain personally experienced caused him to reflect on his approach to business school leadership. His argument is that like animals in a tsunami, deans must remain grounded and listen to warning signs to remain safe by moving to higher ground. Business school deans should be alert to what faculty members are saying and writing, particularly in turbulent times when organizational mindfulness can avert disaster (Ray et al., 2011).

National Border Lockdowns

The prolonged closure of national borders heralded a particularly critical time for deans of business schools in Australia and New Zealand. Foreign students contribute significantly to Australia's export income (Brumby, 2021) but the global status of Australian business schools (QS and ABDC, 2021) was severely affected by national border lockdowns (Bothwell, 2021) during the COVID-19 pandemic. Flows of international students and collaborations between Australian and overseas schools in research, teaching and other activities were restricted.

This resulted in considerable numbers of layoffs, increased teaching loads for top management scholars, and an increased focus on the domestic student market. At the same time, there were innovations such as stackable and flexible degrees as well as local industry collaborations to recover from tough economic conditions.

At UTS Business School in Sydney, Carl Rhodes moved from Deputy Dean to Dean during a national lockdown. He reflects on this experience and its consequences:

> Business schools were hit particularly hard as a third of all international students who come to Australia enrol in business degrees (ABDC, 2021). As a result, for Australian business schools the most pressing issues arising from COVID included 'funding of research activities, maintaining the health and wellbeing of school staff, and reimagining what teaching and learning would look like in the "new normal"' (QS and ABDC, 2021). In particular, the negative impact of the pandemic on university finances led institutions to lay off teaching staff, close subjects and courses, shut departments and even merge faculties (Price, 2021). Some have argued that business schools are witnessing the end of their status as the 'cash cows' in their parent universities, calling their very existence into question (Hogan et al, 2021). Others have suggested that Australian universities in general are fast on the way to becoming 'just another knowledge provider', with nothing differentiating them from corporate competitors.
>
> (Ross, 2021)

Nevertheless, Rhodes was able to reframe this crisis in positive terms:

> This period has also been an opportunity to re-think about our longer-term future and our purpose as a business school in a public university of technology. Business school executives have been complicit in enthusiastically embracing 'the use of journal lists and associated crude measures of performance' (Harley, 2019). This directs teaching and research in business schools away from addressing inequality, climate, racism, sexism, and other major problems facing the world today (Harley and Fleming, 2021) which require collaborative approaches. Mark Scott (2021), Vice Chancellor of the University of Sydney, has called for greater collaboration between co-located universities in Sydney to present a more united front in seeking support from the federal government to address these grand challenges. There are, however, emerging alternative models based on an idea of the 'business school for public good' (Kitchener and Delbridge, 2020) that takes seriously the need to question economic orthodoxy and contribute to fairness and equality in society (Fotaki and Prasad, 2015). The question that we can only answer positively through real innovations and willingness to changes is: can business schools contribute to meeting the grand challenges of the present era?
>
> (Waddock, 2020)

Such critical incidents provide serious wake-up calls for business school deans to revisit the curriculum and the role of management education in society with renewed vigour.

Brexit

In the UK, Brexit was a national political shock (Davies et al., 2017, Davies, 2021) with far-reaching implications. The outcome of the Brexit referendum was a historical inflection point when business school deans in the UK were forced to reflect on threats to globalizing forces in the sector. At the time, critical management scholars argued that Brexit represented nationalism and anti-intellectualism (Bristow and Robinson, 2018). Following Brexit, Finn (2018) called for the reinstatement of 'trust between academic citizens, their institutions and the broader publics they serve'. He quoted Robbins who chaired a report on higher education in 1963, which stressed the need in higher education for responsible citizens with open minds and warned about the negative aspects of nationalism:

> Above all, we should set our forces against the intrusion into science and learning of the anti-social forces of nationalism…Without weakening the sense of duty to their local society, we must seek to make our young men and women citizens of that republic of mind which knows no frontiers.
> (Robbins, 1966)

A key message is that business school deans should not globalize or internationalize at the expense of localism and civic engagement. They should integrate differences and develop an international mindset. Sandra Dawson, former Director of Cambridge Judge Business School, stresses this point (YouTube, 2011b):

> A shared purpose is what keeps us all together… It's extraordinary what you can learn and how you can help each other by realizing that many of the issues that you face are faced by others. [In a] changing international world … always look outwards rather than inwards.

In the next section, we explore classical critical incidents that might be expected in a business school dean's role.

Archetypal Situations

Deans discussed six types of critical incidents that might be expected to exercise them. These included convergence on a strategy; communicating; establishing the right culture; driving change with a degree of autonomy and support; mediating with the central university; and pursuing entrepreneurial opportunities.

Strategic Planning

First, business school deans talked about significant periods when they had to synthesize a business school's strategic positioning. This was based on the mandate they were given on arrival and on consultations. For example, George Bain vividly recalled Patrick Barwise saying to him, 'George, you've just repeated back to us what we told you.' This was immediately after Bain had given his inaugural presentation to staff at London Business School. Other deans talked about being hired following a phase of strategic drift in a business school's history.

Deans talked about critical times when they had to converge on a particular strategy to gain support: 'There was onus on the dean to express and articulate a sort of coherent strategy that people would buy into' [Robin Wensley, Warwick Business School].

Championing a business school's strategy entails effective and timely storytelling skills: 'It's really trying to find the right place and where the narrative of the school gets the most traction' [Jane Houzer, London South Bank University]. This also requires ongoing conversations: 'You have to have people engaged in the constant dialogue and debate which shifts and changes and explore those strategic priorities and refine them' [Jane Houzer].

Communicating

Second, deans were conscious of the important occasions when they had to champion and communicate the school's vision as leaders and figureheads. Critical points included accreditation body peer review team visits. As a business school's chief spokesperson and disseminator of its impact, deans were conscious of the need to communicate in positive language internally and externally. Deans developed storytelling skills to embed a school's strategy in conversations with advisory board members, potential donors and other key stakeholders. Waller at the University of Arkansas emphasizes that the dean is a cheerleader: '[p]art of a dean's role is to sing the praises of the faculty' (Waller and Caldwell, 2021).

One new dean had been anxious about communicating with a philanthropist for the first time as part of the fundraising strategy. In contrast, when Sandra Dawson was asked how she responded to a rejection when asking for funding she commented: 'I see a "no" as a deferred yes. I'm always optimistic that we can find a shared sense of purpose. After all, everyone wants to be part of a business school with high quality teaching and research.'

Informal communications in chatting with people about their research were key motivators for some deans: 'We had some really good people. You could have a good chat with everyone' [Robin Wensley].

Some deans gained valuable market intelligence and insights about the mood of the business school in small talk with people at all levels, in corridors, staff lounges and significant 'water cooler moments' (Wu et al., 2011). These encounters may appear incidental and inconsequential but are critical for deans to know what is really going on: 'He's very good at small talk, down-to-earth, chats with everyone' [About Howard Thomas].

Being communicative and approachable was seen as an important aspect of the business school deanship.

Business School Accreditation Events

For some business school deans, business school accreditation visits can loom in their calendars as major ordeals when they need to communicate confidently about the school they lead. For other deans, accreditation events are well organized by professional service staff who tell the dean what they need and which meetings to attend.

Peer review team visits can be a valuable source of intelligence and help deans to provide a united front. They can boost a dean's confidence with external endorsement of quality and accreditations differentiating the brand with evidence of the business school belonging to an elite club (Bell and Taylor, 2005). On the other hand, failed accreditations (Lejeune and Vas, 2014) can represent triggers in a business school dean's career when strategies and practices and their own leadership is questioned. A failed accreditation can result in a watershed when the dean steps down (Alajoutsijärvi et al., 2018): 'OBS [Oulu Business School in Finland] went through a change in the school's top management, when the dean, exhausted by the adversity involved in the accreditation project, decided to resign, and he was succeeded by the former vice dean.'

Charles Harvey, who was a business school dean four times (Royal Holloway, UWE, Strathclyde, Newcastle University), emphasized the importance of celebrating victories such as success in accreditations, rankings and publications as key moments to celebrate: Celebrating your victories is very, very important. You notice I use the word 'victory' because you're at risk so often.

Deans' Dinners

George Bain used to tell a joke: 'What's the difference between a business school dean and a supermarket trolley? You can get more food and drink into a dean but they're harder to steer.' While hosting and participating in social events might not appear onerous, they can be exhausting and difficult to delegate when key stakeholders expect to see the head of a business school. Michael Osbaldeston commented from his experiences (of leading two business schools with a focus on executive education) on the high-energy levels and stamina required: 'Night after night, you have to turn up at social events, hand shaking events, bragging about how wonderful the place is.'

These incidents can be challenging for deans who are introverts and others with young families. An acting dean talked about endless rubber chicken dinners in the university when he was frequently asked to explain what a business school is to people from outside the sector. Several deans stayed on campus during the week so that they were available for networking and could switch off with their families on weekends. Arnoud De Meyer of Cambridge University enjoyed college dining as part of networking within the university when he lived in university accommodation. Barbara Allan, a business school dean in London, used her weekly commute from home as a buffer and limited herself to two or three evening events during the week to pace herself.

Organizational Culture and Community Building

Third, many deans reflected on memorable points in their tenures when they had challenging conversations about enabling the right culture of good citizenship, hiring and developing talent, counselling underperformers, forming their inner cabinet, advisory board and building teams. Potential threats to their credibility as intellectual and responsible leaders – as role models – was evident from instances of incivility and dissent. Deans also recalled successful conversations when a sought-after academic agreed to join the business school and talented individuals agreed to take on leadership roles.

Hiring and Developing Talent

In his deanships, Howard Thomas was conscious of hiring faculty members with appropriate motivations to contribute citizenship and a sense of community in the business school, not self-interested business school professors who lack a sense of service (Piercy, 1999) and who behave like semi-independent contractors:

> As a dean I have tried to hire well-rounded individuals, not solely on the basis of their publication records. I recruit faculty also based on their character and their motivations to contribute actively to developing the business school institutionally as good citizens. My motto was 'to hire the best athletes and let them run'. I do not see any value in hiring 'academic mercenaries' or in chasing individuals who are reluctant to move from existing jobs.

He sought to appoint rounded academics, good organizational citizens who nurture others' careers within their own business school. This contrasts with academic mercenaries who are self-interested careerists focused on maximizing their personal income (Sturdy and Gabriel, 2000) and brand rather than contributing to goodwill and the well-being of the business school.

Deans grapple with decisions about growing or buying in talent:

> Deans face a stark choice. Do they invest in the slow process of building international researchers or bow to ... the Chelsea FC [Football Club] model? In making that decision they need to consider the sustainability of the strategy they choose. In buying international academics they are competing with the American schools with billion-dollar endowments, in a country with lower tax rates and a lower cost of living than the UK. Also, like individual academics, deans have to ask themselves 'do I play the national game or strive for true, unambiguous international excellence?'
> (Saunders et al., 2011) [John Saunders, Aston Business School]

There is a global talent pool for deans to hire top researchers: 'What kept me awake at night if anything was the challenge of hiring top faculty members' [Arnoud de Meyer, Cambridge Judge Business School].

Bain at WBS recalled times when: 'It was particularly rewarding to help a colleague who had hit a brick wall in their careers to come unstuck.' A colleague of George Bain we interviewed commented on the critical incident of Bain appointing two highly capable individuals externally to marketing professorships although only one position had been advertised: 'George persuaded the university to allow him to appoint both Robin Wensley and Peter Doyle. He was the only academic leader I worked for at Warwick who really harnessed professorial talent to build the institution.'

Ken Freeman, who had not previously worked in academia, appreciated the pressures on management faculty to publish (Miller et al., 2011). He ensured that senior well-published professors were fully involved in hiring and performance evaluation processes and that he took responsibility for being involved in difficult conversations.

Forming the Dean's Cabinet

Decisions about who to include in the dean's senior team also represent critical incidents. One dean was pleased that she achieved a self-organizing team in a small private business school that was part of a group which included private schools. The chair of the business school board did not approve of this form of shared leadership and only wanted to work with her.

Rolf D. Cremer reached a critical point in his leadership role when he realized that his trust in his colleagues' motivations to behave responsibly was misplaced in a context of allegations of fraud. His experiences were distressing and demotivating as he tried to stabilize the business school's finances:

> I am naturally trusting and think the best of people, that they are intrinsically motivated and responsible. This leads to a somewhat specific lesson. I regard it as essential to build one's own leadership team. I should have suspected that the unusual and weird business model could not possibly be the result of one single person at the top, let alone the allegations of embezzlement – which in fact were never proven anyway. Rather it was the result of an inner circle of people in the institution who worked closely together. On reflection, I would advise a dean that if someone has unsuccessfully applied for your job, you should move them on.
>
> (McGregor, 1960)

Change Agency

A fourth type of critical incident related to deans involved in juggling, innovating, restructuring, overhauling curricula, closing programmes, handling disturbances and students' complaints and faculty resistance, as well as space constraints.

Curriculum Development

Deans spoke about the need to be forthright and straightforward when driving change following consultations so that goals were unambiguous. One critical incident for Ken Freeman was when he was challenged by a senior colleague in an open meeting. Freeman was quite candid in his response:

At Boston University, the decision to revamp the undergraduate curriculum was voted down the first time but it was a close thing. Some faculty said this was a big defeat but we went back and improved the proposal and it was accepted. One senior professor stood up to me in a meeting in front of all staff resisting the change. I told him that I had consulted widely and that I welcomed his contributions. But if he didn't want to get on the bus with us, I would be happy to support him to move somewhere else. He did get on board subsequently.

[Ken Freeman, Questrom School of Business, Boston University]

Business school deans explained how they were motivated to reform the curriculum based on business school students' concerns about social responsibility: 'Our current students are motivated to contribute to issues of climate change, corporate social responsibility, and social justice in the curriculum' [Heather McLaughlin].

Students' Complaints

Student complaints can rapidly escalate into critical incidents. It is important for deans who are very busy to step up responsively when appropriate to collaborate on solutions: 'I'm an enthusiastic optimist so I always think there will be a solution and I always feel one can get people involved' [Sandra Dawson, Cambridge Judge Business School].

Sandra Dawson emphasized her role as a key communicator amongst multiple stakeholders: 'See yourself in the middle of a variety of stakeholder relationships. Keep in contact with your supporters in industry'. She talked about rapidly responding to student complaints by convening meetings with students immediately to resolve issues jointly and to communicate that she cared about the student experience.

It took Swansea University a long time to address staff and student complaints about Nigel Piercy, Dean of the School of Management, in a culture where he frequently denigrated his colleagues and students (BBC News, 2015). This resulted in discussions amongst parliamentarians at the Welsh Assembly (The Times, 2015) about university governance.

Facilities

While business schools have at times been accused of isolationism in occupying shiny (Parker, 2018), iconic buildings that are set apart from the rest of the university campus, several deans we spoke with were exercised by crunch points before the COVID-19 pandemic when they lacked suitable space for growing numbers of students and new hires. In a few cases, promises of new buildings were unrealized and when this dawned on deans they felt disappointed.

Some deans inherited space problems which were pressure points:

> My predecessor set many hares racing. It was like a runaway train, George Bain worked at an enormous pace to move the school to the next level. My role was to consolidate these initiatives. For example, we needed more teaching space for the growth in student numbers and I had to persuade the university to provide this. So, I focused on continuity and change.
> [Robin Wensley, WBS]

Other deans felt like victims of their own success as they first had to increase student numbers and income before space was allocated in subsequent budget rounds. Ken Freeman was forced to use space creatively in Questrom School of Business at Boston University when he faced a crisis of student growth and complaints about inadequate facilities. The lack of physical space was negatively impacting on the business school faculty and student experiences:

> In the first six months, I met the Provost every three to four weeks for half an hour. Then I only met the new provost on an exceptional basis. She gave me more autonomy than other deans. Those of us who survived did not mind meeting her less frequently. Indeed, she gave the business school significant cash, $25m, to retrofit the space we had, to make it more creative. I had to contribute $5m from the business school's surplus but this seemed a fair deal four years into our mission. It was tough because we were bursting at the seams which is a better scenario than having spare capacity. This was a high-class problem. We carried out lots of creative work to maximise every square inch of space.

Deans had to balance their drive to relieve pressing space constraints in the business school with patience in navigating university approval processes: 'I tried hard to be inclusive and patient about the faculty office refurbishment for co-working space. Eventually, this was agreed by the central university as we were unable to provide offices for new staff' [Heather McLaughlin, Coventry University].

McLaughlin experienced a crunch point when there was a lack of capacity for office space for new faculty members pre-pandemic. She was creative in developing with non-professorial staff state-of-the art co-working spaces to stimulate creative collaborations amongst academics:

> The experience of negotiating with the university to invest in attractive and well-used modern co-working spaces demonstrated commitment to

employee well-being and quality of working life. I enjoyed collaborating on the project and seeing others take a lead in implementing creative ideas. Key learning points were to communicate the clear benefits of the change, to be fair, inclusive, and supportive, and sufficiently flexible to accommodate the professoriate's preference for the status quo. Clearly, the pandemic has significantly changed attitudes to workspaces and digital offices.

McLaughlin drew on her values about equitable working conditions to deal with resistance to her idea to create state-of-the-art working space for members of faculty. She was passionate that this would facilitate multidisciplinary collaborations and impact to serve the business school's wider goals:

> My approach to the estates problem was to consult widely on creating state-of-the-art co-working spaces for all the academics. My ambition was to encourage cross-disciplinary collaborations across different research groups. To my surprise, the professors were highly resistant. Despite the exciting suggestions that non-professorial staff provided, the professors insisted on remaining in their dull, old-fashioned offices. I persisted with holding regular meetings with a diverse range of staff, taking on board their ideas, and negotiating with the central university for laptops, brightly painted and inspiring co-working space. I was pleased to see that several individuals were passionate about the project. Although I did not win the full battle to convert all the academics to the idea of co-working space, I felt that we achieved small wins and a much better sense of community which supported our goal of more interdisciplinary working and mutual support.

Ken Freeman was stoical about recalling instances when a new building for the business school was promised but not agreed although he was shown a potential site by a senior university administrator: 'I was patient about the delay with the central university providing a new building the president promised. It was never delivered, however, relations remained amicable.'

Andrew Pettigrew at Bath School of Management experienced a similar realization when early talks about a new building did not materialize during his tenure. He, too, remained on good terms with the head of the university despite this non-event.

Co-working and social spaces present opportunities for deans to facilitate knowledge-sharing and serendipitous opportunities for new ideas. The loss of frequent in-person interactions following the COVID-19 outbreak has been exacerbated in some business schools by deans agreeing to repurpose staff office space for student use. This may discourage faculty members from voluntarily coming into the university at all.

Boundary Spanning

Business school deans are classic middle managers and boundary spanners. Bain was skilful in harnessing professorial talent and negotiating university politics to bring people on board. He illustrates the argument by Rosser (Rosser et al., 2003) and her colleagues that deans benefit from network centrality institutionally which enables them to build coalitions:

> By virtue of their midlevel placement within the higher education organizational structure [deans] are in the center of controversy, conflict, and debate; they play the role of coalition builder, negotiator, and facilitator…with overtones that are more political and social than hierarchical or technical.

University-based business school deans reflected on crucial meetings when they had to comply with or negotiate financial contributions to the centre. Bain talked about taking his 'rottweiler' accounting professor to such meetings to ensure a degree of transparency in interrogating the university's accounts. One dean talked about his role as 'chief compliance officer', another saw himself as 'chief defender' as he engaged in standoffs about the business school being held accountable for overseas student recruitment while central administration wanted to be responsible for determining related expenditure. Deans at the start of their tenures were often enthusiastic about offering to help the university and ensure smooth operations and integration at the university–business school interface. Others later in their tenures were more wary about critical meetings where they had to bid for resources to be allocated in competition with other parts of the university. At times, deans were conflicted about which committees to attend or chair. Charles Harvey, a business historian, commented: 'I tend to prioritise committees that the vice-chancellor is chairing to ensure we remain visible.'

University Meetings and Issue Selling

Critical incidents involving deans presenting proposals at central university meetings tested deans' communication, persuasion and impression management skills. Some business school deans were skilled political operators who rose to the pressure of high-stakes committee meetings. Robert Dyson (who led SIBS part-time for three years and WBS on an interim basis) observed: 'You have to be brief and well briefed.'

> For one dean, there were welcome opportunities in being put on the spot to justify the case for investment in the business school within the university. Robin Wensley at WBS found that centralized university governance and feedback from peers helped him to hone his arguments: 'When we were centralised, it required you to argue your case to a different community

and to persuade a group of senior peers who were not part of the business school.' It was interesting that individuals commented about Robin Wensley's conversational approach to his deanship, including in negotiations: 'With Robin, every negotiation was a conversation.' In contrast, conversations with George Bain at WBS were seen as key points for him to negotiate: 'With George, every conversation was a negotiation.'

Both approaches were appreciated, with Bain seen as the architect of the school in the 1980s in taking it to a new level of excellence and Wensley succeeding him for a phase of continuity and consolidation.

Entrepreneurial Activities

Finally, deans as entrepreneurs struggled with major turning points in their careers as they sought to recognize opportunities, take on risks, and create benefits through new or different activities to change values (Drucker, 1993). For example, Nora Colton at University College London chose to become the inaugural dean of a business school start-up during the COVID-19 pandemic in a leading research-intensive public university which is almost 200 years old rather than take on a more senior traditional cross-university role.

Typical Events

In this third section, we explore daily incidents which may not seem critical yet can wear deans down. These include endless meetings, emails, constantly communicating and challenges with transitions in the role.

Diary, Time and Energy Management

Managing their Outlook calendars was a major challenge for many deans. Some asked their personal assistants (PAs) to filter routine requests, to block out time for them to think, and avoid arranging back-to-back meetings in different locations that were hard to reach on time. One dean who was trying to finish a book hid in the British Library and gave his PA strict orders not to disturb him unless the vice-chancellor called. Robin Wensley (WBS) commented:

> At some critical point in every dean's tenure they realise they've bitten off more than they can chew. I realised early on that I would only be able to do the job with the help of some very good colleagues who were willing to provide support. I remember one time when I was booked to attend a

conference overseas for a week and it was cancelled. I decided to keep the conference in my diary so I could take some time at home just to think without being interrupted by meetings.

Another dean's PA talked about critical moments when a dean stood on the threshold of his office conflicted about which international meeting he could attend. For example, whether he could leave one meeting early to catch a flight in time to attend the second half of another meeting. During the pandemic, we talked to a dean in Egypt who was on multiple Zoom and MS Teams calls at the same time. Clearly, there are trade-offs between high levels of concentration in a meeting and being visible in a range of important meetings.

Effective committee and meeting chairing skills are vital for deans to get things done. George Bain (WBS) reflected on his approach:

> I run meetings in a very structured way and I'm a very forceful chairman. I warn people when I start, unless they know me well, that I'm going to push and push and push. What I'm always trying to do is to capture a point, sum up and see if people really agree.

While some individuals may view meetings as ritualistic and tedious, deans must understand that 'all the meeting, the talking, the form-filling and the number crunching…Getting things done involves the nitty-gritty, often tiresome and repetitive routines of strategy' (Whittington, 1996). Indeed, one PA said of the business school dean she worked with:

> When I take the minutes of meetings that the dean chairs, we're really clear about what's been agreed and the action points. When he's away travelling, the same meetings just become talking shops. At these types of meetings, I really just don't know what to write in the minutes as nothing seems to get decided when the dean isn't in the chair.

Sandra Dawson (Cambridge Judge Business School) and Robert Dyson (WBS) were seen as particularly effective at chairing meetings. They facilitated useful discussions and conscientiously followed up to ensure action points were implemented. Robin Wensley (WBS) observed that people were relieved when deans were able to stop issues from being constantly raised at important meetings because they were resolved rather than recycled for the next meeting.

While deans' diaries were punctuated by regular meetings with their senior team and the predictable academic rhythms of open days, staff meetings, away days and graduation ceremonies, critical incidents arose when there were difficult decisions to make such as closing or launching courses or research centres.

Experienced deans were mindful of pacing themselves, the importance of delegating non-critical activities and at the same time overcoming institutional inertia of change fatigue. Deans were energized in different ways, e.g., some enjoyed long haul flights so that they could spend time on their own research and to think more clearly away from everyday distractions. Others avoided checking their emails on weekends and holidays for some kind of work-life balance but ensured systems were in place to contact them in cases of emergencies.

One Cannot Not Communicate

Importantly, deans talked about how their throwaway comments could turn into critical incidents and backfire if they were misinterpreted, especially in a context of cancel culture and culture wars. Daily banter with colleagues and corridor conversations with people at all levels appear mundane and inconsequential (Watzlawick et al., 2011). However, chance conversations can raise morale and reduce anxieties, enable deans to gain valuable real-time market intelligence for evidence-based decision-making, and make them seem accessible. There are risks, however, of 'deans being cornered in the corridor and agreeing with the last person they spoke with rather than sticking to agreed policies at important meetings', as one School Manager observed about ad hoc favours being made 'on the fly'.

Several deans emphasized the importance of staff common rooms and making free refreshments available at set times to encourage internal networking and knowledge-sharing. Ken Freeman (Boston University) deliberately relocated the dean's office away from a secluded part of the business school to an internal glass office near the café with an open-door policy. This communicated his accessibility and humility.

However, a balance needs to be struck to avoid being too ready to communicate or for issues to escalate rapidly to the dean's office. Howard Thomas (WBS) pointed out that in tricky situations he would draft an email and sleep on it before reviewing and sending it the next day to avoid hasty decisions. Waller (University of Arkansas) established a regular series of podcast interviews as part of his communications strategies when he was internally appointed as dean. Weekly newsletters and tweets from the dean can look like virtue signalling but they can provide useful sources of regular updates on progress and aspirations. On one occasion, Andy Lockett (WBS) realized the imperative to take time in his busy diary to make a public statement (WBS, 2019) related to controversies about poor student behaviour in the university which he thought were undermining the business school's values. Deans who hide away in their

offices behind closed doors to concentrate on their personal research are suscep-
tible to what Bedeian (2002) called the 'dean's disease', that is insulated from
daily realities. This impedes the quality of decision-making and transparency in
routine activities such as workload allocations (Boncori, 2020) which can lead
to a (perceived) culture of unfairness. Both Heather McLaughlin (Coventry
University) and Ken Freeman (Boston University) wrote one-page strategic
documents annually to ensure these informed everyday decisions.

Deans' Entries and Exits

Finally, announcements of business school deans' appointments, arrivals, ups
and downs and departures represent important points in the individuals' careers and in the histories of the business schools they lead. Transitions over a
deanship can be unsettling (Delbecq, 1996) for the postholder over the various
seasons (Gmelch et al., 2012) of their tenure in any country, institutional context or business school culture. Onlookers might assume that deans are well-
paid and well-supported, however, business school leaders who take seemingly
trivial and unglamorous activities seriously (Alvesson and Sveningsson, 2003)
and treat people with respect while also focusing on the big picture and ostensibly higher stakes events seem well placed to weather mundane events as well
as existential crises.

In the final section of this chapter, we explore internal shocks in the business
school which can make or break deans' careers.

Internal Shocks

Aside from external shocks to their deanships caused by global and national
crises, deans we spoke with mentioned various non-routine internal events
which were wake-up calls that made individuals question their assumptions
and change systems. Several of these critical incidents resulted in meltdowns
and shakeouts with potentially serious consequences for deans' careers.

Fraud Allegations

One particularly traumatic episode that Rolf D. Cremer experienced was a
police raid and his predecessor's arrest on fraud allegations. This happened
before Cremer actually took up his post. The unexpected series of events
meant that Cremer started his position earlier than expected. The distressing

experience of reputational damage caused by events which took place before he joined the business school culminated in him resigning because of stress-related ill health within 22 months. Cremer stabilized the business school while struggling with a major cash flow and reputational crisis but it took a major toll on his well-being. This was despite his extensive experience in business school administration in New Zealand (Massey University) and China (CEIBS).

On a positive note, Cremer reflected on a critical incident much earlier in his career when he was unexpectedly appointed as Dean at the University of Macau aged 37. Fortunately, his counterparts who led other schools in the university were very supportive mentors and friends at that time. Being able to sound out trusted confidants outside the business school and the loyalty of the Chief Financial Officer during the cash flow crisis were key factors in keeping him sane during these turning points in Cremer's career.

External Mergers Resulting from Insolvency

Another interesting example of a critical incident that another experienced business school dean did not foresee was a pensions black hole. Again, fortunately the business school survived. In Ashridge Business School, Kai Peters discovered the 'black swan' pensions deficit, an entirely unexpected event which had significant consequences for the history of Ashridge and his own career. Peters was Dean of Rotterdam School of Management for over three years and CEO at Ashridge for 11 years, a charity specializing in executive education. Following the GFC, a huge pensions deficit emerged which was unsustainable and a merger with Hult International Business School (Financial Times, 2014a) was announced in 2014. Peters had to oversee layoffs and this intense period made him realize the limitations of some advisory board members who saw their roles mainly as 'a nice day out for a good cup of tea'. He became Chief Academic Officer for over two years in the new entity which included a sabbatical and time to write a book. He subsequently moved to the Coventry University Group, a large undergraduate public university, as Pro-Vice-Chancellor of Business and Law. Peters' extensive networks in the business school sector, thought leadership and board and business development experiences enabled him to transfer between very different types of business school. The strategic alliance at Ashridge happened at the same time as the 'merger mania' (Financial Times, 2014b) of Grand Ecole business schools in France because of funding cuts and Arizona State University's takeover (Financial Times, 2014c) of Thunderbird, a private graduate school that was in financial difficulties.

Internal Mergers

Deans also referred to internal mergers generating anxieties. In the case of Bain, he merged the industrial relations (IR) and organizational behaviour research groups to strengthen both units. Andrew Pettigrew said that at the time it seemed like a bloodbath and only Bain could pull this off because he was an IR scholar himself. On reflection, however, Pettigrew understood the logic of reducing vulnerabilities for the separate groups. Other episodes when deans were on the receiving end of school mergers that were decided centrally in the university led to them leaving within two years. For example, in one case the schools of law and business were merged into a faculty and the business school dean was not appointed as faculty dean despite the law academic lacking a doctorate or knowledge of the business school sector. Following a sabbatical, the former business school dean moved to two further deanships. In another business school, a dean felt demoted when his school was merged into a larger university college structure where he no longer reported directly to the head of the university. He also decided to move on and became president of an academic unit with greater autonomy in a more prestigious university.

On a personal level, an acting dean who was upset that she was not short-listed internally for the deanship moved to become dean of another school for the sake of her mental health, even though it entailed weekly commuting. To his surprise, another dean's first term of office was not renewed by a new vice-chancellor/president and he was offered the deputy deanship. He rejected this and after a few months moved to a new deanship despite the disruption involved in relocating his family home.

Retrenchment

'Divestment from research and scholarship' (Komik, 2021) in critical management studies at the University of Leicester Business School when there was a national boycott of the university is another kind of shock wave which Martin Parker (2020) has reflected on as a business school sociologist. When he was head of a management department, Martin Parker also wrote about his increasing discomfort at Keele University during a national higher education funding crisis:

> my reflexive playing at becoming manager rapidly came to feel like an indulgence when jobs and the future shape of the university were at stake. … People no longer joked in corridors, but said that I looked tired. I began to seriously think about trying to get a job elsewhere, and felt increasingly

trapped and depressed by my desire to do an impossible job with a measure of good grace. … Perhaps I am not 'manager' enough to do what seems necessary here by captaining the boat away from the icebergs.

(Parker, 2004)

Change Management

Martin Parker (2014) provided an agonizing account of neoliberalization in a European business school where a new dean announced that a new 'earth shattering change programme' would enable it to 'be *the* leading business school in Europe'. The programme involved dissolving shared governance, implementing strict performance targets based on publishing in top-tier journals, significantly raising tuition fees and overseeing new roles and structures that resulted in high levels of stress and turnover. Parker asked 'why was dissent so muted, and what does this tell us about the capacities of responsibly autonomous professionals to resist the managerialism that they teach about'?

Personal Tragedies

Of course, the unexpected death of a dean (Biddulph, 2006; Bloomberg, 2015; Gleeson, 2015) while still in post or family tragedies that result in them stepping down abruptly are shocks to a business school's stakeholders. The sudden deaths of students in a business school (Byrne, 2012; Allen, 2016; BBC News (2022) or of faculty members are clearly serious moments in a dean's tenure. Deans must drop everything to attend to family members and to make public announcements to reassure their constituents.

Dipak Jain recounts a tragedy he experienced in 2002 when he was dean. He heard that Sky Polega, a great granddaughter of Carl Sandburg (the three-time Pulitzer Prize winner), on the MBA programme at Kellogg School of Management was experiencing a medical emergency on a study visit in an isolated part of Alaska. The school had no insurance cover and the student had no medical insurance:

Sky had a persistent headache, was helicoptered to Anchorage where emergency surgery for bleeding on the brain failed, and she was transferred to Seattle. I flew to meet Sky's mother and reassured her that we would fund all medical and other costs. Soon after I returned to Chicago for an inaugural September class, Sky passed away.

One of my mantras is that 'uncertainty is inevitable but worrying is optional'. You must show compassion and empathy. I contacted Sky's mother and later collected her from the airport, and she met privately with the student who had accompanied Sky to hospital.

This incident could have resulted in the school incurring massive legal costs for professional negligence. We learned, however, that Sky had a serious pre-existing medical condition. The student's family did not blame the university for her death. They established a scholarship in her name.

Of course, we tightened up on safety policies and procedures after this tragedy. My view is that the dean can delegate accountability but not responsibility. By the end of my deanship, I delegated to two deputy deans but the buck always stopped with me. I also believe that if someone asks you for help and you give it, you will receive four times more in return.

Other Critical Incidents

Harassment, Racial and Gender Discrimination

For reasons of confidentiality, business school deans we interviewed rarely talked about issues of harassment and racial and gender discrimination in their own business schools. They were very wary, however, about the prevalence of these issues and potential pitfalls. One dean, for example, expressed concern about James Ellis, former Dean of USC Marshall School of Business. An interim president fired Ellis from his deanship with allegations that he had mishandled and failed to address harassment, racial and gender discrimination complaints (Valbrun, 2019). Students and trustees protested for him to be reinstated. Ellis did not agree to step down from the deanship after serving another academic year, nor did he accept full pay for the remaining three years before going on sabbatical and returning to a professorial role. He refused to sign a non-disclosure agreement. Ellis wrote an op-ed in the *Los Angeles Times* (Ellis, 2019) to voice his concerns about being a scapegoat in a toxic university culture. Ellis stated that he was unaware of 10 years of complaints against the business school that had been reported to the University's Office of Equity and Diversity and about which he had not acted.

Rankings Scandals

The egregious lying and lack of remorse shown by Moshe Porat (Bleizeffer, 2022), formerly Dean at Temple Fox, who was sentenced to 14 months in an US prison (with a $250,000 fine and 300 hours of community service) for rankings fraud has been a particular talking point within the business school community. Although there have been several incidents related to business schools submitting inaccurate data for rankings, this case of faking information over many years is especially shocking.

Faculty Suicides

The suicide of a business school faculty member is especially traumatic for all concerned. Several deans refused to comment about suicides within their own schools that had been reported in the press. For example, workload pressures, inability to take annual leave and long hours were blamed for the death of Malcolm Anderson at Cardiff Business School (Haf Jones, 2019). A professor in the business school acknowledged that staff lacked confidence in the work-load model and managers who were attempting to implement it. At Kingston Business School, Diana Winstanley took her own life. The inquest heard that she had struggled with her new role as a professor and with the technology (BulliedAcademics, 2007).

Additional Challenges

Direct showdowns by deans with the head of the university can present tricky moments in their careers, for instance, about financial contributions, auton-omy and parents' requests to condone students' cheating. Barbara Allan chal-lenged her own boss when he violated university equity, diversity and inclusion policies by appointing a deputy vice-chancellor without due process. She ad-mitted that complaining to the university board about this might appear to be a career-limiting move for any business school dean but she was incensed by the hypocrisy. Nevertheless, she remained on good terms with her male line man-ager while the correct recruitment process was followed, although it resulted in the same man being appointed as an internal candidate. This incident took place shortly before Barbara retired from the deanship at the end of her career so perhaps she had nothing to lose by taking the moral high ground.

Clearly, many students suffer from loneliness (University World News, 2022) and university staff were under great pressure during the pandemic (Lee et al., 2022) lockdowns and continue to be. This has tested their resilience (de los Reyes et al., 2022). Business school deans must remain alert to health and well-being issues (Edwards et al., 2021) caused by their own interventions in driving changes. One executive education dean we spoke with only realized the negative impact on others he made during a casual remark when he read a letter on a development programme in which he had participated. The fallout from Nigel Piercy's very public resignation 'with immediate effect' (BBC News, 2015) at Swansea University is a stark reminder of the importance of deans behaving professionally as role models.

Other examples of very uncomfortable and unexpected conditions deans experienced internally included incidences of faculty disloyalty; incivility in public meetings; theft by a close colleague; violations reported in the national media about research integrity (CBS DK, 2016); and a proven case of sexual harassment by a doctoral supervisor. A particularly dramatic scenario was a palace coup while a dean was overseas. Senior professors who had tried to support the dean confronted the head of the university with an ultimatum for the dean to step down in his second term because of strategic drift. Eventually, the first external appointment to the business school deanship in its history was made with a turnaround mandate.

Evidently, some of the internal crises discussed here were self-inflicted and several might have been avoided had the individuals carried out due diligence. Learning from experience, showing humility, asking for help and being empathetic are key learning points from these significant events. Knowing when to stand one's ground and when to walk away relies on judgement and an understanding of context. Stories of recovery and renewal following critical points in deans' careers in different countries, contexts and different cultures offer hope as business school leaders face new predicaments in uncertain times.

Conclusion

When analysing case studies of critical incidents, there is a tendency to provide instant solutions based on emotions and instinct, to think fast (Kahneman, 2011). However, the examples provided in this chapter imply that, especially in situations that are ambivalent and emotionally sensitive, business school deans should practise the processes that business school professors advocate. These include evidence-based decision analysis and due process and stakeholder and contingency theories. Deans need to judge when they should draw on fast, automatic, emotional and instinctive approaches (system one thinking) to making decisions as well as allowing time for slower, more conscious and deliberative decision-making (system two thinking), depending on the situation (ibid). There is a risk that deans' initial good intentions and energies are diverted by noise and organizational sludge (Sunstein, 2021).

In viewing critical incidents holistically and for long-term positive outcomes, deans should be confident in dealing appropriately with risks of anxiety contagion and scapegoating when they are blamed for events beyond their control. Hasty responses to incidents may prove worse than the incident itself. However, a lack of responsiveness can also lead to dissatisfaction with business school leadership. Both approaches can exacerbate the already high turnover (Moules, 2020) and short tenures of business school deans (Thomas et al., 2013).

The overarching aim of this chapter has been to explain and understand key strategic leadership challenges of business school deans. By reflecting on unique, real-life, critical incidents discussed in semi-structured interviews, we illustrate multiple events and stakeholders at different levels and in different circumstances that have the potential to surprise, shock and distract deans from their core strategic priorities. Importantly, nuanced insights gained from business school deans dealing with critical incidents provide powerful examples of morally responsible business school leadership. We also see examples of irresponsible and unprofessional behaviours and some seemingly impossible situations when a dean's leadership characteristics and style and followers' moral compass are shaken. We hope that by providing examples of business school deans learning from disruptive events, we convey the importance of reflective practices and the value of dialogue to establish professional organizational cultures. The aim is to help business school leaders and their fellow management educators to sustain continuous learning in their own institutions and careers. In that spirit, we invite constructive feedback on the types of incidents related to leading business schools outlined here and suggestions for additional vignettes in different countries, cultures and contexts over time.

A list of helpful Discussion Points for Reflection in relation to some of the events described in this chapter can be found in Appendix 1.

References

AACSB (2022) Innovations that inspire. Tampa, FL: AACSB. Available at: https://www.aacsb.edu/about-us/advocacy/member-spotlight/innovations-that-inspire. Accessed 4 June 2022.

ABDC (2021) Australia's business schools. Australian Business Deans Council. Available at: https://abdc.edu.au/about-us/australias-business-schools/#footnote-1

Alajoutsijärvi, K., K. Kettunen and S. Sohlo (2018) Shaking the status quo: Business accreditation and positional competition. Academy of Management Learning & Education, 17(2) pp.203–225.

Allen, N. (2016) Available at: https://poetsandquants.com/2016/03/14/tragic-death-vanderbilt-mba/. March 14.

Alvesson, M. and S. Sveningsson (2003) Managers doing leadership: The extra-ordinarization of the mundane. *Human Relations*, 56(12) pp.1435–1459.

BBC News (2015) Available at: https://www.bbc.co.uk/news/uk-wales-south-west-wales-33651707. July 24.

BBC News (2022) Available at: https://www.bbc.co.uk/news/uk-wales-south-east-wales-44389004. June 9.

Bedeian, A.G. (2002) The dean's disease: How the darker side of power manifests itself in the office of dean. *Academy of Management Learning & Education*, 1(2) pp.164–173.

Bell, E. and S. Taylor (2005) Joining the club: The ideology of quality and business school badging. *Studies in Higher Education*, 30(3) pp.239–255.

Biddulph, M (2006) Disease drove dean to death. *Oxford Mail*, April 20.

Bleizeffer, K. (2022, March 11) Moshe Porat, former Temple Fox Dean, sentenced to 14 months in prison for rankings fraud. *Poets&Quants*, March 11.

Bloomberg (2015) Milan Polytechnic Business School Dean Spina killed in avalanche. *Bloomberg.com*, February 22.

Boncori, I., L.M. Sicca and D. Bizjak (2020) Workload allocation models in academia: Panopticon of neoliberal control or tools for resistance? *Tamara Journal for Critical Organization Inquiry*, 18(1) pp.51–69.

Bothwell, E. (2021) Australian universities in 'deep trouble' as borders stay closed. *Times Higher Education*, February 3.

Bott, G. and D. Tourish (2016) The critical incident technique reappraised: Using critical incidents to illuminate organizational practices and build theory. *Qualitative Research in Organizations and Management*, 11(4) pp.276–300.

Bristow, A. and S. Robinson (2018) Brexiting CMS. *Organization*, 25(5) pp.636–648.

Brumby, J. (2021) Foreign students are our fourth largest export, even with the pandemic. *The Sydney Morning Herald*, February 19.

BulliedAcademics (2007) Available at: https://bulliedacademics.blogspot.com/2007/02/how-many-silent-witnesses.html

Byrne, J.A. (2012) Available at: https://poetsandquants.com/2012/05/23/the-tragic-death-of-a-harvard-mba/. May 23.

CBS DK (2016) Available at: https://www.cbs.dk/en/cbs-news-en/1867/cbs-initiates-investigation-of-report-on-danish-agriculture. December 12.

Clark, B.R. (1998) *Creating entrepreneurial universities: Organizational pathways of transformation*. Oxford: Pergamon Press.

Coursera. Available at: https://www.coursera.org/certificates/launch-your-career

Currie, G., J. Davies and E. Ferlie (2016) A call for university-based business schools to "lower their walls:" Collaborating with other academic departments in pursuit of social value. *Academy of Management Learning & Education*, 15(4) pp.742–755.

Davies, J. (2014) *Hybrid upper middle manager strategizing practices: Linking archetypes and contingencies in the UK business school deanship*. PhD thesis, Coventry: University of Warwick.

Davies, J. (2021) Book review: British universities in the Brexit moment: Political, economic and cultural implications. *Management Learning*, 52(3) pp.374–388.

Davies, J., K. Alajoutsijärvi and K. Kettunen (2017) Brexit means…, *Global Focus*, 1(11) pp.26–30.

Davies, J., E. Ferlie, H. McLaughlin and H. Thomas (2021) Examining business school leadership. *Global Focus*, 1(15) pp.66–73.

Delbecq, A.L. (1996) What's next after 10 years as dean? Reflections of a reemerging professor. In P.J. Frost and M.S. Taylor (Eds.), *Rhythms of academic life: Personal accounts of careers in academia*. Thousand Oaks, CA: Sage, pp.437–442.

De los Reyes, E.J., J. Blannin, C. Cohrssen and M. Mahat (2022) Resilience of higher education academics in the time of 21st century pandemics: a narrative review. *Journal of Higher Education Policy and Management*, 44(1) pp.39–56.

Drucker, P.F. (1993) *Innovation and entrepreneurship: Practice and principles*. New York: HarperBusiness.

Edwards, M.S., A.J. Martin and N.M. Ashkanasy (2021) Mental health and psychological well-being among management students and educators. *Journal of Management Education*. Available at: https://doi.org/10.1177/1052562920978252

EFMD (2022) Excellence in practice awards. Available at: https://www.efmdglobal.org/awards/eip-excellence-in-practice-award/. Accessed 4 June 2022.

Ellis, J. (2019) Op-Ed: James Ellis: Setting the record straight about my departure from USC. *Los Angeles Times*, June 30

Ethier, M. (2021) The biggest b-school scandals of 2021. *Poets&Quants*. Available at: https://poetsandquants.com/business-school-news/the-biggest-b-school-scandals-of-2021/. Accessed 4 June 2022. December 27.

Financial Times (2014a) Available at: https://www.ft.com/content/c12b55b2-0368-11e4-817f-00144feab7de. July 4.

Financial Times (2014b) Available at: https://www.ft.com/content/7ddf8044-0859-11e4-9afc-00144feab7de. September 14.

Financial Times (2014c) Available at: https://www.ft.com/content/ff9afc6e-89c6-11e4-8daa-00144feabdc0. December 22.

Finn, M. (2018) *British universities in the Brexit moment: Political, economic and cultural implications*. Bingley: Emerald Group Publishing.

Fotaki, M. and A. Prasad (2015) Questioning neoliberal capitalism and economic inequality in business schools. *Academy of Management Learning & Education, 14*(4) pp.556–575.

Fragueiro, F. and H. Thomas (2011) *Strategic leadership in the business school: Keeping one step ahead*. Cambridge: Cambridge University Press.

GatesNotes (2020) Available at: https://www.gatesnotes.com/Energy/Climate-and-COVID-19. August 4.

GBSN (2020) Moving the HBS MBA online: A conversation with Srikant Datar. YouTube, April 20. Available at: https://www.youtube.com/watch?v=K5Gm4wHxgrw

Gleeson, B. (2015) University of Liverpool professor dies in motorcycle crash. *Liverpool Echo*, April 15.

Gmelch, W.H., D. Hopkins and S. Damico (2012) *Seasons of a dean's life: Understanding the role and building leadership capacity*. Sterling, VA: Stylus Publishing, LLC.

Haf Jones, C. (2019) Lecturer's widow hits out at Cardiff University workload. *BBC News*, February 20. Available at: https://www.bbc.com/news/uk-wales-47296631

Harley, B. (2019) Confronting the crisis of confidence in management studies: Why senior scholars need to stop setting a bad example. *Academy of Management Learning & Education, 18*(2) pp.286–297.

Harley, B. and P. Fleming (2021) Not even trying to change the world: Why do elite management journals ignore the major problems facing humanity? *The Journal of Applied Behavioral Science, 57*(2) pp.133–152.

Harris, R. (2003) The case against cases. cfo.com. Available at: https://www.cfo.com/human-capital-careers/2003/04/the-case-against-cases/

Hogan, O., M.B. Charles and M.A. Kortt (2021) Business education in Australia: COVID-19 and beyond. *Journal of Higher Education Policy and Management*, doi: 10.1080/1360080X.2021.1926616

Hogan, O., M.B. Charles and M.A. Kortt (2022) The market's filthy lesson: Disruption for business and management education in Australian public universities. In R. Koris & A. Örtenblad (Eds.), *Debating the legitimacy of business schools*. London: Macmillan, pp. tbc.

Kahneman, D. (2011) *Thinking, fast and slow*. Basingstoke: Macmillan.

Kets de Vries, M.F.R. (2021) *Leadership unhinged: Essays on the ugly, the bad, and the weird*. Basingstoke: Palgrave Macmillan.

Kitchener, M. and R. Delbridge (2020) Lessons from creating a business school for public good: Obliquity, waysetting and wayfinding in substantively rational change, *Academy of Management Learning & Education, 19*(3) pp.307–322.

Komik, O. (2021) Available at: https://economicsociology.org/2021/01/28/condemning-the-university-of-leicester-standing-for-political-economy-and-critical-management-studies/. January 28.

Kruse, S.D. (2020) Department chair leadership: Exploring the role's demands and tensions. *Educational Management Administration & Leadership*, 50(5) pp.739–757.

Lee, M., R. Coutts, J. Fielden, M. Hutchinson, R. Lakeman, B. Mathisen, D. Nasrawi and N. Phillips (2022) Occupational stress in university academics in Australia and New Zealand. *Journal of Higher Education Policy and Management*, 44(1) pp.57–71.

Lejeune, C. and A. Vas (2014) Institutional pressure as a trigger for organizational identity change: The case of accreditation failure within seven European business schools. In A. Pettigrew, E. Cornuel and U. Hommel (Eds.) *The institutional development of business schools*. Oxford: Oxford University Press, pp.95–125.

Lennick, D. and F.K. Keil (2005) *Moral intelligence*. Upper Saddle River, NJ: Prentice Hall.

Mavin, S. and M. Yusupova (2020) Gendered experiences of leading and managing through COVID-19: Patriarchy and precarity. *Gender in Management*, 35(7/8) pp.737–744.

McGregor, D. (1960) Theory X and theory Y. In D.S. Pugh (Ed.), *Organization theory: Selected readings*. London: Penguin, pp.1–14

Miller, A.N., S.G. Taylor and A.G. Bedeian (2011) Publish or perish: Academic life as management faculty live it. *Career Development International*, 16(5) pp.422–445.

Moules, J. (2020) Business schools grapple with a high turnover of deans. *Financial Times*, March 2.

Naudé, P. (2021) *Contemporary management education: Eight questions that will shape its future in the 21st century*. Cham: Springer.

Parker, M. (2004) Becoming manager: Or, the werewolf looks anxiously in the mirror, checking for unusual facial hair. *Management Learning*, 35(1) pp.45–59.

Parker, M. (2014) University, Ltd: Changing a business school. *Organization*, 21(2) pp.281–292.

Parker, M. (2018) *Shut down the business school: What's wrong with management education*. London: Pluto Press.

Parker, M. (2020) The critical business school and the university: A case study of resistance and co-optation. *Critical Sociology*, 47(7–8) pp.1111–1124.

Pazzanese, C. (2020) Departing business school dean recalls a consequential decade. *Harvard Gazette*, December 16.

Pettigrew, A. and K. Starkey (2016) From the guest editors: The legitimacy and impact of business schools—Key issues and a research agenda. *Academy of Management Learning & Education*, 15(4) pp.649–664.

Piercy, N.F. (1999) A polemic: In search of excellence among business school professors: Cowboys, chameleons, question-marks and quislings. *European Journal of Marketing, 33*(7/8) pp.698–706.

Podolny, J.M. (2009) The buck stops (and starts) at business school. *Harvard Business Review, 87*(6) pp.62–67.

Price, J. (2021) Australian universities are dying and no one is coming to save them. *Sydney Herald*, May 18.

QS and ABDC (2021) *The future of Australian business schools. Results from the 2020 Australian business school survey.* Canberra: ABDC. Available at: https://abdc.edu.au/wp-content/uploads/2021/03/qs_abdc_fobs13.pdf. Accessed 6 June 2022.

Ray, J.L., L.T. Baker and D.A. Plowman (2011) Organizational mindfulness in business schools. *Academy of Management Learning & Education, 10*(2) pp.188–203.

Robbins, L. (1966) The university in the modern world. In L. Robbins (Ed.) *The university in the modern world.* London: Macmillan, pp.1–16.

Ross, J. (2021) Universities 'just another knowledge provider' by 2030: Report. *Times Higher Education*, August 15

Rosser, V.J., L.K. Johnsrud and R.H. Heck (2003) Academic deans and directors: Assessing their effectiveness from individual and institutional perspectives. *The Journal of Higher Education, 74*(1) pp.1–25.

Saunders, J., V. Wong and C. Saunders (2011) The research evaluation and globalization of business research. *British Journal of Management, 22*(3) pp.401–419.

Scott, M. (2021) *Prof. Mark Scott AO, Vice Chancellor, The University of Sydney*, September 8. Available at: https://www.youtube.com/watch?v=jhuB9-TF-JU

Sturdy, A. and Y. Gabriel (2000) Missionaries, mercenaries or car salesmen? MBA teaching in Malaysia. *Journal of Management Studies, 37*(7) pp.979–1002.

Sunstein, C.R. (2021) *Sludge: What stops us from getting things done and what to do about it.* Cambridge, MA: MIT Press.

Symonds, M. (2021) Making health a priority at business schools. *Forbes*, October 3.

The Times (2015) Available at: https://www.timeshighereducation.com/news/nigel-piercy-resigns-dean-swanseas-school-management

Thomas, H., L. Thomas and A. Wilson (2013) *Promises fulfilled and unfulfilled in management education: Reflections on the role, impact and future of management education.* Bingley: Emerald Group Publishing.

Tufano, P. (2020) A bolder vision for business schools. *Harvard Business Review*, March 11.

Twitter (2018) Available at: https://twitter.com/algore/status/1075797921608712193. December 20.

UN (2015) *The 17 goals*. New York: United Nations. Available at: https://sdgs.un.org/goals. Accessed 4 June 2022.

University World News (2022) Available at: https://www.universityworldnews.com/post.php?story=20220609110221496. June 9.

Valbrun, M. (2019) Revolt over dean's ouster. *Inside Higher Ed*. February 19.

Waddock, S. (2020) Will businesses and business schools meet the grand challenges of the era? *Sustainability, 12*(15) pp.2–11.

Waller. M.A. and S. Caldwell (2021) *The Dean's list. Leading a modern business school*. Fayetteville: University of Arkansas.

Watzlawick, P., J.B. Bavelas and D.D. Jackson (2011) *Pragmatics of human communication: A study of interactional patterns, pathologies and paradoxes*. London: WW Norton & Company.

WBS (2019) Available at: https://www.wbs.ac.uk/news/statement-by-dean-andy-lockett/. February 4.

Whittington, R. (1996) Strategy as practice. *Long Range Planning, 29*(5) pp.731–735.

Wu, L., S. Aral, E. Brynjolfsson and A.S. Pentland (2011) Water cooler networks. *Essays on social networks and information worker productivity*. Available at: https://dspace.mit.edu › handle › 759082523-MIT

Yarrow, E. and J. Davies (2022) Delegitimizing women management scholars' underrepresentation in the research impact agenda. In R. Koris and A. Örtenblad (Eds.) *Debating the legitimacy of business schools: Attacking, rocking and defending the status quo*. London: Macmillan.

YouTube (2011a) Available at: https://www.youtube.com/watch?v=HzWMgxW7JTQ

YouTube (2011b) Available at: https://www.youtube.com/watch?v=KZOC3oHNlkQ

Zhang, L (2021) Shaking things up: Disruptive events and inequality. *American Journal of Sociology, 127*(2) pp.376–440.

4
How Do Deans Learn?

Introduction

The business school dean's role is exceptionally challenging on many fronts. We would, therefore, expect deans to have a strong commitment to learning. We assume that they appreciate both formal and informal, personal, incidental and professional leadership development opportunities to gain a better understanding of their roles. They may be too busy, of course, to benefit fully from their own medicine!

The dean is a custodian and ambassador for the business school. He or she must guard against being consumed by distractions such as endless emails and meetings that add little value to the mission. This can be achieved by deans building effective teams, delegating and sustaining a professional organizational climate where individuals and organizations flourish.

March observed that 'leadership involves a delicate combination of plumbing and poetry' (Podolny, 2011). He also emphasized the need for beauty, joy and passion as values that should support leadership development. Yet to achieve organizational goals, business school deans need to learn to do much more than merely fix things or speak fine words.

Deans must learn to operate at the intersection of dynamic institutional structures and systems while developing themselves, others and their institutions. We know that management learning is situational, experiential (Kolb, 1983) and social and that leadership is relational, contextual, reflexive, political and ethical (Liu, 2017). Hence, business school deans must understand personalities and preferences, relationships and networks (Bolden et al., 2008). They increasingly need to learn to deal with woke behaviours (Rhodes, 2021) and culture wars. So, how can prospective and current deans be developed in an increasingly complex, challenging (Seale and Cross, 2016) and turbulent environment?

DOI: 10.4324/9781003178125-4

Our interviews with business school deans and our analysis of media reports demonstrate the importance of deans' self-management and awareness during identity transitions. Allies, mentors and executive coaches can help during different phases of a deanship. Deans can learn to manage their priorities, emotions (Heffernan and Bosetti, 2020) and energy to ensure they add value. Eisenhower's (Gray, 2021) matrix of time and task management in terms of what is urgent and important is one of the useful tools taught in business schools that deans might find challenging to apply in practice.

Business school deans know that they must build effective teams, as well as a sense of community and belonging while delegating appropriately, as they 'can't do it all'. At the same time, they must remain in touch with sector trends and listen to and act on internal feedback. It is critical that business school deans make time for reflection, self-care and networking to avoid overload, burnout and a lack of focus. This is necessary to support organizational development as well as a dean's own career. Deans must be mindful about their own well-being and strategic about their employability. Some of our interviewees talked about the need for an exit strategy when starting a deanship. Others spoke about never having a career plan, with 'one thing leading to another' serendipitously.

Importantly, strategic leadership is about making decisions for the long term and stakeholder engagement. This involves managing conflicting demands and resources to gain and sustain competitive advantage in a changing context. It helps if business school deans understand the qualities of strategic leadership, their scope for decision-making – within institutional constraints – teamwork and what influences their own leadership style (Samimi et al., 2022). How do they learn to promote culture change that engenders trust, respect, optimism and well-being? How do they deal with stresses, paradoxes and successes over time? How do business school deans understand systems, provide support, collaborate and sustain their own concentration and mental energy when there are so many demands on their time? This is in a context, following the coronavirus pandemic, where there is a shift to hybrid working and calls for innovative educational models.

Howard Thomas's adage 'there's no meaning without context' suggests national, institutional and cultural influences affect deans' learning and development. In some countries, business school deans must learn to navigate ministry of education approval for academic appointments (Zhang et al., 2020). In other countries, fundraising and philanthropic activities are well established and require additional support (Shackelford, 2021). In many universities, business school deans must learn to deal with managerialism (De Vita and Case, 2016) and organizational inertia while they personally drive initiatives such as responsible management education (Doherty et al., 2015).

Deans may experience critical incidents, such as institutional mergers, differently depending on the receptive contexts and resistance encountered. Deans also develop through learning moments from internal shocks related to misconduct, misfortune, cash flow problems and unavoidable changes. Reading about various scandals, losses and inequities can also offer important awareness of how deans might have behaved more responsibly and ethically. Appendix 2 provides examples of critical events/challenges at multiple levels. It also suggests lessons that business school deans might draw from these incidents. Learning from experience is not automatic, of course; people sometimes learn the wrong lessons, and learning may be partial and happen intermittently (McCall, 2004). However, reflections on critical incidents can help deans to understand strengths and weaknesses in systems and processes and their own behaviours. Reflections on critical episodes can complement 360-degree appraisals, formal mentoring and coaching activities and other professional development interventions.

Deans new to the role can learn from insights into academic leadership success shown in Table 4.1. A wide range of leadership scholarship (Reynolds and Vince, 2004; Starkey and Tempest, 2009; Howorth et al., 2012; Nabi et al., 2017; Harney and Thomas, 2020) is available to business school deans. For example, understanding critiques about the liberal arts, civil society, (social) entrepreneurship, critical management education and action learning can help deans to deal with the design challenge (Simon, 1967) of business schools in bridging management scholarship and practice. Deans need to learn to address the gaps between the rhetoric of branding and rankings (Gioia and Corley, 2002) and the realities of grand challenges (Gatzweiler et al., 2022). They must sustain personal and organizational legitimacy and impact. Business school deans have to ensure that students are equipped for the changing nature of work and for jobs that do not yet exist.

Clearly, deans learn from a range of seemingly never-ending on-the-job tasks and responsibilities. These include strategic planning, shaping organizational culture and creatively forming the senior leadership team. Other critical activities need attention such as curriculum design, improving facilities, dealing with complaints as well as chairing committees to manage and implement strategic change. However, it is also important that deans communicate meaningfully with staff, faculty and students. Regular newsletters and face-to-face meetings allow for deans to communicate about successes, new resource allocations and future strategic directions to create a positive learning environment and sense of community.

In the following sections, we first consider business school deans' leadership styles. These influence how deans are socialized in the role and how they gain

Table 4.1 Criteria for academic leadership success

1. Able to set a clear direction, ambitious, high standards, articulate, courage, positive attitude, team person, role model, good listener, positive energy, effective decision maker, boosts morale, builds trusting relationships.

2. Understands and respects academic culture, demonstrates expertise in understanding academic leadership.

3. Acknowledges, appreciates, values and respects colleagues, students and other key stakeholders and treats them with dignity to encourage belonging and inclusion.

4. Shares the truth with compassion, passionate, deals with conflict, proactive, demonstrates a high degree of morality, integrity, commitment and empathy.

5. Ready to take risks, accountable, follows policies and procedures, honest, demonstrates integrity, inspiring, confident and approachable, ability to trust and empower others and deal with conflict.

6. Communicative, consultative, collaborative, engaged. Seeks to be understood and to understand others.

7. Openly seeks and shares information and knowledge as appropriate.

8. Connects, develops and maintains positive relationships and collaborations through social and other media.

9. Organizational (re)design skills and able to build a sense of community.

10. Develops people and future generations of leaders.

11. Passionate about learning, reflective, culturally sensitive. Highly willing to learn, unlearn and relearn, to be creative, innovative and entrepreneurial, challenging the status quo while respecting history.

12. Successfully navigates boundary and self-identity work to achieve organizational and personal objectives, e.g., income generation and financial targets, reputation, quality, grand challenges, employability, impact, credibility, career goals.

Source: Zafar et al., 2019.

confidence in communicating and implementing strategic intent. We highlight how business school deans acquire new knowledge, understand the rules of the game and develop their leader(ship) behaviours and skills over their tenure. Second, we emphasize the value of the often overlooked period between individuals accepting and starting a business school deanship. During this time, a dean designate can synthesize information, acclimatize and develop their profile so that they can hit the ground running. Third, we discuss how (aspiring) deans make sense of the role. Once in position, how do deans overcome barriers and champion and facilitate organizational changes in management education and wider society? Finally, we discuss post-deanship trajectories which show how deans sustain legitimacy and impact through continuous personal and professional development.

Leadership Styles

Ewan Ferlie (Davies et al., 2021) has argued that studying differences in deans' leadership styles using leadership theories taught in business schools is important. Indeed, deans and their senior leadership teams are influential in designing and delivering management education to current and future leaders and employees globally.

While business school deans may understand theories about leadership styles, be they autocratic, democratic, paternalistic or laissez-faire, they experience knowing–doing gaps and expectations change over time. Individuals must reflect on the extent to which they adapt their leadership styles to the expectations of a deanship within a particular business school. We certainly do not advocate forms of transformational leadership (Andersen, 2015) that stifle and disrespect others' voices. One business school dean we talked with believed that he was a hired gun to clear out 'dead wood'. Another dean commented that the head of the university, a scientist, knew little about business schools. While other candidates for the role expected to be told what to do, this individual was appointed because he had thought through (on the 'back of a serviette') what the strategy might be.

Naturally, business school deanships differ in terms of job titles, size and scope. Learning to be a dean is influenced by different ideologies in various business schools as well as by institutional cultures, regulators and public attitudes in different countries and contexts. Deans must learn to communicate narratives that are plausible from individual, business school, university and external perspectives to gain buy-in for a strategy and its implementation. Deans may underestimate the difficulties of coping with multiple self-identity and organizational identity transitions. Planned and opportune learning activities and support through mentoring and coaching can develop a dean's resilience and emotional and moral intelligence. This requires hard work, asking good questions, listening, observing and learning from others. It also involves un-learning and for deans to develop new routines and perspectives.

Amanda Goodall (2009) contends that higher education leaders must act as standard bearers, with expertise and credibility to signal the importance of research success. Matt Waller's (Waller and Caldwell, 2021) trajectory from visiting assistant professor to acting, then substantive business school dean il-lustrates a traditional insider appointment. In contrast, Scott Beardsley (2017), a non-traditional dean with three decades' experience in management consul-tancy, completed a professional doctorate in education shortly after his dean-ship at Darden was announced.

Notably, in some situations, business school deans' jobs have been diminished by internal faculty and college mergers. In other cases, their jobs have been enlarged by external mergers. There are common lessons to be learned from the lived experiences of business school deans and from new developments in broader ecosystems (such as new players like Quantic School of Business and Technology). There are also very localized lessons for deans to take onboard in order to embed university-based business schools meaningfully in their own institutions while innovating to differentiate themselves in the marketplace.

We are seeing a focus on STEM subjects in universities. This offers business school deans a real opportunity to work with science-based schools on post-graduate and executive STEM/MBAs and design creative partnerships in on-line executive education. Questrom School of Business offers an online MBA with edX (IBL News, 2022); the GetSmarter partnership works with SDA Bocconi School of Management, University of Stellenbosch Business School, Harvard Business School and Cambridge Judge Business School. Other sce-narios may involve business schools being absorbed into larger academic units to cross-subsidize other disciplines. This may entail the business school dean losing control of the sub-brand and reduced autonomy. In such cases, business school deans may find themselves having to adjust to reporting to a faculty dean of social sciences rather than the head of the university. This results in former business school deans feeling demoted.

In one recent scenario, Soumitra Dutta, Dean of Cornell SC Johnson College of Business, suddenly stepped down (Byrne, 2018) following a merger controversy (Foderaro, 2016) and the appointment of a new president and provost. Four years later, he relocated for a new deanship at Oxford University (Byrne, 2022). In other situations, we have seen deans coping with the near demise of independent business schools that were established around the end of World War II, e.g., Henley Business School (Anderson, 2008) and Thunderbird School of Global Management (Bleizeffer, 2022). Both business schools were later absorbed into public universities. In contrast, we have seen entrepreneurs and global influencers such as Santiago Iñiguez de Onzoño (former Dean of IE Business School, a long-time member of EFMD's board and former chair of AACSB) gaining significant responsibility by creating IE University, where he is now President.

Making Sense of the Business School Deanship

The time between accepting an offer of a deanship and taking up the position is often overlooked. Yet it can provide valuable learning opportunities. Externally appointed and novice deans often experience a steep learning curve. So, taking time to become familiar with key documents, listening to a variety of stakeholders, preparing a vision and public announcements of gratitude, and taking a holiday before transitioning into a deanship are all important steps. The learning which incoming deans gain during this phase can help to avert an induction crisis brought about by failing to adjust.

Accepting an offer to become a dean involves balancing the hopes and expectations of the new hire to shape a school's strategy with an appreciation of the institution's culture, context and governance arrangements. A new dean must learn to uphold the existing academic culture and values by influencing others rather than by adopting a command-and-control approach. At the same time, business school deans must manage performance and ensure changes for long-term sustainability. An incoming dean must balance continuity and change, scholarship (personal and collective), and other higher education management goals and objectives. He or she needs to recognize current strengths and the potential for developing themselves and others in an academic unit that is pluralistic and complex. Deans in other university schools, especially in schools that do not have links with the professions, may not appreciate the challenge business school deans experience in constantly catering for the needs of both management scholars and management practitioners.

Deans' Leader and Leadership Development

Day (2000) suggests that

> [l]eadership development can be thought of as an *integration* strategy by helping people understand how to relate to others, coordinate their efforts,

build commitments and develop extended social networks by applying self-understanding to social and organizational imperatives. This is as much about development as it is about leadership, multi-levels and changes in context over time within the leader and between the leader and followers.

(Day et al., 2014)

In considering deans' development, it is important to compare expectations with actual experiences (Davies and Thomas, 2009). These vary in different situations over time depending on type of institution, individual dispositions and changes in the business school sector as well as broader organizational and societal contexts. Bryman and Lilley (2009), both management scholars and former heads of a school of management, asked leadership scholars what they expected from their own leaders. They found that academics valued university leaders who are sensitive to context, honest, trustworthy and develop people to reach goals beyond those they felt capable of achieving. Leadership scholars appreciated university leaders who took a genuine interest in others and made time to consult them with a clear sense of values and direction. Importantly, academic staff stated that they respected leaders who gave them time and space to carry out research, facilitated collegiality and called out unprofessional behaviours. At the same time, leadership scholars recognized that academic faculty members are difficult to manage, as their primary allegiance is typically to their discipline. In the end, deans must learn to navigate institutional politics successfully to drive through change and get things done despite organizational inertia.

Evidently, deans operate from a middle position in university-based business schools. In some institutions, they are expected to incentivize others' research productivity while sustaining their personal research profile. Deans are not only managing the business school but their own careers, upwards and externally. It is important that leader and leadership development experiences provide the time and space for business school leaders to reflect on their own behaviours and actions. At the same time, they must differentiate the school in the marketplace while integrating the business school within the university and local communities.

Clearly, there are many types of deans (e.g., serial, novice, interim, acting deans, individuals from under-represented groups and disciplines and work experiences) in different types of business school and country contexts and cultures. They are all in the learning business and should be lifelong learners and reflective practitioners. However, the pressures of the job mean they may neglect their own professional development. This observation is a reminder that business school deans need to understand management education as a subject and as an object of scholarship. They need to ensure that they make sufficient time for 'learning by doing' on the job, reflecting on experiences, and critically evaluating data and feedback. They need to be aware of developing new models and mindsets, the value of social learning, experimenting and innovating. Business school deans need to take advantage of formal and informal learning opportunities to support evidence-based decision-making and considered approaches to developing themselves, others, and their organizations. Interestingly, writing about business and management education can help business school deans make sense of their own roles (Dawson, 2008; Fragueiro and Thomas, 2011).

So, how do deans learn formally and informally as leaders, develop leadership in others and facilitate organizational development? The business school dean's role can be highly interactive (Thomas and Thomas, 2011). Ostensibly, a business school dean has access to colleagues who are experts on leadership and management development and who can theorize about the intellectual, social, relational, emotional, mental and physical well-being challenges entailed in devising and delivering strategy. Deans can build networks and a sense of community through dialogue and engagement with a wide range of stakeholders. But the business school deanship can also be a very isolating experience.

Deans can benefit from a range of formal leadership programmes. They can participate in workshops designed for executives, customized activities for cohorts of business school deans or university leaders in general and benefit from degree programmes such as MBAs in Higher Education. The rationale for individuals to participate in executive education might be to signal to executive search firms that they belong to a particular cadre.

Executive education for business school deans allows them to network with peers and to accelerate their learning through benchmarking and knowledge exchange. Some see deans' development programmes as a form of therapy, where participants make confidential soundings about their ideas. The strengths of these formal learning opportunities are that they give participants time away from their busy jobs. However, these experiences can be constrained by a form of 'group think' about conservative norms in the business school sector, or heroic stories from top schools that participants find hard to translate to their own institutional context. Moreover, there are increasing sustainability concerns relating to reductions in the carbon footprint for international travel to workshops and conferences.

There is a lack of longitudinal studies to measure the returns on investing in developing business school leaders. Nevertheless, we have seen positive evaluations of cohort programmes for business school deans (Davies, 2012). These evaluations report valuable opportunities to share knowledge, to reflect candidly on difficult experiences and plans, to network and gain exposure to different models. Such programmes offer time and space for deans to interact and engage in debates about trends as well as the details of their own immediate challenges. Graduates from the International Deans' Programme (IDP) which was developed for EFMD and ABS (now CABS) have supported each other on business school advisory boards and exchanged WhatsApp messages about negotiating salaries and personal crises of confidence. IDP graduates have also developed partnerships between their respective universities. Participants of the IDP mentioned that they benefited from developing their competences, connections and sector and self-knowledge in a supportive and challenging community of peers. The IDP included visits to different business schools. There was time for psychometric assessments, reflections and social activities. Case studies and confidential conversations with participants candidly discussing their real-world challenges in action learning sets were complemented by one-to-one personal development.

Our own approaches at EFMD to designing the aims and objectives of cohort programmes for business school deans globally have been based on our surveys and interviews with business school deans, observations during and following appointments, and research on what business school deans do. We have seen successive deans in one business school arriving with enthusiasm and then being worn down over time with the same struggles for autonomy and recognition. Typically, they struggle at times, despite their appetite for continuous professional development (CPD) and networking, to learn in the business school community. This suggests that despite excellent leadership development opportunities, the systems, politics and cultures in which deans are operating play an important role in their success.

We also recognize the risks of such development programmes becoming echo chambers. There is a risk of experienced deans showcasing models of success that are no longer sustainable. Participants might be tempted to follow 'me too' strategies, engaging in defensive and compliant behaviours to play safe rather than accelerating riskier innovations.

Clearly, EFMD is committed to experiential learning, reflective practice and formal education to prepare business school leaders and to improve the quality of leadership. Formal training can be complemented by learning ad hoc on the job, in teams, from asking good questions, and from consulting and listening carefully. Basing future decision-making on experimentation, reflection and evidence-based research becomes a constant dynamic process.

The strengths of dedicated cohort programmes for aspiring or current business school leaders consists of scene setting, knowledge exchange, making connections, developing confidence and confidants, and sharing common experiences in different countries, contexts and cultures. These programmes help deans to realize they are not alone in terms of their own identity development and workloads. By gaining an overview of the history of business schools, of current trends and models of business and management education, and of some of the criticisms of the sector, participants in deans' programmes can be clear about the identity of their schools and distinctive strategies. Participants can sound out their peers on various dilemmas and the competitive positioning of their institutions. At social events, they start to feel comfortable about reflecting on their professional and personal challenges. We can also help them to understand different career paths and to think about an exit strategy from the deanship at some point. Many participants on development programmes such as the IDP and EFMD's Strategic Leadership Programme (SLP) make career-long connections.

Can development programmes for business school deans really help them to become effective? We highlight the key elements which can contribute to the success of focused networking programmes for (aspiring) business school deans in Table 4.2. These insights are based on our personal experiences (Davies, 2012) of designing and delivering the International Deans' Programme for EFMD and ABS (now CABS) in different continents and for the Association of Asia-Pacific Business Schools. The table is based on cohort programmes offered by EFMD (Cremer, 2018) and good practices for organizing inclusive events (BAM and CABS, 2021). It closely reflects EFMD's three-day SLP (EFMD, 2022a, 2022b).

Relevant Life and Career Experiences

Business school deans spoke about experiences in their lives that influenced their desire and ability to lead. These included working in a family business, after school and during vacations, which helped them to understand the world of work and develop a work ethic. Deans we interviewed also talked about the influence of their parents and the value of volunteering. For instance, George Bain (Association of Business Schools, 2011) spoke about watching his father leave for manual work on the Canadian Pacific Railway at 6am daily. This taught him the importance of hard work and discipline. Bain volunteered as a Canadian naval cadet where he learned to respect other cadets' space. He felt this was a valuable lesson for his subsequent experiences in mediation and arbitration. Bain also commented on the discipline of practising the piano at home in exchange for playing outside after school which developed his negotiating skills. Several deans reflected on the value of team sports. Howard

Table 4.2 Elements of an ideal programme for business school deans

Purpose

To build leadership capacity, networks, legitimacy, positive impact and share knowledge and experiences in the business school sector.

Benefits

Focused, trusted networking, knowledge and experience sharing, confidence building, socialization into the business school community to provide high-quality and impactful management education. Space to think about solving challenges, gain insights, build lasting peer relationships, understanding opportunities, risks.

Participants and diversity

Around 20 newly appointed deans/directors general who have overall responsibility for a business school/school of management. Some associations may include deans at later stages in their tenures and aspiring deans. Ensure diversity in terms of participants and speakers such as geographical representation (including the Global South), gender, ethnicity, type of business school.

Moderator

Established current or former business school dean with international experience who works with an organizer from the business school association to design, develop and deliver the programme. An effective facilitator with current understanding of the sector who provides group and one-to-one support with plenty of interactions within the Chatham House rule.

Learning outcomes – by the end of the programme participants should be able to understand

- the role and evolution of the business school deanship in different contexts, expectations challenges.

- relevant knowledge, skills and behaviours in the role, e.g., managing oneself, strategic and inclusive leadership, negotiating, decision-making, conflict management, performance management, marketing and communications, public relations, fundraising, benchmarking.

- the business school sector ecosystem; competitive positioning, branding, business school identity, mission, vision, values and strategic choices within the business school and broader landscape.

(Continued)

Table 4.2 (Continued) Elements of an ideal programme for business school deans

- how to build practical skills in developing relationships with key internal and external stakeholders.

- develop confidence in capacity building and managing change through team building, managing people, finances and other resources effective to achieve organizational objectives.

- challenges in managing self, teams, organizational development (governance, advisory board, structures, committees), reputation, quality and an inclusive culture in the business school with faculty, professional service staff, students and other key stakeholders to ensure institutional sustainability and address grand challenges (e.g., the UN's sustainable development goals).

- issues in being a change agent, effectively and efficiently balancing a portfolio of research, teaching, executive education, consultancy (using fair and transparent workload models), curriculum development, collaborations, well-being.

Duration, timing, location

Three-day module face-to-face. Deliver immediately before a deans' conference. From Tuesday evening networking dinner until Friday afternoon in a business school or business school association. Recommend a hotel with preferential rates for delegates to book. Some programmes include multiple modules and locations.

Preparatory activities

Establish LinkedIn and WhatsApp groups, share biographies – experiences, expertise, non-work interests, b-school profiles. Psychometric assessments with feedback from a coach. Option for mentoring. Readings.

(Continued)

Table 4.2 (Continued) Elements of an ideal programme for business school deans

Schedule and activities

Start with dinner. Guest speaker/panel presentations in plenary interspersed with small group work. Participants present their own challenges based on 'What could I have done better?' Gain feedback throughout to adapt the programme if necessary. Day 1: welcome, introductions, overview, establish a culture of trust, open discussions about live on-the-job challenges using action learning sets. Encourage light-bulb moments. Group photograph shared on LinkedIn, Twitter, on web site, in annual report. Days 2 and 3 also include icebreakers, sharing stories and challenges with participants presenting individually to the group and guest speakers who ask questions and make suggestions. Reflections, action planning at the start and end of each day. Regular breaks, lunch and dinner (possibly with a speaker) with free time after dinner. Optional: b-school tour; social event; meet a dean's senior management team, students, vice-chancellor/president, advisory board chair.

Topics – examples

B-school landscape, different models; accreditations; trends, criticisms; transitions, identity and boundary work; resources; communications; dealing with resistance; managing upwards; managing conflict; technology; future of work; faculty development; performance management; executive search firms, careers.

Follow-up activities

Invite participants to speak at or host future programmes/events; facilitate alumni activities; ongoing mentoring, buddying and coaching. Collect testimonials to promote the programme. Keep in touch.

Thomas emphasized lessons from playing rugby linked to teamwork and the role of coaches in developing a 'collective spirit'.

Defining moments in some deans' early life experiences included winning scholarships to public school and for a life-changing MBA experience in a top US business school. At the beginning of his career, Robin Wensley learned valuable lessons in an apprenticeship role while assisting Harold Rose, a distinguished economist, on a national report about the expansion of UK business schools and improving their intellectual understanding. Peter Tufano was asked to help evaluate faculty outputs at Harvard Business School when he was a young academic. This was useful for his later position as a business school dean at Oxford University in managing research performance and faculty development.

Experiences in industry, for instance, being seconded to lead or develop a new operation, were seen as useful preparation for a later role as a business school dean. Shocks, such as the loss of a parent at a young age, were viewed by several deans as critical factors that enhanced their sense of responsibility, drive and motivation to make a difference. Within academia, setbacks and successes, working with inspiring mentors, publishing (sometimes with co-authors who misrepresented their work) and navigating relationships within communities of practice were all regarded as character building. Business school deans also discussed the value of mentors who act as role models. Mentors can support deans to make sense of their personal dispositions, career intentions and contextual challenges. They advise deans about decision-making, action planning and navigating different degrees of autonomy and faculty resistance. Assigned or informal mentors can cultivate deans' leadership skills, awareness and self-esteem and can reduce anxiety with confidential just-in-time support. Opportunities to take on academic leadership roles early in their careers were also helpful in developing skills required for a business school deanship. For instance, Howard Thomas talked about heading the doctoral programmes at London Business School in his late 20s.

Table 4.3 illustrates typical responsibilities listed in job descriptions for business school deans.

Deans as Lifelong Learners

The world of work is changing at such a pace that if business school leaders do not prioritize their own learning and development, they will be left behind. They need to be lifelong learners, continually acquiring new knowledge and experiences to sharpen their own skills, impact and employability.

Table 4.4 presents an interesting array of contributions by John H. McArthur, seventh Dean of Harvard Business School for over 15 years from 1980 (HBS Communications, 2019). We suggest that contemporary business school deans might be inspired by and learn to emulate some of these approaches in quite different contexts.

Figure 4.1 illustrates the phases of a dean's tenure during which they must learn to deal with various transitions. For example, individuals must move from being a regular scholar to become a public figure in the dean's office (Gmelch, 2004). Figure 4.1 is based on the work of Gmelch and his colleagues (2011). They characterize beginning 'deaning' as springtime, gaining confidence as summer, sustaining energy during the fall of a dean's tenure and the end of a tenure as

Table 4.3 Examples of key responsibilities of business school deans

(1) As a senior academic leader, to be ambitious in setting strategic direction and leading the operational management of a school and its constituent academic areas aligned with the university's vision and strategy.

(2) Participate in the university's strategic and operational decision-making as a member of the university's executive board, and as an ex officio member of academic council and other committees and working groups. Contribute to key decision-making in the university's best interests, taking an institutional view.

(3) Lead strategic creative and innovative cross-university initiatives and projects as agreed with the university president/vice-chancellor or their deputy.

(4) Take ownership and champion the collective decisions of the university's executive board and committees. Communicate and implement these decisions effectively with staff and students in the school.

(5) Ensure breadth, quality, standards, develop and enhance portfolio, the quality of the student experience and outcomes.

(6) Ensure high-quality research outputs and impact to enhance research culture and the school's reputation.

(7) Embed enterprise and innovation activities across the school and to ensure the quality of those activities.

(8) Manage evaluations of the quality of the school's provision by accrediting and other external bodies.

(9) Develop workforce plans that recruit and retain a diverse workforce that account for emerging skills/student demand and deliver new digital and distributed course content.

(10) Agree and monitor targets for student recruitment and retention and income generation, monitoring performance to ensure targets are met.

(11) Lead the school's financial management, fundraising, agree and meet budget targets in liaison with the school's director of finance.

(12) As the school's budget-holder, lead in allocating and controlling devolved resources, e.g., transparent academic workload allocations.

(Continued)

Table 4.3 (Continued) Examples of key responsibilities of business school deans

---

(13) Provide inspirational leadership and effective management to ensure academic and support staff and student engagement, well-being and development including mentoring, succession planning, and aligning goals with strategic objectives.

(14) Line manage research/subject group heads, head of the business school, head of the law school, deputy/associate/assistant deans, school manager … including mentoring, setting objectives, conducting performance and development reviews.

(15) Develop and manage appropriate organizational and administrative structures and evaluate their effectiveness in the business school.

(16) Chair the school's executive committee and ensure effective communications.

(17) Ensure compliance with university policies and procedures.

(18) Assess and manage risk and escalate matters where necessary.

(19) Accountable for health and safety in the school.

(20) Undertake any reasonable tasks required by the vice-chancellor/president or his/her deputy.

(21) Ensure constructive working relationships with members of the university's executive team, heads of central services, counterparts in other faculties, direct reports, members of the deans' advisory board, and external stakeholders.

---

winter. Figure 4.1 also integrates the five seasons of a CEO's tenure enumerated by Hambrick and Fukutomi (1991), who viewed the stages as responding to a given mandate followed by experimenting, settling on and sustaining a priority and ending with dysfunctional behaviours unless the individual can inject new ideas into their tenure. This chronological perspective is a salutary reminder that deans must remain alert to the risks of overconfidence and of becoming stale in the saddle. Deans must learn to lead despite the pressures of the 'dean's squeeze' (Gallos, 2002) and the 'dean's disease' (Bedeian, 2002) of groupthink, which threatens an open mindset as their tenure progresses. Moreover, length of tenure is an important consideration in terms of a dean's learning curve. An ideal tenure might be seven to eight years (Fragueiro and Thomas, 2011),

Table 4.4 Achievements of John H. McArthur, Dean of Harvard Business
School 1980–95

Early childhood: Grew up in a working-class environment in Canada,
worked part time in a local sawmill.

Formal learning and scholarship awards: MBA, DBA – scholarship award

Community of practice: Six decades at Harvard Business School. Developed
multi-disciplinarity, diversity.

Personal skills valued by others

Energy, passion, vision, consensus building, caring about others, transforming
lives. Encouraging others to 'dream big deans' through their intellectual
ambitions, skilled negotiator, tough-minded, considerate, warm, generous,
kind, fundamentally decent, quiet, never interested in impressing others.

Intellectual contributions: Intellectual foundations and development at
HBS.

Stories about his character

'One employee who was seriously injured in a car accident was astonished to
receive a visit from McArthur in the hospital even before his family could get
there.'

'He generously thanked people for their efforts on behalf of the School,
sending handwritten notes. … McArthur also was there for members of the
HBS community in good and bad times.'

Environmental management

He banned most vehicles from Soldiers Field, creating green spaces, directed
the planting of thousands of flowers and many trees.

Impact: Greater Boston region, organizations and institutions globally,
including Canada, his home country.

Track record in different roles: Scholar, teacher, administrator.

(Continued)

Table 4.4 (Continued)   Achievements of John H. McArthur, Dean of
Harvard Business School 1980–95

Curriculum innovations

Comprehensive MBA curriculum review, greater student diversity in terms of
gender, home country, and socio-economic background; changes in student
workload and faculty assignment patterns; stronger focus on teamwork,
skill-building, and field-based learning. Social Enterprise Initiative,
entrepreneurship, leadership, ethics, strategy.

Talent management

Recruited and promoted outstanding faculty from broader disciplines, adding
more women and minorities. Helped faculty members with their careers,
created a centre for emeritus professors.

Organizational development

Strengthened research, enhanced executive education, ethics and social
enterprise initiatives, oversaw major campus master planning, launched
Harvard Business School Press and restructured the School's publishing arm
for thought leadership globally. Helped to design non-denominational chapel
to support spiritual values.

Income generation: Increased endowed professorships, annual research and
course development budget, HBS endowment.

Recognition

Honorary doctorates from seven universities, Officer of the Order of Canada,
Lifetime Achievement Award from the National Association of Corporate
Directors. John H. McArthur Fellowships in Medicine and Management were
established. Honorary Coach of the hockey team at Harvard College.

**Contributions to other organizations (beyond a mere public relations
exercise)**

Committee memberships, corporate directorships, consulting posts in
business, government, education, and health care organizations around the
world. Member of the Future of the Canadian Financial Services Sector
Task Force. Founding board member Canada Development Investment
Corporation.

(Continued)

Table 4.4 (Continued)   Achievements of John H. McArthur, Dean of
Harvard Business School 1980–95

Community service: Chaired Boston's Brigham and Women's Hospital for
many years and drove through its merger.

Outreach

Promoted tutoring, sports, field trips for local schools; HBS alumni clubs
and associations, summer programmes for under-represented groups in
corporations.

Stakeholder management

Trustee in Bankruptcy of the Penn Central Transportation Company,
represented and protected interests of complex stakeholders.

Post retirement

Supported the President of the World Bank, actively involved in boards,
e.g., in Canada, Turkey, particularly healthcare, and helped several start-ups.

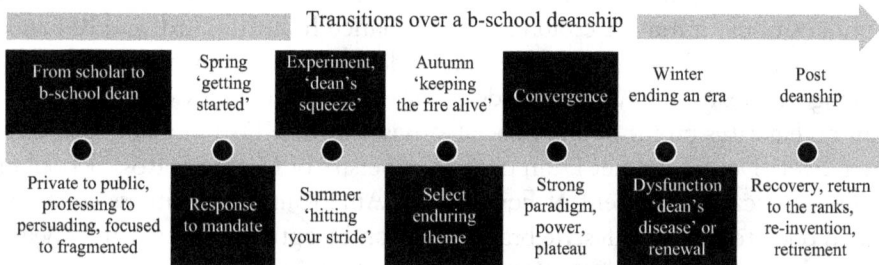

Figure 4.1 Seasons of a dean's tenure.
Source: Authors' synthesis of Gmelch et al. (2011) and Hambrick and Fukutomi (1991).

although the typical length of a term of office is around 6.8 years (mean average) according to AACSB survey data (AACSB, 2021).

Appendix 3 illustrates learning opportunities following a first business school
deanship. It is based on media reports such as *Poets&Quants* and our observations and interviews.

Post Deanship

Post-deanship trajectories include repeating the role in the same or different
business school, interim, deputy or advisory roles. Some deans may develop

a profile that enables them to gain promotion as a faculty dean, more senior general academic leadership roles, or head of the whole university. Others may take a sabbatical to re-group their ideas, return to the benches as a regular faculty member, move to a satellite campus (possibly overseas) or into a specialist accreditation/quality assurance role internally or in a business school association.

Peter Lorange went as far as founding his own business school, which he subsequently sold. Other post-deanship activities include becoming an emeritus to support faculty members. Some former deans exit the business school sector and become executives in industry, offer consulting services, advise governments or mentor other deans. There may be a combination of faculty teaching roles and accreditation support roles, non-executive directorships or special projects. Some continue to volunteer on recruitment panels for deans and accreditation peer review teams and as fellows for business school and other membership associations. Journal article reviewing, undertaking commissions, charity work or coaching business owners may be part of a phased retirement that leads to a full retirement focused on travelling, family or dealing with ill-health, for example.

As part of his career planning, before he stepped down as President (European) at CEIBS, Dipak Jain became honorary Vice-Chancellor of Jio Institute. This is a philanthropic initiative established by Reliance Industries Ltd. and Reliance Foundation. He felt it was very important to decide his next move before formally leaving the deanship. After serial deanships over 25 years, Howard Thomas is now an emeritus professor and Special Advisor to EFMD's President, Eric Cornuel. Scott DeRue, former Dean of the University of Michigan Ross School of Business, became President of Equinox, an American luxury fitness company which operates several lifestyle brands. We can be optimistic that former deans can find interesting opportunities to continue learning and giving back to universities, supporting their own or others' organizations and development.

Conclusion

In evaluating how business school deans learn, we have emphasized individual leadership styles, sense-making processes and the influences of specific life and career experiences. We assume that deans have ready access to scholarship on leader and leadership development from which they can benefit as lifelong learners. As strategic leaders, deans need to develop their understanding of the personalities, experiences and biases within the top team in the business school. They need to appreciate the limits to their own agency in strategic and other decisions and how to build teams and institutional capabilities while motivating individuals (Samimi et al., 2022).

Yet deans may suffer from cobblers' children syndrome – too overly preoccupied with others' learning and development to pay attention to their own needs or to faculty leadership development. University leaders may believe that they can buy in rather than grow their own business school leaders. Understanding how deans learn and variations in styles (Davies et al., 2021) can help capacity building in the business school sector.

We hope that business school deans feel empowered beyond mere compliance with institutional and business school sector norms. We also hope that university leaders understand the need to invest in business school leadership and succession planning (Amann, 2021). Ultimately, a key priority for a business school dean's balanced scorecard (Kaplan and Norton, 2005) in different national and institutional contexts, cultures and countries has to be taking their own medicine for self, team and organizational learning and innovation.

References

AACSB (2021) *Deans survey participant report 2020–21*. Available at: https://www. aacsb.edu/-/media/publications/research-reports/deans_survey_2021_report.pdf? rev=401c3d1a8f914e6db3928015dfe607ce&hash=6C57F04C2ADECF-10B7230ACEC785BCB2

Amann, W. (2021) *Building a leadership pipeline for deans in business schools*. Little Rock, AR: Walnut Publication.

Andersen, J.A. (2015) Barking up the wrong tree. On the fallacies of the transformational leadership theory. *Leadership & Organization Development Journal, 36*(6): pp.765–777.

Anderson, L. (2008) Henley and Reading University reveal merger plans. *Financial Times*, January 9.

Association of Business Schools (2011) *Professor Sir George Bain*. YouTube. Available at: https://www.youtube.com/watch?v=HzWMgxW7JTQ

BAM and CABS (2021) *All welcome guide to inclusive, accessible and sustainable organising of events*. London: BAM.

Beardsley, S.C. (2017) *Higher calling: The rise of nontraditional leaders in academia*. Charlottesville, VA: University of Virginia Press.

Bedeian, A.G. (2002) The dean's disease: How the darker side of power manifests itself in the office of dean. *Academy of Management Learning & Education, 1*(2) pp.164–173.

Bleizeffer, K. (2022) New Temple Fox Dean: Ranking scandal 'could never happen again.' *Poets&Quants*, March 23.

Bolden, R., G. Petrov and J. Gosling (2008) *Developing collective leadership in higher education.* London: Leadership Foundation for Higher Education.

Bryman, A. and S. Lilley (2009) Leadership researchers on leadership in higher education. *Leadership, 5*(3) pp.331–346.

Byrne, J.A. (2018) Cornell B-School dean abruptly resigns. *Poets&Quants*, January 12.

Byrne, J.A. (2022) Former Cornell Dean named to lead Oxford Saïd Business School. *Poets&Quants*, January 12.

Cremer, R. (2018) Stepping into the role of the dean. *Global Focus, 3*(12) pp.10–14.

Davies, J. (2012) Inciting exciting insights. *Global Focus, 6*(3) pp.42–45.

Davies, J., E. Ferlie, H. McLaughlin and H. Thomas (2021) Examining business school leadership. *Global Focus, 1*(15) pp.66–73.

Davies, J. and H. Thomas, (2009) What do business school deans do? Insights from a UK study. *Management Decision, 47*(9) pp.1396–1419.

Dawson, S. (2008) Building a business school at the heart of Cambridge. In Aspatore (Ed.), *Business school management. Top educational leaders on creating a strong school reputation, offering competitive programs, and thriving in the educational marketplace.* Boston, MA: Thomson Reuters/Aspatore, pp.157–174.

Day, D.V. (2000) Leadership development: A review in context. *The Leadership Quarterly, 11*(4) pp.581–613.

Day, D.V., J.W. Fleenor, L.E. Atwater, R.E. Sturm, and R.A. McKee (2014) Advances in leader and leadership development: A review of 25 years of research and theory. *The Leadership Quarterly, 25*(1) pp.63–82.

De Vita, G. and P. Case (2016) 'The smell of the place': Managerialist culture in contemporary UK business schools. *Culture and Organization, 22*(4) pp.348–364.

Doherty, B., J. Meehan and A. Richards (2015) The business case and barriers for responsible management education in business schools. *Journal of Management Development, 34*(1): 34–60.

EFMD (2022a) Strategic Leadership Programme for deans. Available at: https://www.efmdglobal.org/learning-networking/professional-development/strategic-leadership-programme-for-deans/

EFMD (2022b) Strategic Leadership Programme for deans 3. Available at: https://events.efmdglobal.org/events/strategic-leadership-programme-for-deans-3/

Foderaro, L.W. (2016) February 15. Cornell's plan to merge hotel school gets an icy reception. *New York Times*, February 15.

Fragueiro, F. and H. Thomas (2011) *Strategic leadership in the business school: Keeping one step ahead.* Cambridge: Cambridge University Press.

Gallos, J.V. (2002) The dean's squeeze: The myths and realities of academic leadership in the middle. *Academy of Management Learning & Education*, 1(2) pp.174–184.

Gatzweiler, M.K., C. Frey-Heger and M. Ronzani (2022) Grand challenges and business education: Dealing with barriers to learning and uncomfortable knowledge. In A.A. Gümüsay, E. Marti, H. Trittin-Ulbrich and C. Wickert (Eds). *Organizing for societal grand challenges*. Bingley: Emerald Publishing Limited, pp. 221–238.

Gioia, D.A. and K.G. Corley (2002) Being good versus looking good: Business school rankings and the Circean transformation from substance to image. *Academy of Management Learning & Education*, 1(1) pp.107–120.

Gmelch, W.H. (2004) The department chair's balancing acts. *New Directions for Higher Education*, 126(Summer) pp.69–84.

Gmelch, W., D. Hopkins and S. Damico (2011) *Seasons of a dean's life. Understanding the role and building leadership capacity*. Sterling, VA: Stylus.

Goodall, A.H. (2009) *Socrates in the boardroom: Why research universities should be led by top scholars*. Princeton, NJ and Oxford: Princeton University Press.

Gray, D. (2021) What makes successful frameworks rise above the rest? *MIT Sloan Management Review*, 62(4) pp.1–6.

Hambrick, D.C. and G.D. Fukutomi (1991) The seasons of a CEO's tenure. *Academy of Management Review*, 16(4) pp.719–742.

Harney, S. and H. Thomas (2020) *The liberal arts and management education: A global agenda for change*. Cambridge: Cambridge University Press.

HBS Communications (2019) *John H. McArthur dies, was Business School dean from 1980–95. Harvard Business School*, August 23. Available at: https://news.harvard.edu/gazette/story/2019/08/john-h-mcarthur-business-school-dean-from-1980-95-dies/

Heffernan, T.A. and L. Bosetti (2020) The emotional labour and toll of managerial academia on higher education leaders. *Journal of Educational Administration and History*, 52(4) pp.357–372.

Howorth, C., S.M. Smith and C. Parkinson (2012) Social learning and social entrepreneurship education. *Academy of Management Learning & Education*, 11(3) pp.371–389.

IBL News (2022) Over 300 students will graduate from BU Questrom's online MBA, May 23. Available at: https://iblnews.org/over-300-students-will-graduate-from-bu-questroms-online-mba/

Kaplan, R.S. and D.P. Norton (2005) The balanced scorecard: Measures that drive performance. *Harvard Business Review*, 83(7) pp.71–79.

Kolb, D.A. (1983) *Experiential learning: Experience as the source of learning and development*. Englewood Cliffs, NJ: Prentice Hall.

Liu, H. (2017) Reimagining ethical leadership as a relational, contextual and political practice. *Leadership*, *13*(3), pp. 343–367.

McCall, M.W. (2004) Leadership development through experience. *Academy of Management Perspectives*, *18*(3), pp. 127–130.

Nabi, G., F. Liñán, A. Fayolle, N. Krueger and A. Walmsley (2017) The impact of entrepreneurship education in higher education: A systematic review and research agenda. *Academy of Management Learning & Education*, *16*(2), pp.277–299.

Podolny, J.M. (2011) A conversation with James G. March on learning about leadership. *Academy of Management Learning & Education*, *10*(3) pp.502–506.

Reynolds, M. and R. Vince (2004) Critical management education and action-based learning: Synergies and contradictions. *Academy of Management Learning & Education*, *3*(4) pp.442–456.

Rhodes, C. (2021) The woke business school. *The PRME blog*, October 1. Available at: https://primetime.unprme.org/2021/10/01/the-woke-business-school/

Samimi, M., A.F. Cortes, M.H. Anderson and P. Herrmann (2022) What is strategic leadership? Developing a framework for future research. *The Leadership Quarterly*, *33*(3). Available at: doi.org/10.1016/j.leaqua.2019.101353

Seale, O. and M. Cross (2016) Leading and managing in complexity: The case of South African deans. *Studies in Higher Education*, *41*(8) pp.1514–1532.

Shackelford, D.A. (2021) Observations from a professor serving as dean. *The Accounting Review*, *96*(5) pp.403–410.

Simon, H.A. (1967) The business school: A problem in organizational design. *Journal of Management Studies*, 4 pp.1–16.

Starkey, K. and S. Tempest (2009) The winter of our discontent: The design challenge for business schools. *Academy of Management Learning & Education*, 8(4) pp.576–586.

Thomas, H. and L. Thomas (2011) Perspectives on leadership in business schools. *Journal of Management Development*, *30*(5) pp.526–540.

Waller, M.A. and S. Caldwell (2021) *The dean's list: Leading a modern business school.* Fayetteville: University of Arkansas Press.

Zafar, S.T., W. Hmedat, D.S. Chaubey and A. Rehman (2019) An exploration of academic leadership dynamics: A literature review, *International Journal on Leadership*, *7*(1) pp.35–43.

Zhang, X., X. Zheng and Y. Xi (2020) How governmental agencies legitimize organizations: A case study on Chinese business schools from 1977 to 2014. *Academy of Management Learning & Education*, *19*(4) pp.521–540.

5

The Future of Business Schools and Management Education

Looking Back and Moving Forward

Introduction

It is clear from all the evidence in this book that business and management studies has established itself strongly as a successful field of study in global higher education. It has always attempted to be both practical and responsive to the needs of all its stakeholders: namely academic, business, government and society. Yet, as we have seen, it has consistently been criticized about issues of legitimacy, identity, role and purpose.

In particular, critics argue that business schools often research the wrong things, e.g., focusing on theoretical rather than more practical, applied topics; they teach the wrong things, e.g., focusing more attention on analytical, mechanistic management tools than the softer skills of management, empathy and leadership; they tend to stress philosophies of free market economic and shareholder capitalism as statements of intent and purpose; and, finally, they question the significance of their practical impact on business and government policy. Were these critics correct and are business schools not fit for purpose?

What, therefore, were the key concerns of business schools and their deans pre-COVID (up to early 2020)? And how should they now modify their approaches in the current crisis and redefine their strategies for achieving meaningful future impact and societal value?

Over the past 50 years, the North American model of management education became arguably the dominant model worldwide. It was developed from the so-called Gordon-Howell Foundation Studies in the early 1960s. However, perhaps the main concern among leading scholars and deans has been that management as a field became trapped by adopting the dominant logic of a North American paradigm which does not necessarily reflect the global

DOI: 10.4324/9781003178125-5

diversity of educational needs, and approaches, of countries with distinctive cultures, norms and contexts. For example, Paul Schoemaker (2008), a well-known strategy academic, noted that

> the traditional paradigm of business schools (rooted in the Gordon-Howell Studies of the 1960s) with its strong focus on analytical models and re-ductionism, is not well suited to handle the ambiguity and high rate of change facing many industries today. Business educators have always faced the dilemma of academic rigour pitted against practical relevance (notwithstanding Kurt Lewin's astute observation that 'nothing is as prac-tical as good theory').

Pfeffer and Fong (2004) also point out that business schools 'stand accused of promulgating ideas and an ethos that have led to corporate scandals such as Enron'. This criticism was reinforced by the late Sumantra Ghoshal (2005), in asserting that business schools, by propagating and teaching amoral theo-ries (based on shareholder capitalism) that destroyed sound moral and ethi-cal management practices, had contributed both to corporate failures such as Enron and the growth of irrational exuberance associated with financial behav-iour before the Global Financial Crisis (GFC). From a historical perspective, Rakesh Khurana (2007) notes that business schools began their evolution with great promise in producing moral business leaders following management as a profession, to ultimately create a cadre of 'myopic career technocrats – "hired hands"'.

There have also been a wide range of environmental disturbances ranging from the Asian financial crisis of the 1980s to the current global COVID-19 pan-demic that have shaped the conduct of business schools. Three disruptions were particularly significant: first, the advent of the rankings era (in 1987), which turned business schools into businesses 'embalmed' in managerialism and a winner-takes-all mentality; second, the GFC of 2008/09 which surfaced the lack of a moral and ethical imperative in managerial behaviour, and finally, the global pandemic which has created a major disruptive jolt to the processes and practices of management education.

Therefore, it is important to understand how business schools reacted to some of these major changes. In all of these instances, the dean's challenge was to re-evaluate their school's purpose, reflect on re-framing a curriculum anchored in financial and economic theories, and develop a new, more broadly based education vision. Students, particularly those in Europe, were increasingly ad-vocating a vision of businesses maximizing stakeholder not shareholder value and directing greater managerial attention towards societal and economic val-ues and impact.

Hence, we now turn to considering how deans reacted to how key environmental forces, pre-COVID, such as the media rankings explosion and the GFC re-shaped the strategic agendas and debates of their business schools prior to the unexpected event of the global pandemic.

Rankings, Dotcoms, Enron and the Aftermath of the Global Financial Crisis: What Challenges Were Faced by Business Schools?

As Andy Policano noted in 2005 when he was Dean of the Business School at U.C. Irvine,

> Few people can remember what it was like before 1987 – what I call the year before the storm. It was a time when business school Deans could actually focus on improving the quality of their schools' educational offerings. Discussions about strategic marketing were confined mostly to the marketing curriculum. PR firms were hired by businesses not business schools … The storm of rankings changed everything. In simple terms, and for better or worse, the advent of rankings in 1987 marked the dawn of an era of business schools as businesses with the rules of the game laid down by the Foundation Studies.

This meant that competition, and competitive advantage, was now determined through the voice of the media rankings and the criteria that shape these rankings, such as the quality and research capabilities of faculty and their academic publications in so-called A* (top) journals, often identified as the 'holy grail' of business faculty attainment (despite the fact that the impact of their research on practice is often minimal). The 'tyranny of the rankings' (Khurana, 2007) is that they divert attention to performance on a narrow range of key performance indicators. For example, business school reputation is determined by high-quality student placement and students' subsequent rate of salary progress as well as the extent of rigorous research measured by A* publications.

Thus, academic faculty were hired for their status as specialized research academics rather than for their classroom or instructional skills. This allowed curricula to become much more specialized, often with a finance/economics concentration, and less focused on general management and leadership skills; hence, fewer and fewer schools taught general management. And in so doing, business schools redefined their mission and purpose to become university 'cash cows', resolute advocates of shareholder capitalism and builders of ever more opulent new business school facilities. Taken together, the criticisms of Ghoshal, Pfeffer, Spender and others were that business schools had lost a sense of their role in business and society by emphasizing managerial behaviour and leadership practices that led to the collapse of companies such as Enron in the United States and Parmalat in Europe, as well as leading to the collapse of a number of companies in the dotcom boom.

Both Starkey and Thomas (2019) and Khurana point out that the lessons of economic and business history were never more evident than in this period. They pointed to the wise words about business school deanship of Wallace Brett Donham, the second and very highly regarded Dean of Harvard Business School (HBS) in the 1930s, who argued that business schools needed to broaden their horizons and to not exist solely for the benefit of an elite minority. In his view, they should make a much wider contribution to the economy and society by focusing on social problems and social systems – broad ecosystems – rather than on individual companies. However, the philosophy of the Foundation Studies of the 1960s moved away from broad horizons and led to what Augier and March (2011) described as the golden era of US business schools, in which risk-taking behaviours and questionable management practices had probably led to irrational exuberance and the disruption of the GFC. The demise of the well-established financial institution, Lehmann Brothers, and the bankruptcy or near collapse of finance and banking institutions was the inevitable outcome.

The EFMD publication *Securing the Future of Management Education* (2014) summarized the views of both the EFMD Board and the evidence drawn from the extensive stakeholder interview study undertaken on behalf of EFMD (Thomas et al., 2013a, 2014). Following Donham's early arguments while leading HBS in the 1930s and the insights gained from the EFMD interview study, David Oglethorpe (2015), the Dean at Cranfield, implied in a blog that there was a belief, following many years of financially motivated, risk-driven business education, that management schools were compliant in the events leading up to the GFC. Quoting not only the 2014 study but also the 2012 EFMD Board Manifesto on the future of management education, he noted the EFMD advice for deans was that 'issues of ethics, moral responsibility and sustainability should be embedded in the core curricula as well as in the broader practices of schools'.

However, he pointed out that while the notion of corporate social responsibility (CSR) (as a catch-all phrase for ethical, moral and sustainability dimensions) was important for business and business schools it tended also to polarize opinion among deans. Further, pointing to a survey undertaken by the Academy of Business in Society and EFMD in 2013, he indicated that while ESG (environment, society and governance) goals had moved to the mainstream of management education and research, the formulation of an appropriate ESG response by schools through integration of such goals into their mission, values and purpose was much less evident.

This mirrored the findings of both the 2013 and 2014 research books *Promises Fulfilled/Unfulfilled* (Thomas et al., 2013b) and *Securing the Future* (Thomas et al., 2014) in which not only the inclusion of ESG goals but also addressing the impacts of technological change was seen to be marginalized in business school curriculum developments. This was viewed as further evidence of incremental rather than innovatory curriculum change. Deans were seen as rather cautious, making incremental rather than more radical adjustments to the status quo paradigms.

However, subsequent evidence from the Business Education Open Innovation crowd-sourcing Jam of 2014/15 (held virtually with research facilitation) at the Questrom School in Boston University (2015/16) (Carlile et al., 2016) threw up many strong sentiments about the need for change and more radical innovation in management education. In fact, it specified ten key areas for change and a range of ideas for handling them in curriculum design. These ideas were the subject of many subsequent conferences from Boston University's Jam 2.0 to the regular conferences of EFMD, AACSB and CABS (UK) – in which business schools turned the mirror on themselves and seemed to acknowledge that their curricula and agendas were at a 'tipping point' or on the cusp of a second curve for growth and change, as Charles Handy described the situation in his book *The Second Curve* (Handy, 2015).

Yet instead of leading change and reacting to the signals of impending change indicated by an upcoming turning point and the strategic crossroads for business schools, deans seemed to be either unwilling or unable to change. Most administrators seemed to be satisfied by the strength of their status quo paradigms, rankings and accreditation standards as well as pointing to strong market demand for their programmes. In essence, they were ignoring the realities of a new business environment in which the virtues of stakeholder capitalism and issues such as globalization, sustainability and community values were being widely discussed. Indeed, a quote from AACSB in a 2011 report partially explains the tendency towards incrementalism in the decade following the GFC (Peters et al., 2018).

> Business schools have been slow to take disruption seriously ... Compared to the business environment, higher education tends to be more tightly rooted in tradition and tends to encounter more inertia than business in the 'face of change'.

Simply put, over this period, business school faculty and important researchers in fields such as strategy and business economics were successfully studying and teaching about transitions in businesses facing major disruptions in areas such as online shopping and retailing largely driven by the combined forces of technological and global innovation. They also researched businesses with new providers in the digital culture, such as Uber and Airbnb. Yet while these lessons were learned in a business environment which was changing in a rapid fashion, most business schools continued their strategies and existing business models in a traditional, somewhat conservative manner. Deans were wilfully blind to changes 'inside' their own 'business school industry', ignoring many valid criticisms about their own value, identity and legitimacy and were generally not willing to consider major disruptions in their own models of delivery despite the increasing presence of for-profit higher education institutions and online education companies entering their marketplace. Nevertheless, towards the end of the decade, around 2018/19, there were increasing signals and pressures for re-imagining management education and for a series of more extensive changes in the model of management education.

So, while the shifting economic and social development landscape of the previous 50 years could perhaps have stimulated disruptive and ground-breaking innovation in the field, it clearly did not. This reflects in part the challenges created by the growing diversity of management education offerings globally across cultures, countries and contexts and the attendant difficulty of changing the status quo because of resource constraints and problems associated with educational and economic development in many emerging markets.

However, the various iterations of the Questrom Education Jam (Jam 1.0 in the United States, and particularly Jam 2.0 which focused closely on identifying the critical issues in 10 developing market locations worldwide) highlighted key challenges and a range of ideas for addressing them (see 'Crowdsourcing', Freeman and Thomas 2015, 'Global Focus and Open Innovation', Carlile and Thomas, 2020, *Global Focus*). These included the following contrasts, questions and themes: contrasting strong business school competition with the associated lack of collaboration; creating business schools' distinctive identity and differentiation in the marketplace; specifying the dimensions, and areas, of meaningful societal impact for a business school; questioning whether innovation and entrepreneurship research and teaching can stimulate and enhance economic change and development; can an ethical and moral compass be taught, and implemented in emerging market environments of rampant fraud and corruption? Does capitalism work for everyone? Do issues of access and affordability of management education have to be addressed globally? How can inclusive growth be achieved given societal inequality and social/financial exclusion? How can leaders and leadership qualities be shaped and taught? How do we produce global mindsets in environments of increasing populism and nationalism? How do we narrow the 'digital divide' as technological change transforms societies? How do we ensure the growth of lifelong learning and continuing upskilling in management education practices? How should business schools evolve in terms of form, purpose and mission as societies evolve?

The critical question for deans was clearly how these themes and issues should be addressed as they considered changes in their models of management education. This led to a focus on a number of important implementation problems that may arise in designing new models of management education; particularly, first, the 'willingness to pay' exhibited by students and 'customers' given high programme tuition prices; second, the potential disruption from non-traditional management education suppliers, and third, increased competition from the strategies and strategic groups of business schools which might lead to the potential closure of some non-competitive management schools. We examine each of these in turn.

'Willingness to pay'

Brandenburger and Stuart (1996), in a highly cited paper in the field of competitive strategy, note that the added value of a 'firm' will find an upper boundary based on market conditions and the customer's 'willingness to pay'. Translating the context of this paper to management education leads to the question of whether and how much students, businesses or parents are willing to pay for the tuition fees charged by business schools. For example, domestic business undergraduate degree fees are currently £9,250 per year in the UK, with perhaps £10,000 a year for living costs, leading to a total of around £60,000 for a three-year undergraduate degree (overseas students might pay an additional fee of between one-third and one half more than that over the three-year period). Note, these fees are increasingly perceived as an access barrier for many students despite the availability of student loan programmes. For a one-year MBA programme, tuition costs might be £30,000–£50,000 irrespective of living costs (with overseas students again paying a significantly higher fee). The fee levels for tuition in the United States at both undergraduate and MBA levels are substantially higher.

Therefore, while fees will continue to rise, business schools must continually face the question of how much they will be able to charge for tuition in a competitive environment, and this calculation must be based on the 'willingness to pay', which is the maximum a 'customer' would be willing to pay for the programme. Competitive advantage for a given business school relative to another occurs when the value spread between the 'willingness to sell' (i.e., the lowest point at which the school can offer a programme) and the 'willingness to pay' is greater (note also that 'willingness to pay' and rising tuition fees raises a question about social justice, namely, access to and affordability of management education).

Competitive Pressures

New entrants, or third-party providers with alternative learning methods often with just-in-time information, raise the issue of at what point will traditional, physical business education be substantially disrupted. Examples were already emerging of entrants such as the for-profit school Hult International Business School (2003), with campuses in Boston, London, Shanghai, etc., and a broad programme portfolio with their programmes accredited by both EFMD/AACSB, proving to be strong competitors.

The Gies Business School at the University of Illinois at Urbana-Champaign decided to completely close its MBA programme over five years ago and replaced it with an online MBA programme designed in partnership with the Coursera platform at a tuition price of $22,000, which has been very successful. More recently, in September 2020, the Questrom School in Boston University launched an online MBA to complement its full-time MBA. This online MBA, costing $24,000, designed using the research background and results obtained in the BU Jams and a partnership with EdX, has also done extremely well in market acceptance by attracting over 800 students in two cohorts in academic year 2020/21. Note that both of these programmes have been very well reviewed on the *Poets&Quants* website (alongside other online offerings from the Kelley School at Indiana University and UNC, Chapel Hill).

Of course, distance learning courses have been around for some time. In the 1970/80s, Warwick Business School launched its own Distance Learning MBA in parallel with its full-time offerings. It has attracted a large number of students and is in the top 5 of distance learning programmes in the *Financial Times* ranking of such programmes (indeed, it was number one in the 2020 rankings).

So, there are, and were, examples of business schools innovating with distance/online offerings before and after the GFC. However, their innovation processes and programme designs differed. For example, Illinois and Boston University partnered with Coursera and EdX platforms respectively, whereas Warwick innovated and designed its programme in-house. All of these programmes successfully answered the question of schools being able to teach management education at scale. So too did Britain's Open University, a pioneer in this field, in developing a highly regarded and successful online programme using its own Future Learn platform design. (Note that the attraction of such distance learning programmes is the 'value for money' pricing and enhanced access and flexibility for working students.)

Strategic Groups and Strategic Options for Business Schools[1]

In a competitive business school marketplace, it is clear that elite schools such as Harvard, Wharton, Stanford and Chicago in the United States and INSEAD and London Business School in Europe have different strategic options available to them than other publicly funded or privately funded business schools. This leads to the question of what strategic options should each type of business school consider to achieve sustainable competitive advantage in its own marketplace environment.

As the future of management education has become more uncertain, with real growth in government funding declining, business schools have relied on the revenue from quite large increases in tuition fees for both undergraduate and graduate programmes. As stated previously, this rapidly increasing (rising/escalating) price tag calls into question whether students will be 'willing to pay' increasingly high fees with the attendant political and public policy issue of the access to, and affordability of, business education for all educationally qualified and able students irrespective of parental/family income. Therefore, the range of strategic options varies in relation to the nature and character of the business school.

Three broadly different categories of strategic groups emerge from a review of governance and reputation issues, namely, publicly funded, 'elite, and private schools'.

Publicly funded schools are both the most common and financially constrained. Often, they are found within large universities and may have relatively little strategic freedom or autonomy. They will tend to focus on undergraduate and digital platform or alliance types of programmes. Their postgraduate courses will often face declining enrolments because of competitive pressures.

On the other hand, elite schools top the business school rankings and are highly regarded because of their brand reputation and substantial endowment resources. Their brand characteristics enable them to attract the best quality students and offer scholarships to the most able and financially deserving students. They have many strategic options available and continually enhance their brand image and global reputation as they develop partnerships and alliances with similarly strong schools and organizations across the world.

<u>Private schools</u> rely on tuition fees and private funding. Their challenge is to find a strong, well-defined market position based on location, brand and distinctive competitiveness. In essence, analysis of current strengths, distinctive capabilities and special areas of competence alongside careful assessment of needs and market demands should provide clear competitive advantages.

If schools, whether public, elite or private, have a good portfolio design they will be better able to drive innovation and build a sustainable business model. Yet, apart from the three key implementation issues of model design, 'customers' willingness to pay' and increased competition, there were other questions about next steps, such as how schools might build innovation processes to create meaningful organizational change. Another was how to increase industry engagement to encourage project-based, participative student-centred learning. This would enable meaningful learning about insightful management principles in practice.

Hence, at this point (2019), deans were ready to start a transformational change journey to re-engineer and redesign their programmes and activities and offer more radical solutions for the future of their educational journeys.

While there was much for deans to praise, and much promise, in recent debates about management education, there was also strong pressure to abandon incrementalism and to innovate to close the theory–practice relevance gap and blunt Hamel's (1996) assertion that 'what we examine in the business school is a little bit like being a mapmaker in an earthquake zone. Never before has the gap between our tools and the reality of emerging industry been larger.'

It was seen as increasingly important to recognize the global strength and relevance of the undergraduate business programme and the relative inattention afforded its design and curriculum development in comparison to the MBA. Therefore, it was argued that renewed attention should be given to liberal management education models in this context (Harney and Thomas, 2020). Further, there was clear evidence globally of a student shift in attitude towards issues of social inequality, inclusive growth and sustainability. There was much greater acceptance of CSR and a focus on stakeholder value rather than shareholder value maximization as goals of management education. This shift would certainly stimulate the creation of more purposeful, balanced, holistic models of management education.

Whilst all the elements of transformational change in management education were evident in this 2019/20 period, it took the onset of COVID-19 to finally disrupt the status quo and force deans and university administrators to create more innovative, imaginative and entrepreneurial schools. A pathway fundamentally embedded in league and ranking tables was about to change.

2019/20 Conclusions and the Calm before the Arrival of the Pandemic

Before moving onto a discussion of what schools did after COVID-19 arrived, it is important to ask why many deans were conservative and cautious about change in the decade after the GFC.

Why were Deans and faculty so resistant to radical, innovatory change? One possibility is that a culture involving a mixture of complacency about past success and a historical inertia and aversion to risky change in a financially successful and rewarding business school environment impeded radical model change.

It is clear that many strategic moves had been advanced in the 2019/20 period, indicating the potential for more innovative responses and models. They included the following, which provided some of the potential thinking frameworks for future strategizing:

- Increasing strategic differentiation within 'strategic groups'

- University-based business schools making new strategic moves because of increasing pressure from the university

- Continuing investments in new learning platforms and alliances, e.g., Coursera, EdX, Future Learn

- New delivery models for continuing lifelong learning and executive programmes

- New business models from outside players

- Consolidation and merger/acquisition activity as the signature MBA programme declines in popularity

And then, in February/March 2020, the pandemic spread from China to Europe, to the Americas and across the world.

Whatever the reasons for incremental change in the historical context, the pandemic created a crisis situation that brought about immediate change in issues such as technology-enabled learning and more inclusive, accessible and affordable programmes of instruction. Simply put, the crisis disruption forced transformational changes in institutional behaviour. For example, in the *Times Higher Education Supplement* (8th May, 2020), two academics (Devinney and Dowling) asked 'Is This the Crisis Higher Education Needs to Have?' They argued that the crisis provided the opportunity for decision makers to abandon expedient, short-term 'muddling through' strategies and design visionary, innovative pathways for the future. Further, in an article following a similar theme in the *Economist* (8th August, 2020, entitled 'Uncanny University: COVID-19 could push some universities over the brink', Briefing Section), the authors argued that higher education was in trouble even before the pandemic, and the sudden impact of the crisis had cut revenue generation, forced staff cuts and put a hold on new facility development. It also provided the opportunity to rethink and redesign business models for the future.

Changes in Business School Models Post-Pandemic

In a recent book (Thomas, Lorange and Sheth, 2013a, p.140) the authors argue 'that management education in general, and well-established business schools suffer from the bad habits of good institutions (e.g. leading firms) and especially from denial, complacency, being impervious to change, competency dependence and internal turf wars anchored in functional disciplines'. They believed that business schools would need to go through the transition of a crisis management process before they can embrace change and adapt to a rapidly changing environment. We illustrate this crisis management approach and framework in Figures 5.1 and 5.2.

Figure 5.1 illustrates the value of a crisis management approach. It suggests that if business schools continue to practice 'status quo' management and take an 'inside out' perspective, they are likely to decline, or even disappear, over time. However, a crisis such as that occasioned by a pandemic should lead to an urgent 'wake-up call', requiring transformation (outside in) of the business school following an opportunity-driven perspective, perhaps by leveraging technology and globalization drivers in order to create new processes, routines and organizational structures.

Figure 5.2 shows how by broadening the market and mission of a business school new opportunities and strategic options emerge. For example, pre-pandemic most business schools embraced philosophies of shareholder value (profit defines purpose) and typically on-campus face-to-face learning models. After the pandemic, it suggests that they should broaden their strategy by embracing stakeholder value philosophies (purpose-triple bottom line defines profit) and focus on opportunities such as global education for all sectors as the target markets, facilitated by online learning models and platforms.

Note that Figures 5.1 and 5.2 provide clear examples of what is required for transformational change in a crisis situation.

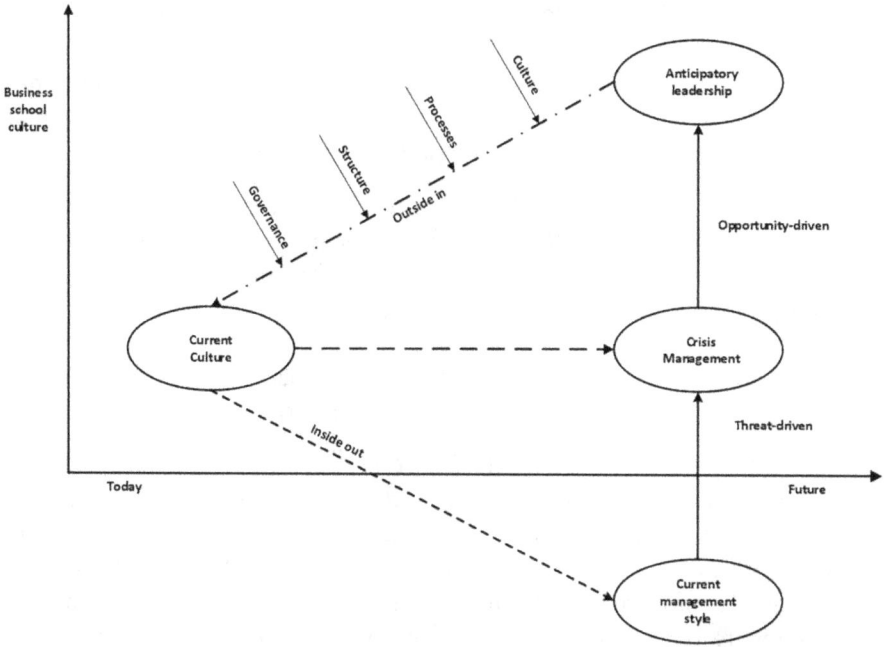

Figure 5.1 Threat versus opportunity-driven transformation.
Source: Howard Thomas.

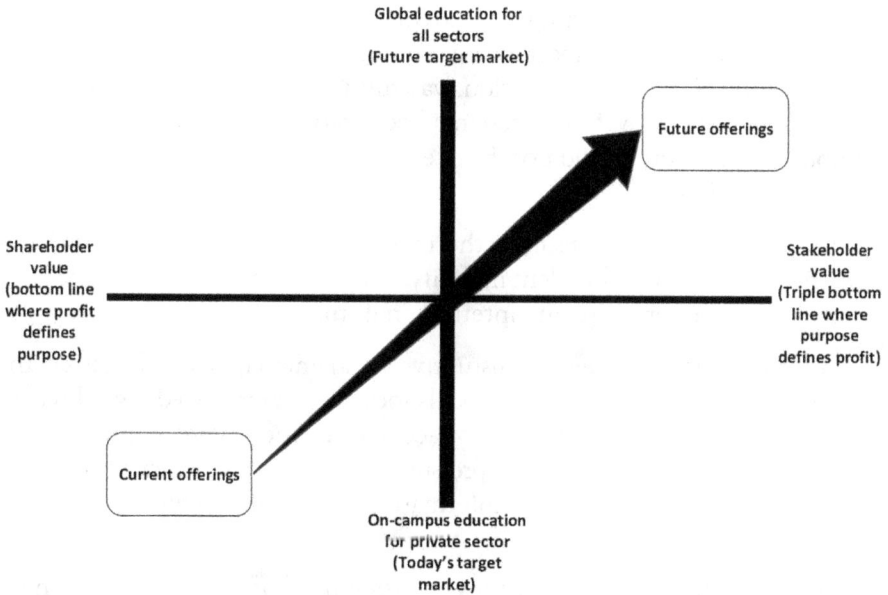

Figure 5.2 Broadening the market and the mission of business schools.
Source: Howard Thomas.

Business School Responses

How did business schools actually respond to the pandemic crisis? The most common response was to shift to a system of remote online learning using platforms such as Zoom, Microsoft Teams and Cisco WebEx.

A blog authored by Magdalena Wanot entitled 'Business Schools Impact During the COVID-19 crisis' (17/02/2021 EFMD) summarizes the results of a survey of 100 schools on the impact on the schools' internal and environments and their projections for the future. The main findings were as follows:

- The headline is that four in five business schools are confident that they have sustained or increased their impact during the pandemic.

- In terms of *dimensions of impact*, almost 50% of the schools indicated that their financial impact has decreased, with greater falls in revenue in private schools than in public schools. Apart from significant revenue decreases, 30% of schools have seen a decline in student numbers, whereas nearly 50% of schools have seen decline in executive education as well as decline in graduate employability and student pressure about tuition fee levels. The relatively good news is that schools' images and societal/economic impacts have remained stable.

- In terms of *internal challenges*, by far the most significant was schools' adjustment to remote learning. This involved aligning faculty skills to remote delivery and making important investments in online technologies. A further problem in implementation was the issue of 'have' and 'have nots' in the student body. Some students had laptops and internet available at home whereas others did not. Hence, there was a 'digital divide' in home-based learning.

- In terms of *external challenges*, the main areas were in international student recruitment and student mobility. There were also 'spillover' effects in placements, internships and international study abroad programmes.

- In terms of *future scenarios*, disruptive pandemic change will hasten the development of new business models focusing on enhanced digital teaching and its relationship to face-to-face learning/networking. Interestingly, despite increased competitive pressure, schools stress the need for more widespread collaboration and information sharing in the future.

Finally, as business schools look forward, they must address the urgent need to address the societal role and responsibility of the sector. Students and faculty are increasingly focusing on schools' impact on their local regions and country/cultural environments whilst adopting a holistic, interdisciplinary perspective on issues such as social justice, inequality and access to and affordability of management education. It should be noted that similar themes, particularly the rapid adoption of online education delivery, were reported by 100 dean delegates at a 2020 AACSB Deans conference and reported by Tricia Bisoux in *BizEd* magazine (18 March, 2020, 'Business Education's Rapid Response to COVID-19').

What became apparent very quickly was that the widespread adaption to online, remote management education, and particularly the sharp disruptive change in technology-enabled learning, necessitated careful strategic thinking about the way in which online methodologies were implemented. First, because schools have wide differences in global cultures, contexts and countries, particularly in stages and levels of social and economic development, there could not be a 'one size fits all' approach in the transition to new forms of teaching and instruction. It was evident to all concerned that teaching online is different (and requires training) and that the human face-to-face factor is missing. Consequently, it was argued that creative, so-called hybrid models would need to be designed. These hybrid models would attempt to blend online and face-to-face learning to achieve an effective balance between face-to-face and well-designed online learning.

The underlying issues were engagingly described by Simon Kuper ('Universities are on a learning curve', 16/17th May, 2020, *FT.com*/magazine) in the following excerpts:

> Six months ago, few of the world's academics had taught an online course. Now they're almost all doing it. I asked dozens of them about their experiences. My conclusion: online education won't replace the in-person variety, but will complement it. University teaching after the pandemic will be blended: a mix of both methods.

> ... Most academics I heard from aren't enjoying teaching online. They plunged into the global experiment untrained ... The human factor is lacking: Zoom kills most jokes: ...

> ... But blended education could expand the university market to all ages, classes and countries.

Kuper also argues that blended education could be extremely important for 'life-long' education and that technology companies such as Zoom and Microsoft have already and will certainly introduce new interactive technologies and features that will make their platforms more intuitive and enjoyable for both the instructor and the student.

Indeed, Santiago Iñiguez de Onzoño, now President of IE University but previously Dean of the Business School at the highly regarded Instituto de Empresa (IE) Business School in Madrid (Spain), was one of the early adopters of blended learning around ten years ago. In an article in *Global Focus* (Vol. 10, Issue 1, 8th March, 2017) entitled 'The Future is Blended', he argued that conventional face-to-face teaching can be augmented and enhanced using technology, such as online learning, in the management education process. For Iñiguez, whose blended learning programmes at IE are seen as innovative and progressive, 'the key instructional and pedagogical question' is not whether blended learning is the future or whether classroom teaching is more effective than online teaching but rather, 'what is the optimal blend of online and face-to-face teaching' (see also Iniguez [2011] 'The Learning Curve'). Indeed, IE was one of the innovators of the 'flipped' classroom and designed a very impressive blended learning technology platform which formed the core of an approach for enhancing blended learning programmes at the MBA and Masters level.

It is always useful to draw on examples to show how different schools have used a range of technology-enabled blended platforms to address the crisis alongside face-to-face programmes. We draw on experiences at the Gordon Institute of Business Science (GIBS), a postgraduate and executive education business school at the University of Pretoria, located in Johannesburg, South Africa, Singapore Management University in Singapore and Questrom School of Business, Boston University.

GIBS, like many other institutions, had to adapt to the change to a digital mode of working very quickly. This was more readily achieved because the school had made significant investments in technology to enable both online delivery and working from home. Consequently, it had built a culture that fostered experimentation, a 'can-do' attitude and a strong emphasis on regular and open communication that had created an environment of effective, strategic execution. This execution process involved 'trial and error' on a continuous basis to determine the methods of digital instruction that suited individual professors and resulted in a satisfactory student experience. The Associate Dean for postgraduate programmes (MBA, DBA, etc.) at GIBS, Professor Louise Whittaker, noted that GIBS' reputation as an outstanding teaching institution was based on the use of the Socratic Method to foster interaction and collaboration in learning. She drew a distinction between distance and contact learning and emphasized that GIBS is very much a 'contact' institution, which is very hard to achieve online. This forced them to pay considerable attention to the design of their blended courses and solutions to enhance digital instruction by adding video material and live interactions with business leaders, giving greater meaning to the online courses and concepts. They found that executive programmes, and particularly customized company programmes, could be redesigned from, say, a one or two-week duration face-to-face course to, say, a duration of two hours per day over a longer time period to allow the design to accommodate work patterns, involve senior executives and design ongoing experiential projects as part of the learning process. In fact, they found that many executive audiences actually favoured online methods and enjoyed the experience greatly. This flexibility in the mode of learning was also evident in the feedback from MBA programmes. As time has evolved since the onset of the pandemic in early 2020, GIBS has used its dynamic capabilities in technology-enabled learning and interactive face-to-face teaching to design blended learning models that offer students both flexibility in learning using online approaches with valued engagement through faculty interaction. Finding the balance between online and in-person teaching was seen as the key to designing their concept of the GIBS business school of the future – one with a strong emphasis on face-to-face learning where faculty interaction and student networking is valued, but is enhanced by a creative blend of digital learning and experiences including, perhaps, virtual reality or gamification approaches.

While GIBS (founded in 2000) operates in a somewhat fragile economic environment in South Africa, Singapore Management University (SMU) (also founded in 2000) operates as a full service (undergraduate → postgraduate → executive education) management university with over 10,000 students in a very strong city-state economy in South East Asia. A full description of SMU's Business School is given in an article by Richard Smith (in *Global Focus* Vol. 14 'A business school disrupted: A view from Singapore'). He notes that 'after the much earlier SARS outbreak the Singapore government ensured that universities have risk management plans that include a pandemic response'. These had included preparation readiness of faculty for online teaching and the adoption of face masks and social distancing measures very early in 2020.

The success that the university had in managing the pandemic can be attributed to a number of factors (see Thomas, Wilson and Lee 2022). The first involved strong coordination and communication efforts with faculty, staff and students to foster an effective community spirit. The university had a Crisis Executive Group (President, Provost and senior management) which liaised constantly with the Singapore government for advice and communicated regularly by email with the university community: it was a 'steering core' which navigated the crisis effectively.

A second important factor was the technological preparedness of the university, making a swift transition to an online environment possible. SMU had developed a business continuity plan in 2014 (following a government edict) that included a requirement that all faculty familiarize themselves with online pedagogical tools and to deliver one section of a semester-long course online.

A third factor, which emerged as the pandemic evolved, involved the provision of online rather than face-to-face exams. Each faculty member, therefore, worked with a designated SMU IT staff member to design 'foolproof' online exams. The IT staff played an influential role in this; so much so that IT staff took a lead in helping SMU design successful virtual student admissions and other university ceremonial events such as convocation and graduation.

As 2020 moved on, Singapore was very successful in containing the coronavirus and was allowed to open the campus in the autumn of 2020 to deliver hybrid classes (with face-to-face classes live-streamed to an online audience). In the summer months of 2020, IT staff once again took the lead role in updating classroom technology (and seating designs) to build the university capacity to deliver hybrid classes.

As 2020 moved into the first semester of 2021, some smaller classes were delivered on the campus (which was now open but on a closely monitored basis), while hybrid classes were offered in all other cases.

It should be noted, in conclusion, that much of SMU's success in managing the pandemic crisis was generated by the strong central coordination efforts of the senior management steering team and the open communication channels that fostered trust in the university administration, with strong support from SMU's Information Technology Services unit.

Boston University's Questrom School of Business pivoted just as quickly, and, in April 2020, directed undergraduate students to return home, cancelled in-person classes for the spring semester and summer sessions, moved to remote teaching and minimized laboratory research.

Subsequently, in the autumn of 2020, the University offered the opportunity of hybrid classes (mixing face-to-face with online) with on-campus presence (protected by regular COVID-19 testing) or the option of fully online remote instruction.

What was interesting from the viewpoint of the Business School was that in the 2019/20 academic year, in the light of the BU Jam and other market surveys, the Dean, Susan Fournier, and Associate Dean, Paul Carlile, worked with colleagues and in partnership with EdX to produce a fully online MBA at a cost of $24,000, which was launched in February 2020 with a projected cohort of 150. (In fact, demand was so strong and of such quality (see *Poets&Quants*) that 400 were admitted), and a second cohort planned for September 2020 also achieved an exceptional quality enrolment of 400.

It should be noted that the underlying programme design was a high-quality, carefully designed, powerful and innovative hybrid learning model delivered at scale by the EdX platform. This certainly attracted strong attention in the business school community and could be creatively adapted for all programmes with F2F content in due course.

Conclusion: Rethinking Paradigms, Business School Futures and Model Innovation

The experiences of business schools during the pandemic have led to many conversations in virtual professional and academic conferences over the last year in which paradigm shifts, questions and ideas about business school futures and preparations for those futures have been debated.

We next examine, and summarize, some of the main assumptions, questions and innovations in business school futures that are in the mainstream of current debates.

As we saw in the 2019/20 (pre-COVID) period, there was some convergence of mainstream arguments that would guide the design of new models of management education. These provided some initial guidance post COVID, but what was clearly uppermost in many discussions about handling COVID-19 was the overarching team and community spirit that had been strongly unleashed leading to meaningful change in many schools as they sought to quickly adapt to digitally based remote learning forms of instruction. While some faculty initially found this mode of instruction stressful and time-consuming, they appreciated the regular communications and advice from deans, IT personnel and senior administrators, who generated a generally collaborative leadership culture. This required skills of planning, flexibility, determination and resilience in order to make decisions and solve problems relating to steps forward.

A key lesson learned was about the role of 'leader(s)' and the 'crisis steering committee' in building a different form of collaborative leadership. In many schools, faculty, in the pre-pandemic context, were less involved in shaping their schools' processes and identity. But in the current situation, faculty worked in a more holistic fashion, collaborated effectively across disciplines and demonstrated leadership across different levels of the school. Transformative change was possible because problem-solving in a 'crisis' required important skills of flexibility, agility, empathy and respect for others as well as creative idea generation through interdisciplinary interaction. This in itself has reshaped ideas about leadership roles in schools and the need for leadership training in moving the organization forward in terms of strategic positioning, design of programme portfolios and direction for the longer term in relation to the schools' identity and image.

There has also been a lesson learned, in that a decade after the Global Financial Crisis and with the advent of the current pandemic, the world had become much less inclusive in terms of social justice and the 'gap' had widened between rich and poor (Piketty, 2014). Rather than social inclusion, inequality, insecurity and exclusion from technological and economic advancement has led to a sense of de-globalization and the rise of nationalism, populism, Trump, Brexit, and the rest, in many countries. Many students and business faculty now felt that some reorienting of shareholder capitalism towards a more inclusive, social democratic form of stakeholder capitalism was overdue in terms of curricula development and the management of tri-sector collaboration, i.e., across business, government and society. Indeed, books on inclusive growth (Thomas and Hedrick-Wong, 2019), reimagining capitalism (Henderson, 2020), the entrepreneurial state (Mazzucato, 2013), and others, have recently emerged from leading business schools highlighting the global challenges of inequality for business and society.

These developments also mandate recognition of the diversity in management schools across countries, cultures and context, and taking on board the best features and lessons learned from each 'global' learning environment. This implies a much deeper collaboration and partnership – as equals – between schools in more developed and less developed regions. In short, there can be no 'dominant' paradigm of management education but instead a range of business models that reflect a broad range of differences. Indeed, it is not only business school collaboration across regions and countries that is essential but also collaboration within universities to address the 21st century grand challenges of society. For too long, the models of management education, anchored in media rankings and reputational contests, have promoted a competition 'fetish' – that is, the winner is the school which achieves distinctive identity through developing long-term sustainable competition advantage, yet it hardly ever shares its advantages meaningfully by collaborating with other less fortunate schools not possessing large government funding or private endowment resources.

Beyond leadership, collaboration and other means of viable co-operation, the main future themes most often discussed currently are about knowledge generation through research, knowledge dissemination through teaching and instruction and knowledge acquisition through meaningful practical linkages with business, government and society. And even more importantly, how to tackle issues of equality, diversity, harmony and integration in society in a global sense.

Rather than providing a checklist of issues in each of these areas, we would prefer to focus on key themes. The first of these is how to *generate meaningful impact* in at least three areas – society and social responsibility in assessing the grand challenges facing society, e.g., poverty, inequality; the generation of business/ industry/government partnerships through experiential internships, project-based learning and joint research projects; and, finally, through our pedagogical impacts on educational quality and blended learning.

The second is determining how to handle *life-long learning*. We all know that the 'shelf-life' of a university degree is becoming shorter because of digital and technological transformation. We, therefore, need to examine whether we can move from three-to-four year undergraduate degree patterns to so-called 'stackable' degrees earned in 'bite-sized' modules of, say, three months each year over a five year period, interspersed with internships and on-the-job learning. The degree is then essentially the certificate earned over the five years, which might also include wide use of digitally-based blended learning approaches.

The third theme, which clearly follows on, is to examine what may be needed for each of the *degree programmes in our product portfolio*. For example, do our undergraduate programmes need to include three or four years of face-to-face instruction? Or could we restrict the face-to-face element to the first two years, during which we embrace principles of liberal management education (encouraging learning through group class interaction), and make the third year a series of project-based learning experiences (graded) with business, government and society? We could also design undergraduate programmes with a first-year face-to-face core programme with the subsequent two years flexibly designed around a mixture of on-campus courses, online blended learning modules and internship/international or study-abroad projects. Similar structural arguments could be made for postgraduate and executive education programmes by offering a menu and a diet of on-campus face-to-face, remote learning and company/government projects and internships.

We strongly believe that these kinds of programme design options will become more common. Indeed, with ongoing technological advances, we can envisage a blended-learning, 'bite-sized' educational model offering the ability to educate many individual students lacking any university training in continents such as Africa. This could be achieved through an online, well-designed programme focusing on 'core' business management tools and techniques (e.g., accounting, finance, economics, marketing, operations management and people management skills), leading to an accredited qualification (endorsed by government and universities with funding from either governments or private sector resources).

In summary, the pandemic offers academics and deans in management education the opportunity to (i) re-evaluate their models and re-think their assumptions about issues such as the place and form of learning; (ii) introduce the necessary improvements in pedagogy, for example, more inspiring technology-enabled instruction tools; (iii) address the appropriate mix of students – international, local and virtual – and to achieve global 'mindsets'; (iv) hire a more balanced faculty with a sound range of skills – so-called 'academic athletes' or 'ambidextrous academics' – who can handle multiple tasks effectively and satisfactorily; (v) think about the future design and vision for what a university degree should be; (vi) establish what the student experience should involve – face-to-face or blended learning or a flexible mix of academic learning, internship and study-abroad activities, assuming their purpose is to produce mature, skilled and ethically grounded graduates. This all adds up to a thorough and insightful review of what the future identity, image, reputation, value and distinctive differentiation of the school, both as an individual entity as well as its impact and contribution to the success of the societies in which it operates, should be. It is also abundantly clear that business schools are being urged to integrate ESG goals into their curricula and to foster increased diversity in their administrators (deans), faculty and staff (see *Financial Times* report on Responsible Business Education, April 12th, 2021).

Note

1 See McGee and Thomas (1986) and Cattani et al. (2017).

References

Augier, M.E. and J. March (2011) *The roots, rituals and rhetorics of change: North American Business Schools after the Second World War.* Stanford, CA: Stanford Business Books

Bisoux, T. (2020) Business Schools' rapid response to COVID-19. *BizEd*, March 18. Tampa, FL: AACSB Publications.

Brandenburger, A.M. and H.W. Jr. Stuart (1996) Value-based business strategy. *Journal of Economics and Management Strategy*, 5(1), pp.5–24.

Carlile, P.R., S.H. Davidson, K.W. Freeman, H. Thomas and N. Venkatraman (2016) *Re-imagining business education: Insights and actions from the business education jam.* Bingley: Emerald Publishing.

Carlile, P.R. and H. Thomas (2020) How to develop collaborative projects that drive innovation. *Global Focus*, 14(2), pp.39–43.

Cattani, G., J.F. Porac and H. Thomas (2017) Categories and competition. *Strategic Management Journal*, 38(1), pp.64–92.

Devinney, T. and G. Downing (2020) Is this the crisis higher education needs to have? *The Times Higher Education Supplement*, May 14.

The Economist briefing (2020) *Uncanny university: COVID-19 could push some universities over the brink*, August 8.

Freeman, K.W. and H. Thomas (2015) Crowd sourced. *Global Focus*, 9(3), pp. 24–27.

Ghoshal, S. (2005) Bad management theories are destroying good management practices. *Academy of Management Learning and Education*, 4(1), pp.75–91.

Hamel, G. (1996) *Competing for the future*. Brighton: Harvard Business Review Press.

Handy, C. (2015) *The second curve: Thoughts on reinventing society*. London: Penguin Random House.

Harney, S. and H. Thomas (2020) *The liberal arts and management education: A global agenda for change*. Cambridge: Cambridge University Press.

Henderson, R. (2020) *Re-imagining capitalism*. Cambridge, MA: Harvard Business School Press.

Iniguez, S. (Ed.) (2011) *The learning curve*. London: Palgrave Macmillan.

Iniguez, S. (2017) The future is blended. *Global Focus*, 11(1), pp.8–11.

Khurana, R. (2007) *From Higher aims to hired hands: The social transformation of American Business Schools and the unfulfilled promise of management as a profession*. Princeton, NJ: Princeton University Press.

Kuper, S. (2020) Universities on a learning curve. *FT.com magazine*, May 16/17.

Mazzucato, M. (2013) *The entrepreneurial state: Debunking private and public sector myths*. London: Anthem Press.

McGee, J. and H. Thomas (1986) Strategic groups: Theory, research and taxonomy. *Strategic Management Journal*, 7(2), pp.141–160.

Oglethorpe, D. (2015) The socially responsible business school: Corporate compromise or competitive advantage? *EFMD blog*, January 29.

Peters, K., R.R. Smith and H. Thomas (2018) *The business of business schools*. Bingley: Emerald Publishing.

Pfeffer, J. and C.T. Fong (2004) The business school business – Some lessons from the US experience. *Journal of Management Studies*, 41(8), pp.1501–1520.

Piketty, T. (2014) *Capital in the twenty-first century*. Cambridge, MA: Belknap Press.

Policano, A. (2005) What price rankings? *BizEd*, September-October, Tampa, FL: AACSB Publications.

Schoemaker, P.J.H. (2008) The future challenges of business: Re-thinking management education. *California Management Review*, 50(3), pp.119–139.

Starkey, K and H. Thomas (2019) The future of business schools: Shut them down or broaden our horizons. *Global Focus*, 13(2), pp.44–49.

Thomas, H. and Y. Hedrick-Wong (2019) *Inclusive growth: The global challenges of social inequality and financial inclusion*. Bingley: Emerald Publishing.

Thomas, H., M. Lee, L. Thomas and A. Wilson (2014) *Securing the future of management education*. Bingley: Emerald Publishing.

Thomas, H., P. Lorange and J. Sheth (2013a) *The business school in the 21st century: Emergent challenges and new business models*. Cambridge: Cambridge University Press.

Thomas, H., L. Thomas and A. Wilson (2013b) *Promises fulfilled and unfulfilled in management education*. Bingley: Emerald Publishing.

Thomas, H., A. Wilson and M. Lee (2022) *Creating a new management university: Tracking the strategy of Singapore Management University (SMU) in Singapore (1997–2019/2020)*. London: Routledge.

Wanot, M. (2021) Business schools' impact during the COVID -19 crisis. *EFMD blog*, February 17, 2020.

Postscript

Recent Conversations, Debates and Dialogues about the Future of Management Education

Post-COVID, it is clear that the tenor, and tone, of current debates has a much stronger student and societal flavour, which suggests that businesses need to address the views of all stakeholders. They should be more proactive in addressing critical social and environmental challenges such as inequality, social and financial exclusion, climate change and social and economic impact. It is agreed that businesses must act with greater social responsibility and not simply try to reward shareholders and maximize shareholder wealth (Kate Reilly, 2021, https//time.com/6105006/mba-programs-changing). This theme was addressed thoroughly during the most recent virtual annual conference of EFMD in 2021, with the Conference Chair, Nicola Kleyn, Dean of Executive Education, Erasmus University, Rotterdam and the CEO of EFMD, Eric Cornuel, giving blog summaries and dinner speeches about the most current and pressing issues faced by deans of leading business schools.

Kleyn's summary ('Looking Back on the 2021 EFMD Annual Conference' https://blog.efmdglobal.org/2021/11/01/) focused on the underlying theme of 'not business as usual'. Several issues emerged: first, the need for a more humanistic ethos in management education; second, the changes that may be required to make our faculty more valuable, e.g., providing them with enhanced skills in research, teaching and societal service necessary to improve the collaboration between academia and management practice; third, that significant innovatory effort will be needed in this rapidly changing marketplace for both new programmes for new learners and the redesign and modification of existing programme offerings; fourth, management educators must clearly demonstrate the social and economic impact of our knowledge generation activities; fifth, the need to leverage technology to improve technology-enabled learning and

DOI: 10.4324/9781003178125-6

build hybrid programmes that encourage a balanced mix between physical student interaction and online remote learning; sixth, there is a need to create research that satisfies both academic and practical audiences. There is a dominant view that there is little business school impact on thought leadership for management practitioners relative to the very strong focus on academic research targeted to so-called A-journals; the focus on competition and competitive advantage between business schools has significantly reduced collaboration and the sense of community across business schools.

Eric Cornuel, in a speech to Erasmus faculty following the EFMD conference, noted that the pandemic disruption of COVID-19 has thrust management education into an important and creative period of transformation and change. This dramatic shift has accelerated a process of deeper reflection on the mission and values of business and management education and its role and impact on societies and ecosystems.

He noted, in particular, that the rise of nationalism and inequality globally has unleashed a lack of trust among ordinary citizens about the actions of politicians, big business and elites. This is borne out in the results of the prestigious Edelman Trust Barometer survey. This lack of trust started with the societal burdens that followed the immoral and unethical actions of the financial sector during the Global Financial Crisis (GFC). Citizens felt that they and not the financiers, had shouldered the 'after-effects' of the GFC.

According to Cornuel, ordinary citizens began to feel that the financial sector was above the law and they became disenchanted, anxious, stressed and angry and resentful because a 'precariat' (precarious proletariat) emerged who did not enjoy 'stable employment, rising income or a sense of belonging'. They distrusted political leadership and the capitalistic system and pointed to societal changes such as 'shrinking middle class' and 'stalling economic mobility' as clear evidence for their distrust in political and business governance. This distrust elevated their desire for changes in the dominant shareholder value business model towards a broader, stakeholder and more socially responsible perspective.

Given these societal challenges, Cornuel, as a leader in management education, notes the importance of this paradigm shift for business schools towards the stakeholder, socially responsible framework that EFMD has strongly advocated in its manifestos and writings since the GFC. He emphasizes that a particular focus must be to reform the principles of the dominant research model in business schools towards both rigour and relevance and not simply academic rigour (typified by so-called A* journals). Faculty members must become more engaged, working on interdisciplinary, applied projects as well as more theoretically focused projects. This engaged scientific scholarship should aim to attack practical management challenges, societal grand challenges such as inequality and climate challenges and generate new academic themes. Engaged scientific scholarship should thus 're-nobilitate the role of faculty' as advocates of engaged scholarship and as co-producers of knowledge in partnership with business, government and society.

This enhanced faculty role should also encompass 'life-long learning', in which faculty become involved in re-skilling and upskilling managers through short, focused courses after initial business school training and hence become mentors and coaches to managers during the evolution of their managerial careers.

In conclusion, Cornuel advocates an optimistic – and logical – pathway for the future of management education involving more international collaboration and cooperation with a greater focus on societal issues and impacts.

Many of the themes identified by Nicola Kleyn and Eric Cornuel have also been expressed in other recent contributions including the following:

- Robert S. Fleming (in an AACSB post/article, September 10, 2021, 'Remembering the Past as we Prepare for the Future' on the 20th anniversary of the 9/11 attacks on the USA) addresses the need for students to be taught future-oriented skills such as handling crisis management, foresight skills and scenario thinking in confronting uncertain futures, and visionary, agile business leadership skills such as empathy, team/group working, dialogue and critical and analytic skills in solving 'wicked' problems effectively.

- Wilfred R Vanhonacker (in an AACSB post/article, September 15, 2021, 'The Unbundling of Business Education') identifies four trends in the dynamics of business education, namely, digital transformation, shorter attention spans for educational intervention, the importance of life-long education and a move towards shorter forms of training. Taken together, he argues that business education is unbundling and becoming a world of shorter courses and micro-credentials. This implies the design of a new education paradigm driven by digital transformation and market dynamics, towards a 'degree' based on a range of shorter micro-credentials that address the skills needs of both the individual and the organization over a life-long managerial career. Such degrees, somewhat evident in recent years, have been called 'stackable' degrees.

- Andrew Hoffman, a Professor of Sustainable Enterprise at the University of Michigan (in an EFMD *Global Focus*, December 2, 2021, entitled 'The Engaged Scholar') has a simple message which should resonate with scholars who want to inspire and bring their work to the broad set of public audiences, namely business, government and society, and hence enacts the role of an academic service to society. In his words, 'I want my research, teaching and outreach to have a positive impact on the world around me. Citation counts, A-level publication and an h-index pale in comparison to that simple outcome.'

- Bert de Reyck, incoming Dean at the Lee Kong Chian School of Business, Singapore Management University (in a short article published by SMU's Office of Technology Transfer, 'The 21st Century Business School: Creating Meaningful Impact', November 15, 2021) has a similar vision to Hoffman's in creating a culture to inspire and deliver real-world impact. He envisages three areas, namely, digital transformation, entrepreneurship and sustainability which can significantly stimulate the search for meaningful impact in the business school environment.

Finally, we provide a summary of the dialogue and debate about the future of business schools led by Howard Thomas at the recent virtual annual conference of AABS (the African Association of Business Schools). It was agreed generally that the COVID-19 pandemic was the 'tectonic shift' that had captured the attention of university leaders and had radically transformed conversations about the future of management education on the African continent.

A summary of the key points that emerged from the AABS dialogue and debate follow, that enrich and amplify the discussions from previous 'more developed economy' business educators:

- *Mission/Vision/Purpose*
  What can you do? What might you do? What should you do? To address the urgent need for management training in the context of a diverse, relatively young population in most African countries.

- *Identity*
  Africa, as a continent of around 54 countries, has a wide range of cultures and contexts. Management education needs in Africa vary widely, and there is no 'one size fits all' model that fits every context, need and culture.

- *Impact*
  Research in Africa needs to address meaningful impacts, e.g., addressing the challenges in the economic development of African growth and focusing on the important developmental role for entrepreneurship, alongside foreign direct investment and aid, in generating growing companies and economies in Africa.

- Technology
  Digital technology was seen as an important enabler of economic growth through the rapid adoption of technology-enabled learning. The challenge is to provide access to and affordability of management education to African students. This will require creatively mixing the physical aspects of learning with the strong growth of digital modes of online remote learning in a scalable, efficient manner.

- Era of Imagination
  There was a widespread perception that this was a time to reimagine educational approaches. This would include:

  - Merging competition and collaboration between business schools in Africa by linking schools together to partner with leading international schools, businesses (e.g., big tech, Google, Apple, etc.) and government to provide finance and educational mentorship in the process of growing African schools.

  - Co-producing knowledge and research with businesses, governments and civil society, thereby encouraging practical academic research.

  - Using technology to create new processes of learning, including experiential project-based learning and new patterns of work in a technology-driven economy.

Even more recently, Susan Fournier and Howard Thomas in *Global Focus* Volume 2, 2022, reflected on a 'Zero-based Cultural Perspective on Dealing with Hybrid Reality of Teaching in Business Schools'. With the permission of EFMD, a large part of the article is summarized here.

> It is clear that management educators have accepted the mandate that both online and hybrid forms of instruction will be required as management education moves forward. The critical implementation question is how we, as leaders, confront and solve the complex set of managerial issues and challenges associated with students and faculty adapting to new, redesigned business school models and organisational cultures as we proceed forward into that future.

Zero-Based Culture

It is important to examine these new existential realities using the concept of a 'zero-based culture' for reshaping management education. This means exploring a new business school future without being encumbered by incremental changes to existing knowledge, practices and approaches: in essence, a 'clean slate' approach. The zero-based culture allows deans and senior managers to reinvent and rethink their frameworks with a new set of refreshing insights and with an openness to question existing approaches.

Given the background landscape of where management education might be heading and the canvas of opportunity offered by our concept of 'zero-based culture,' we identify and examine five core issues, some larger in their existential impact than others, but all important in moving forward into the hybrid reality that our world of higher education has become.

Culture of the Business School

The quote attributed to Peter Drucker 'culture eats strategy for breakfast' highlights the problems brought on by the new hybrid reality and its attendant need for cultural re-examination. The shift of faculty to online learning and the increased opportunities of delivering programme experiences remotely by definition changes, and potentially degrades, the residential culture on which virtually all business schools have been historically based. Taken to the extreme, we risk losing our very identities as vibrant residential hubs for teaching, research and learning. Will the business school simply become a 'technology platform' organization with no longer any need for well-endowed and furnished buildings?

Evidence already exists of newly emergent habits that dilute known positives from 'water cooler' conversations, individual and group lunches, and serendipitous coffee meetings on collaboration, relationships and innovation. In Zoom, we now subsist with 'appointment-only TV' (and we know what happened to that!). The Zoom culture, with highlighted yellow squares for every star, the perilous 'leave button' at everyone's fingertips, and active side-bar chats erodes the collective identity that binds us together. Multitasking has risen to new heights in the 'video-off' world of Zoom; meetings have become podcasts that serve as background for other, more important goings-on.

As research productivity rises, we see faculty increasingly 'absent' from servicing collective activities in, for example, doctoral student mentorship, faculty meetings, student events and work groups. Teaching faculty, more likely to be in their offices for reasons of increased teaching loads, and the staff who are mandated to be there, confront daily the visible status signals of empty tenure-track offices. The cultural divide widens.

The result? Transactional cultures. The prioritization of the individual over the collective. The rise of the 'egosystem' (the omnipotent, entitled) among faculty in place of communal cultures that orient us towards service, the collective, a team-oriented, shared vision and culture, the overall greater, common good.

The cultural problem exacerbates when hiring for online teaching shifts to part-time professionals who have less, and maybe, little, connection to the school.

Building a strong culture in this hybrid environment won't work via zoom games, virtual cocktail hours, and 'Wednesdays in the Office'. Good business schools rely on steady staff-student interactions, hands-on project-based learning, and the inspirational moments that occur in a serendipitous fashion in face-to-face interaction.

Academic Integrity and Learning Assessments

Online teaching has clearly disrupted our traditional approaches for controlling integrity and providing feedback to students on their attainment of learning goals and skills development. The system is failing or at least challenged significantly, particularly as we move to online learning models at scale where competencies cannot easily be assessed. The key question is whether online learning can ever come close to the benefits of one-to-one interactions that occur from immersive learning via case discussion and experiential project collaborations. These interaction-based benefits are also enhanced by students' participation in extra-curricular activities such as case competitions, finance investment clubs and career treks. Can we validate that online programmes achieve the same learning goals? Do we see the same grade distributions in online and residential degree environments? Is cheating more rampant in online environments (the answer is yes)? How do we achieve grading at scale while remaining true to the value of depth and application and context? It is not yet clear that online programmes deliver the same learning as their full-time residential degree counterparts. Are we bold enough to find out the truth?

Market Segmentation Particularly in the MBA Market (and the Erosion of the Part-time Market)

The Boston University Questrom School of Business has a proud history in reimagining management education. Iterations of the Questrom Jam (Jam 1.0, 2015) with a Global Remote Learning Jam, and Jam 2.0 (2015–2019), which focused on critical issues in ten developing/emerging market locations, highlighted ongoing challenges and generated clear ideas from crowdsourcing (*Global Focus*, Freeman et al., Volume 9, 2015) and Open Innovation (*Global Focus*, Carlile et al., Volume 14, 2020).

In 2019/2020 – before the pandemic, and using insights drawn from the BU Jams and as well as market evidence from Questrom's MicroMasters™ programmes, Dean Susan Fournier and Senior Associate Dean Paul Carlile worked with colleagues to develop, produce and launch a fully online MBA (OMBA) at a cost of $24,000, in partnership with edX. Demand was so strong (in a segment with an average age of 37 and 12 years of working experience) and the programme of such quality (*Chronicle of Higher Ed* 2019) that aggressive enrollment targets were doubled. Subsequent cohorts also overdelivered (with current enrollment at over 1700). The underlying programme design was innovative, high-quality, carefully designed and powerful: a hybrid-learning model delivered jointly at scale by edX and BU.

According to sound marketing logic, all products – academic programmes included—should address defined segments with tailored value propositions, and managers should draw meaningful and sharp lines between these segments in terms of the products and augmented services provided. This was the clear logic that guided BU's development of the Questrom OMBA.

The MBA degree is arguably the most coveted postgraduate degree in the world, and demand for it, while counter-cyclical, remains very strong. Online MBAs added to the portfolio can help hedge these risks. How should a dean analyze the facts when even though there exists latent pent-up demand for the MBA degree, portfolio management challenges arise in relation to other segments of the MBA market, namely, the full-time MBA (FT MBA) and the part-time MBA (PT MBA, offered in the evening or weekends for working professionals) when lower-priced online MBAs are in play?

These challenges become most stark when online MBAs challenge the PT MBA in the MBA portfolio of degrees. Exacerbated by COVID and a migration to online teaching in part-time residential programmes, flexibility and cost benefits for busy part-time professionals have become more recognized, salient and coveted. As online MBAs derive more credibility and cost advantages, the fundamental value proposition of the PT MBA weakens. While cannibalization of PEMBA at the hands of OMBA has been held at bay at BU through careful product and service differentiation, at what point does the PT market collapse and migrate to flexible and cheaper online degrees?

There are, in some schools, clear signs that the PT MBA market may be shrinking as students migrate online. This can also sound the death knell for the FT MBA offering. In most business schools, such as those in thriving urban areas, PT MBAs are typically built on the backs of healthy FT MBA programmes, with students merged in year-two nighttime electives that can be run at scale. FT MBA programmes are already under tremendous pressure, with heightened competition, threats from declining international enrollments, and the mandate to offer students sizeable scholarship stipends. Further, with the pandemic's dictate for companies to offer employees remote work options, PT MBA students are likely not only to lose their strong connections to their full-time employers but also the habits that get them out of their homes and into the business school to engage in their evening PT MBA classes.

The 'house of cards' may be crumbling. Some schools have already shuttered their FT MBA programmes and with them, their associated part-time cohorts. The challenge is how to craft these market segments creatively so that they coexist with the online MBA.

Degree Programmes as a Core Product

Again following from the Jam experience, Questrom explored and launched in 2017 with edX a MicroMasters™ programme in digital business. The programme involves completion of four online modules with an exam structure that leads to the award of an online credential and credits towards residential degree programmes. This early exploration, together with the entry of other players from the world of tech into the market, such as Coursera, Google and LinkedIn, opened our eyes to look beyond formal degree programmes as the core product of business schools. New attention focuses on so-called badges, micro-credentials and 'stackables'. The new model is one of life-long learning via bite-sized, online continuing education modules for adult learners; content delivered as and when needed to inform the career journey over time.

Two problems linger. One is the tendency to remain driven by degree thinking despite a shift to a new model of learning. Despite [the] embrace of new product offerings, the degree remains the ultimate credential, as with the concept of 'stackables' that can add up to a degree. Some degree territory has been identified as sacred ground but maybe it should not be. Life-long learning micro-credentials have barely taken hold in the undergraduate space, where the majority of business school students are found. Is the undergraduate degree as 'rite of passage' needed by and relevant to everyone, or is there significant growth potential in a certificate approach to this hallmark of higher education?

The second problem is the current failure to identify a profitable business model for life-long learning and continuing adult education in general. What strategies are needed to fill this gap – a gap which is particularly relevant to the development of management education in emerging markets in Africa and Asia? Technology-enabled learning can undoubtedly advance global society by developing low-cost learning models. Skills-mapping platforms – the Airbnbs of higher ed – comprehensive learner records, and alumni-based models that live not in the university's development office but rather in continuing adult education are needed if we are to achieve these goals. A majority of US business schools have dismantled their executive education arms for lack of enrollment. How do we pivot these practices to embrace life-long learning goals?

Education Costs and the 'Tuition Bubble'

Management education is largely a premium product, and tuition and fees remain the dominant funding source for most business schools. This funding model presents major risks and remains a central challenge to the sustainability of our business models in business schools.

Business schools claim an advantage versus many other colleges at the university: the robust popularity and demonstrated ROI of business degrees remains strong. Indeed, well-ranked business schools are currently experiencing increased demand for both undergraduate and master's programmes. However, at the same time, there exists growing pressure from students, parents and policymakers about the unsustainable cost of business education and escalating levels of student debt. Cultural critique about the magnitude and nature of costs in higher education is at an all-time high. Student dissatisfaction with the career outcomes derived from their significant investments is not inconsequential and increased disconnects from business partners at research-intensive universities exacerbate this charge. Still, tuition and fees continue to rise to cover increased costs, even in challenging global economic environments, and the premium price of college tuition deserves a reckoning.

The tuition calculation should of course be based on the 'customer's' willingness to pay' for the programme. A business school's competitive advantage relative to another school occurs when the value spread between the 'willingness to sell' (i.e. the lowest point at which the school can offer a programme) and the 'willingness to pay' is large. Moves to online programmes at scale provide solid economic logic for lower tuition [fees]. It remains unclear, however, whether business schools are willing to invest the significant funds required to build [the] technological, human and marketing infrastructures required to deliver online at scale.

A wave of hundreds of class action lawsuits requesting refunds of tuition dollars in US schools and colleges that shifted to online and hybrid education during the pandemic presents strong evidence of a changing perception of the value of the business school product and consumers' willingness to pay. One question begs an answer: is the product simply the business degree credential, or does the residential experience provide tangible and significant value beyond the credential?

Concluding Thoughts

In this chapter, we have outlined how technological changes, notably those that involve hybrid (blended) technologically-enabled learning, present real, ongoing, fundamental challenges for business schools as they emerge from COVID.

However, there exist other forces of change that confront business schools today and which require careful consideration and immediate action. Indeed, for the first time in our history, five macro-economic and geopolitical factors are colliding, creating a ripe environment for transformative change. The digital transformation of business and the rise of data as competitive advantage. The global pandemic and consequential changes in the future of work and the workplace. Calls for social justice in relation to movements such as Black Lives Matter and general societal unrest, including a mandate for social impact. Political and geopolitical unrest, exemplified in the Russian invasion of Ukraine and the attempted takeover of the US Capitol Building and entrenched in increased nationalism and de-globalization in the world economy. Add to this various micro-cultural challenges to the higher education landscape, including student access to and affordability of education, anti-business sentiment and charges to reimagine capitalism, pressures against free speech on college campuses, and questions about the relevancy and impact of our academic research. Serious questions have been posed about the purpose of business and the quality/value of higher education and these questions deserve answers.

The siloed nature of the business school landscape and the inherently interdisciplinary nature of our problems and the business/governmental ecosystems that can solve them require us to collaborate and interact more closely as business school leaders. This will inevitably change our missions, values, purposes and responsibilities to society and our key stakeholders.

There is little doubt that these are interesting, exciting and challenging times. It is a privilege to lead business schools in such relentless, high-pressure environments.

Summary

It is clear that debates about the future of management education will continue in an unabated fashion in the current volatile and fast-changing environment. Deans, whether from developed or emerging developing market contexts will increasingly encourage those open debates which will hopefully be facilitated by academic professional organizations such as EFMD, AACSB, AABS, GBSN (Global Business School Network), PRME (Principles for Responsible

Management Education) the UN's Sustainable Development Goals and RRBM (the Responsible Research in Business and Management Community).

These are exciting times. We encourage new upcoming deans as well as organizational leaders to address these challenges and develop a better, even more impactful world for future generations through agile, flexible management education.

References

Fleming, R. S. (2021) Remembering the past as we prepare for the future. *AACSB post/article* 10th September 2021.

Fournier, S. and H. Thomas (2022) A zero-based cultural perspective on dealing with the hybrid reality of teaching in business schools. *Global Focus, 15th Anniversary Issue (forthcoming)*.

Hoffman, A. (2021) The engaged scholar. *Global Focus*, 2nd December 2021.

Kleyn, N. (2021) Looking back on the 2021 EFMD annual conference https://blog.efmdglobal.org/2021/11/01/

Reilly, K (2021) Inside the battle for the hearts and minds of tomorrow's business leaders. *Time Magazine*. https//time.com/6105006/mba-programs-changing

de Reyck, B. (2021) The 21st century business school: creating meaningful impact. *Office of Technology Transfer, Singapore Management University*, 15th November 2021.

Vanhonacker, W. R. (2021) The unbundling of business education. *AACSB Post/Article*, 15th September 2021.

Appendix 1
Discussion Points for Reflection

Critical incidents which deans revealed in our interviews based on rare unforeseen external events, archetypal situations, typical events and internal
shocks prompted the questions below. These might help other business school
leaders and their colleagues to appreciate challenges in the business school
deanship. They can stimulate conversations for participants on leadership development programmes discussed in Chapter 4 about what they might have
done differently.

1. Acting Deans
   Do you consider that acting deans who apply for a deanship internally
   should be interviewed as a matter of courtesy? Should they be included in
   the new dean's team?

2. Executive Search Firms
   What are your views on the roles and behaviours of executive search
   firms?

3. Due Diligence and Negotiating
   What due diligence is necessary and possible when applying for a
   deanship?

4. Negotiating
   In negotiating terms and conditions of a dean's appointment and the
   school's financial contributions to the central university, what are important considerations?

5. Strategic Choices
   What strategic choices do deans have during a recession and other crises?

6. Dean–Central University Relations
   Why do relationships between the dean and head of the university or the
   dean and the head of the university's administration matter?

7. Integration in the University
   How can business school deans develop synergies between the sub-brand and the parent university's brand? (Thomas et al., 2014)

8. Upper Echelons
   How do the dean's personal values and experience affect their leadership style and culture in the business school?

9. Communicating
   How can business school leaders facilitate meaningful and different forms of communications in hybrid working arrangements across academic and professional support staff groups and with other stakeholders such as business school advisory board members?

10. Visibility and Compassion
    How can deans replicate the benefits of 'managing by walking around' to show they care in a digital office?

11. Facilities, Collaboration, Community
    What are your views on business school leaders creating co-working and social spaces to encourage collaborative communities?

12. Community, Empathy, Humanizing the Business School
    How can deans communicate empathy and build a sense of safety, community and purpose in a digital age?

13. Inclusive Leadership
    How proactive are you in communicating values about equity, diversity, inclusion and respect (EDIR) and calling out potential discrimination?

14. Grand Challenges
    How can business school deans support the UN's Sustainable Development Goals through innovative multi-disciplinary and multi-sector collaborations within the university and beyond?[1]

15. Purpose
    What do you consider are the benefits of rethinking a business school's purpose during a crisis?

16. Public Good
    How can business schools operate in directly contributing to 'public good'?

17. SDGs in Business School Operations
    How can business schools better implement the UN's sustainable development goals in their own operations?

18. Personal Well-Being

    How do you manage to gain a sense of equanimity (composure, balance) and personal well-being in a business school leadership role?

19. Mental Health and Well-Being

    How can deans improve their own mental health and well-being more generally in a business school?

20. Ethical Behaviours

    What red lines being crossed would you consider unacceptable in the business school or university?

21. Exiting the Deanship

    In deciding when to step down, what factors such as length of tenure would you consider?

Note

1 See for example: Currie, G., J.Davies and E. Ferlie (2016) A call for university-based business schools to "lower their walls:" Collaborating with other academic departments in pursuit of social value. *Academy of Management Learning & Education*, 15 (4) pp.742–755. George, G., J. Howard-Grenville, A. Joshi and L. Tihanyi (2016) Understanding and tackling societal grand challenges through management research. *Academy of Management Journal*, 59 (6) pp.1880–1895. Miotto, G., A. Blanco-González, and F. Díez-Martín, (2020) Top business schools legitimacy quest through the Sustainable Development Goals. *Heliyon*, 6 (11): p.e05395.

Appendix 2
Examples of Critical Events/Challenges at Multiple Levels and Lessons Learned

Table 1 Individual level

1.1 Executive search firm threatens to blacklist you if you refuse a job offer	Understand the role of executive search firms in higher education (Manfredi et al., 2019); ensure a good fit; be assertive in asking appropriate questions. Seek career advice; do not be rushed into accepting an offer.
1.2 Undertaking due diligence pre-application	Ask questions, sound out networks, trusted confidants; visit; be prepared to withdraw from the recruitment process.
1.3 Interview and recruitment process	Talk about guiding principles in developing a strategic plan rather than focusing on your own achievements, engage with the audience in presentations, avoid negative language about previous employers.
1.4 Negotiating fair terms and conditions before accepting a deanship	Benchmark through peers, b-school associations for a market rate salary; ensure a substantive position after deanship; request support for development and team, research assistants; post-deanship sabbatical. Agree terms in writing – deans serve at the discretion (Gallos, 2002) of the university president/vice-chancellor and new appointees may want different arrangements in the deanship.
1.5 Between accepting and taking up an appointment	Enhance profile with PR announcements, professional photograph, self-branding (AACSB, 2017), plan publicity. Self-education – conduct fieldwork, interview colleagues, read minutes of meetings to improve learning curve.

(Continued)

Table 1 (Continued) Individual level

1.6 Family adjustments – relocation, travel commitments	Discuss implications with family members (Konopaske et al., 2009), e.g., benefits of weekly commuting (100% focus, compartmentalizing work and family); negotiate dual career moves; appreciate disruption to children's schooling if family relocates or refuses to relocate, culture shock. Learning to live on campus with the family as an alternative.
1.7 Acting/ interim deans not shortlisted or appointed	Help contenders to your position to move on with projects and career support, through dialogue, prevent animosity, be prepared for difficult conversations (Reynolds, 2014).
1.8 Identity issues in transition	Accept that people will see you differently in the role, work with a trusted mentor, executive coach, develop a 'thick skin', do not take things personally. Accept that deans are 'a bridge between external stakeholders, school goals and … faculty's own interests and motivations (Thomas and Thomas, 2011)'.
1.9 Decide senior leadership team membership and governance structures.	Examine legacy appointments, cronyism, delegate to trusted colleagues. Interview people 1-1 (Beardsley, 2017), develop terms of reference for advisory boards, develop teams and faculty, role model desirable behaviours, establish transparent systems and culture.
1.10 Relationships with administrative colleagues	Work collaboratively across occupational groups with colleagues supporting each other to reduce stress levels (Basken, 2021). See examples of administrators who have become leaders of universities and of business schools (Ellis, 2022).
1.11 Information overload	Dialogue with close colleagues, pace meetings, committees, e.g., PA filtering emails, doctoral student summarizing committee papers, ask for help (YouTube, 2011a), say 'no'. Delegation, collaboration.
1.12 Dean's visibility	Managing by walking around and learning from corridor conversations (You Tube, 2011b). Deans 'author themselves as research-credible, moral and hardworking (Brown et al., 2021)'.

(Continued)

Table 1 (*Continued*) Individual level

1.13 Financial challenges	Rethink models of fund-raising in public business schools (Bradshaw, 2015).
1.14 Communications crises	Listening. Create, monitor communications and crisis communications plans to gain control (Bieger and Schmid, 2019). Weekly newsletters, set expectations, consultations, (social) media announcements, interviews with journalists. Boost morale (Watson, 2009).
1.15 Imposter phenomenon, crisis of self-confidence	Seek social and emotional support, talk through concerns with mentor, gain validation of success (360-degree feedback), self-talk and positive self-affirmation (Hutchins and Rainbolt, 2017). 'Fake it' until you 'make it' (Cuddy, 2015) – impression management.
1.16 Resistance, incivility	Taking people with you; consulting; 'chillability', ability to switch off.
1.17 Overloaded, overwhelmed, stressed	Discuss vulnerabilities (Ancona et al., 2007), ask for help. Draw on peer-to-peer support (Davies, 2015). Enjoy simple pleasures – family meals, exercise, meditation, reading and resting (Delbecq, 1996).
1.18 Dean's performance	Learn how to prioritize to focus on metrics (Jones et al., 2020) and on what adds value.
1.19 Being fired	Deal with disagreements with new boss (Byrne, 2013), re-invent oneself.
1.20 Contract non-renewal	Being discreet about a dean's reasons for stepping down after one term (Byrne, 2016).
1.21 Merger	Learn from cases of winners (Bradshaw, 2013) and losers.
1.22 Exit and adjustment post deanship	Recognize deanships are finite (Finch et al., 2022); weigh up psychological and economic aspects of exit strategy with colleagues and family members well ahead; support succession planning.

Table 2 Business school level

2.1 Understand different models (Peters et al., 2018), organizational design (Simon, 1967), and debates	Deliberately examine model (Spicer et al., 2021). Developing skills and expertise in bridging management scholarship and management practice (Spencer et al., 2022). Reading (Cornuel, 2022).
2.2 Facilitate management learning	Reflect on experiences not just biographical, chronological, conceptual perspectives without linking to practice (Lorange, 2022). Work with predecessors (Ethier, 2021), blog ideas.
2.3 Meetings, strategy away days to facilitate excellent outcomes	Listening, agenda-setting, avoid talking shops, follow-up. Learn from cases of strategic leadership processes in various contexts.[1] Participate in deans' conference to re-think the value proposition of b-schools (Shinn, 2022).
2.4 Branding the b-school in the university	Ensure brand consultants engage b-school members (Frandsen et al., 2018) to understand faculty ambivalence and cynicism about branding.
2.5 Renaming the b-school	In dealing with donors, understand potential pitfalls in naming (Meley, 2021) the b-school, decolonizing and scholarship initiatives.
2.6 Publicity, reputation, innovation	See innovations spotlighted by accreditation bodies.[2]
2.7 Advisory boards	Learn from effective board management examples (Hardcastle, 2021). Awareness of trends in management education such as stackability, climate consciousness, interdisciplinarity (De Novellis, 2022).
2.8 Claims of bullying, harassment, fraud	Specific criticisms of b-schools may be unjustified so it is important to address claims of discrimination (Rooney, 2020).
2.9 Student/staff death	Deans immediately drop other activities to deal directly (Byrne, 2012) with unexpected deaths and communicate empathy and solidarity.

(*Continued*)

Table 2 (Continued) Business school level

2.10 Poor line management	Ensure careers support (Baruch, 2020). Generativity – support future generations (Doerwald et al., 2021).
2.11 Academic misconduct, contract teaching, scams	Develop awareness of misconduct (Jenkins, 2011) and ensure appropriate procedures.
2.12 Student complaints, e.g., sexual harassment by doctoral supervisor; quality of supervision	Deans need to be mindful about pressures on the student-supervisor relationship (Clegg, 2022) and communicate the importance of professional behaviours and deal swiftly and impartially with complaints.
2.13 Determining accreditations and rankings goals	Recognize the powerful impact of accreditations and rankings on shaping the business school field and businesses as a force for good (Christensen Hughes, 2020) through collaborations and a shared sense of commitment. Learn on the job.
2.14 Meeting targets	Learn from failures. Understanding managerialism in the academy (De Vita and Case, 2016).
2.15 Faculty resistance to changes, restructuring, incivility, vote of no confidence	Understand personal motives, drivers of personal behaviour, personal and organizational power bases, and techniques to influence key individuals (Thomas and Thomas, 2011).
2.16 Closing programmes, research centres, retrenchment, mergers	Working closely with human resources experts, PR, local press, alumni to ensure professional processes in cases of mergers, layoffs (Sunnucks, 2014) to demonstrate empathy and support.
2.17 Growing pains, inadequate facilities, false promises	Place still matters (Hughes, 2019) and when the allocation of suitable institutional space follows tuition fee income, deans can draw on health and safety and reputational issues and with students to improve facilities.

(Continued)

Table 2 (Continued) Business school level

2.18 New orientation, e.g., public value	Making the case for new hires and approaches. Wallace Donham (Acton, 2022), Dean of Harvard Business School in the mid-1920s, hired Elton Mayo and Lawrence Henderson to develop closer social bonds amongst workers for greater community and stability. Learn lessons from the pandemic in facing challenges (Bartleby, 2020).
2.19 Recognising adjuncts, gratitude	Develop student and employee awards, thank you days (Waller and Caldwell, 2021).

Table 3 University level

3.1 Dean on university's senior leadership team	Attend to mediating role institutionally (Davies and Thomas, 2010), potential synergies, communicate b-school ethos and global perspectives, highlighting country differences (Harker et al., 2016).
3.2 New (interim) boss	Recognize this can be a potential trigger for a dean to step down (Byrne, 2015) despite a dean's popularity with students and the board.
3.3 New mandate	Understand priorities[3] and predecessor effect.
3.4 Annual reviews, reports, validations	Systems leadership – ensure systems are fit for purpose and rules are followed (Bradshaw, 2011) compared with other instances of innovating and changing the status quo.
3.5 B-school merged with law/ another unit	Beware of cases where deans have not followed correct procedures (Jongsma, 2011). Consider the location of disciplines, e.g., economics (Heilman et al., 1928) and relationships between them.
3.6 B-school cross-subsidizes STEM	Decide whether or not to work with STEM disciplines for intellectual and research income cross subsidies.
3.7 Dean takes on pan university roles	Communicate better understanding of how deans and b-schools contribute to the broader university (Davies, 2015), improve negotiating skills, inequalities in systems.

(Continued)

Table 3 (*Continued*) University level

3.8 (De)centralization	Some b-schools have gained greater autonomy.[4]
3.9 Relatively high financial contributions to the central university	Accept or be prepared to tackle higher central taxes paid to the central university from the b-school than contributions from other academic units (McKie, 2018). Facilitate system level resilience and agility and collaborations to be on the front foot.
3.10 Opening/ closing branch campus	Read leading journals on management education and the business of business schools, e.g., *AMLE* to understand phenomena such as business bubbles and internationalization (Alajoutsijärvi et al., 2014).
3.11 Unfulfilled promises and inadequate central services, e.g., for executive education	Understand that where there are devolved budgets, b-schools pay for infrastructure (Bouchikhi and Kimberly, 2016) such as buildings, IT, marketing despite paying central overheads for one-size-fits-all services. Be inventive and work with faculty and students for joint problem-solving, appreciate challenges such as the cost-of-living crisis.
3.12 Complaints, risks	Understand views about quality and risks of working with agents and other partners such as private providers (Weinberg, 2013).
3.13 Broad view	Read widely about changes in education, the world of work and society to build capacity, recovery, adaptation and innovation, e.g., journalists and political commentators (Friedman, 2020). Read about leadership[5] and change management tools (Caredda, 2020).

Table 4 Insights on learning to deal with external crises that impact b-schools

4.1 Recession, funding cuts	Accept strict centralized financial controls; ask for help to generate opportunities and revenues; offer help to struggling students (Deveau, 2013); understand risks; solidarity; embed learning from crises in the curriculum (Tangel, 2013).
4.2 Public health crisis	Provide a safe learning environment, appropriate infrastructure; communicate how adversity is being mitigated; re-think delivery modes; re-imagine flexibility; consider enduring changes (Rana et al., 2020).
4.3 Natural disaster, e.g., climate	Deans can collaborate to draw on expertise in business schools related to governance, leadership, marketing, operations, business and organizational transformation and performance measurement to address the climate crisis (Galdón et al., 2022).
4.4 Terrorism	Developing and investing in contingency plans, careful risk management, being empathetic and responsive in a context of radicalism and cyber terrorist attacks (Whitford, 2022).
4.5 External merger	Practise good governance, prioritize, communicate constantly, be hands on, redesign processes and procedures, be passionate and committed to success by involving everyone (Guilhon, 2015). Build new brands, bridge cultural differences, reshape teaching models (Anderson, 2009).
4.6 Accreditations	Accreditations affect activities, identity, and purpose, losing/failing to gain an accreditation can result in de-legitimation (Lejeune and Vas, 2014) and opportunities to learn.

Notes

1 Examples: Fragueiro, F. and H. Thomas (2011). *Strategic leadership in the business school: Keeping one step ahead.* Cambridge: Cambridge University Press. Thomas, H., A. Wilson and M.P. Lee (2022) *Creating a new management university: Tracking the strategy of Singapore Management University (SMU) in Singapore (1997–2019/20).* Oxford: Routledge.

2 For example: AACSB innovations that inspire: https://www.aacsb.edu/media-center/news/2022/04/innovations-that-inspire-2022.

3 For example, after a case of fraud: Bleizeffer, K. (2022) New Temple Fox Dean: Ranking scandal 'could never happen again.' *Poets&Quants*, March 23.

4 Durham university business school became a separate university faculty whereas other business schools have been absorbed into larger academic units, e.g., Birmingham University Business School became part of a College of Social Sciences.

5 E.g., Weybrecht, G. (2022) What kind of leadership are you selling? AACSB, June 15. Randall, L.M. and L. A. Coakley (2007) Applying adaptive leadership to successful change initiatives in academia. *Leadership & Organization Development Journal*, 28 (4) pp.325–335. Niewiesk, S. and E.G. Garrity-Rokous (2021) The academic leadership framework: A guide for systematic assessment and improvement of academic administrative work. *Global Business and Organizational Excellence*, 40 (4): pp.50–63. Books for practitioners by business school faculty, e.g., Colley, J. and D. Spyridonidis (2022) *Unprecedented leadership: Learning to lead in turbulent times*. Cham: Palgrave Macmillan.

References

AACSB International (2017) Why business school deans should have a personal brand. *YouTube*, August 29. Available at: https://www.youtube.com/watch?v=pPh9fRh0bBI

Acton, R.M. (2022) The search for social harmony at Harvard Business School, 1919–1942. *Modern Intellectual History*, First View, pp.1–27. doi: https://doi.org/10.1017/S1479244321000706

Alajoutsijärvi, K., K. Juusola and J.A. Lamberg (2014) Institutional logic of business bubbles: Lessons from the Dubai business school mania. *Academy of Management Learning & Education*, 13(1) pp.5–25.

Ancona, D., T.W. Malone, W.J. Orlikowski and P.M. Senge (2007) In praise of the incomplete leader. *Harvard Business Review*, 85(2) pp.92–103.

Anderson, L. (2009) Schools merger finalised. *Financial Times*, November 17.

Bartleby (2020) The pandemic increases the challenges facing business schools. *The Economist*, May 20.

Baruch, Y. (2020) The changing nature of academic careers in management education in Western societies. In P.R. Kadiyil, A. Forrier, and M.B. Arthur (Eds.), *Career dynamics in a global world*. Cheltenham: Edward Elgar Publishing, pp.162–174.

Basken, P. (2021) Administrators 'help relieve stress burden' on academics. *Times Higher Education*, September 16.

Beardsley, S.C. (2017) *Higher calling: The rise of nontraditional leaders in academia*. Charlottesville: University of Virginia Press.

Bieger, T. and U. Schmid (2019) Take control – seven steps for crisis communications in business schools. *Global Focus*, 3(13) pp.12–17.

Bouchikhi, H. and J. Kimberly (2016) Business schools on the hot seat: Is Darwinian selection in their future? *Le journal de l'école de Paris du management*, 119(3) pp.38–44.

Bradshaw, D. (2011) Copenhagen Business School fires Johan Roos. *Financial Times*, March 28.

Bradshaw, D. (2013) Melbourne Business School wins in merger battle with university. *Financial Times*, May 1.

Bradshaw, D. (2015) Cracks in finances put business schools at risk. *Financial Times*, May 31.

Brown, A.D., M.A. Lewis and N. Oliver (2021) Identity work, loss and preferred identities: A study of UK business school deans. *Organization Studies*, 42(6) pp.823–844.

Byrne, J.A. (2012) The tragic death of a Harvard MBA. *Poets&Quants*, May 23.

Byrne, J.A. (2013) Why the b-school dean was really fired at George Washington. *Poets&Quants*, September 5.

Byrne, J.A. (2015) Ross dean to step down after one term. *Poets&Quants*, May 18.

Caredda, S. (2020) *Models: The Lippitt-Knoster model for managing complex change*, March 3. Available at: https://sergiocaredda.eu/organisation/tools/page/2/

Christensen Hughes, J. (2020) Mounting efforts to transform business school rankings. *Global Focus*, 2(16) pp.12–19.

Clegg, K. (2022) *Building trust in supervisory relationships*. EFMD, April 11. Available at: https://blog.efmdglobal.org/2022/04/11/building-trust-in-supervisory-relationships/

Cornuel, E. (Ed.) (2022) *Business school leadership and crisis exit planning*. Cambridge: Cambridge University Press.

Cuddy, A. (2015) *Presence: Bringing your boldest self to your biggest challenges*. London: Hachette.

Davies, J.A. (2015) *Reflections on the role of the business school dean*. London: Chartered Association of Business Schools.

Davies, J. and H. Thomas (2010) What do deans do? *Global Focus*, 4(1) pp.44–47.

Delbecq, A. (1996) What's next after 10 years as dean? Reflections of a reemerging professor. In P. Frost and M.S. Taylor, (Eds.), *Rhythms of academic life: Personal accounts of careers in academia*. Thousand Oaks, CA: Sage, pp. 437–442.

De Novellis, M. (2022) 5 business education trends to watch in 2022. AACSB, January 25.

Deveau, D. (2013) Global recession forced business schools to focus on exposed warts, silos. *Financial Post*, November 25.

De Vita, G. and P. Case (2016) 'The smell of the place': Managerialist culture in contemporary UK business schools. *Culture and Organization*, 22(4) pp.348–364.

Doerwald, F., H. Zacher, N.W. Van Yperen and S. Scheibe (2021) Generativity at work: A meta-analysis. *Journal of Vocational Behavior, 125* pp.103521.

Ellis, R. (2022) Give administrators a shot at top job, says registrar turned V-C. *Times Higher Education*, April 22. Yvonne Beach, Dean, Bristol Business School, UWE. Available at: https://www.linkedin.com/in/dr-yvonne-beach-093a0630/?originalSubdomain=uk

Ethier, M. (2021) At Cambridge, 3 deans tackle burning questions. *Poets&Quants*, July 14.

Finch, J.H., C. Carson and F. McIntyre (2022) Exit strategies for business school deans. *Christian Business Academy Review, 17*(Spring) pp.49–61.

Frandsen, S., M. Gotsi, A. Johnston, A. Whittle et al. (2018) Faculty responses to business school branding: A discursive approach. *European Journal of Marketing, 52*(5/6) pp.1128–1153.

Friedman, T.L. (2020) After the pandemic, a revolution in education and work awaits. *New York Times*, October 20.

Galdón, C., K. Haanaes, D Halbheer, J. Howard-Grenville, K. Le Goulven, M. Rosenberg, P. Tufano and A. Whitelaw (2022) Business schools must do more to address the climate crisis. *Harvard Business Review*, February 1. Available at: https://hbr.org/2022/02/business-schools-must-do-more-to-address-the-climate-crisis

Gallos J.V. (2002) The dean's squeeze: The myths and realities of academic leadership in the middle. *Academy of Management Learning & Education, 1*(2) p.179

Guilhon, A. (2015) SKEMA. The story of a merger. *Global Focus, 10*(3) pp.46–49.

Hardcastle, S. (2021) Business school advisory boards: increasing engagement, adding value. *Global Focus, 3*(15) pp.52–75.

Harker, M.J., B. Caemmerer and N. Hynes (2016) Management education by the French Grandes Ecoles de Commerce: Past, present, and an uncertain future. *Academy of Management Learning & Education, 15*(3) pp.549–568.

Heilman, R.E., E.L. Bogart, W.H. Kiekhofer, C.O. Ruggles and G.W. Dowrie (1928) The relationship between departments of economics and collegiate schools of business. *The American Economic Review, 18*(1) pp.73–84.

Hughes, A. (2019) 11 of the prettiest business school campuses. *Businessbecause*, April 11.

Hutchins, H.M. and H. Rainbolt (2017) What triggers imposter phenomenon among academic faculty? A critical incident study exploring antecedents, coping, and development opportunities. *Human Resource Development International, 20*(3) pp.194–214.

Jenkins, C. (2011) University of Wales degree and visa scam exposed by BBC. *BBC*, October 5.

Jones, D.R., M. Visser, P. Stokes, A. Örtenblad, R. Deem, P. Rodgers and S.Y. Tarba (2020) The performative university: 'Targets', 'terror' and 'taking back freedom' in academia. *Management Learning, 51*(4) pp.363–377.

Jongsma, A. (2011) DENMARK: Rector resigns over business school fiasco. *University World News*, April 1.

Konopaske, R., C. Robie and J.M. Ivancevich (2009) Managerial willingness to assume traveling, short-term and long-term global assignments. *Management International Review, 49*(3) pp.359–387.

Lejeune, C. and A. Vas (2014) Institutional pressure as a trigger for organizational identity change: The case of accreditation failure within seven European business schools. In A.M. Pettigrew, E. Cornuel, U. Hommel (Eds.) *The institutional development of business schools*. Oxford: Oxford University Press, pp.69–95.

Lorange, P. (2022) *Learning and teaching business: Lessons and insights from a lifetime of work*. Cham: Springer.

Manfredi, S., K. Clayton-Hathway and E. Cousens (2019) Increasing gender diversity in higher education leadership: The role of executive search firms. *Social Sciences, 8*(6) p.168; doi:10.3390/socsci8060168

McKie, A. (2018) UK universities 'bleeding their business schools dry'. *Times Higher Education*, November 5.

Meley, C. (2021) *Bayes Business School rebrand sparks renewed focus on diversity & inclusion*. businessbecause.com, October 12.

Peters, K., R.R. Smith and H. Thomas (2018) *Rethinking the business models of business schools: A critical review and change agenda for the future*. Bingley: Emerald Publishing.

Rana, S., A. Anand, S. Prashar and M.M. Haque (2020) A perspective on the positioning of Indian business schools post COVID-19 pandemic. *International Journal of Emerging Markets, 17*(2) pp.353–367.

Reynolds, M. (2014) *The discomfort zone: How leaders turn difficult conversations into breakthroughs*. Oakland, CA: Berrett-Koehler Publishers.

Rooney, S. (2020) HEC Paris Business School: A systemic education fraud. December 19. Available at: https://blogs.mediapart.fr/srooney/blog/191220/hec-paris-business-school-systemic-education-fraud

Shinn, S. (2022) What's wrong with business schools today. *AACSB International*, February 14.

Simon, H.A. (1967) The business school: A problem in organizational design. *Journal of Management Studies*, 4, pp.1–16.

Spencer, L., L. Anderson and P. Ellwood (2022) Interweaving scholarship and practice: A pathway to scholarly impact. *Academy of Management Learning & Education, 21*(3) pp.422–448.

Spicer, A., Z. Jaser and C. Wiertz (2021) The future of the business school: Finding hope in alternative pasts. *Academy of Management Learning & Education*, 20(3) pp.459–466.

Sunnucks, M. (2014) More layoffs at Thunderbird as business school preps for ASU merger. *Phoenix Business Journal*, July 21.

Tangel, A. (2013) 2008 financial crisis holds lessons for business schools. *Los Angeles Times*, September 19.

Thomas, L., J. Billsberry, V. Ambrosini and H. Barton (2014) Convergence and divergence dynamics in British and French business schools: How will the pressure for accreditation influence these dynamics? *British Journal of Management*, 25(2) pp.305–319.

Thomas, H. and L. Thomas (2011) Perspectives on leadership in business schools. *Journal of Management Development*, 30(5) pp.526–540.

Waller, M.A. and S. Caldwell 2021. *The dean's list. Leading a modern business school.* Fayetteville: University of Arkansas.

Watson, D. (2009) *The question of morale: Managing happiness and unhappiness in university life.* New York: McGraw-Hill.

Weinberg, C. (2013) Thunderbird Business School tries to calm dissent over deal with for-profit. *The Chronicle of Higher Education*, August 2.

Whitford, E. (2022) Cyberattacks pose 'existential risk' to colleges—and sealed one small college's fate. *Forbes*, April 19.

YouTube (2011a) Professor Robin Wensley, *YouTube*, 13 May. Available at: https://www.youtube.com/watch?v=iXtjcL1f7vY

YouTube (2011b) Professor Stephen Watson. The role of business school dean. *YouTube*, 31 May. Available at: https://www.youtube.com/watch?v=c-H5LTErKbM

Appendix 3
Learning Opportunities after a First Business School Deanship

accreditation visits team member	move to different campus/department
charity work	new b-school deanship
coaching	non-executive directorships
consulting	pro-vice-chancellor
deputy dean/dean's adviser	provost
emeritus	quality assurance, accreditation job
faculty dean	recruitment/accreditation panels
faculty development	repeat deanship, contract renewal
faculty role (part-time)	return to the benches
found own business (school)	sabbatical
government adviser	semi/full retirement
industry (not higher education)	university president/vice-chancellor
interim deanship	writing/research project
mentoring deans	

Source: Authors' interviews and analysis of LinkedIn profiles and media reports.

Index

For Product Safety Concerns and Information please contact our EU
representative GPSR@taylorandfrancis.com
Taylor & Francis Verlag GmbH, Kaufingerstraße 24, 80331 München, Germany

www.ingramcontent.com/pod-product-compliance
Lightning Source LLC
Chambersburg PA
CBHW061246220326
41599CB00028B/5554